All About
EXCHANGE-
TRADED
FUNDS

THE EASY WAY TO GET STARTED

OTHER TITLES IN THE "ALL ABOUT" FINANCE SERIES

All About
EXCHANGE-
TRADED
FUNDS

THE EASY WAY TO GET STARTED

SCOTT PAUL FRUSH, CFA, CFP

New York   Chicago   San Francisco   Lisbon   London   Madrid   Mexico City
Milan   New Delhi   San Juan   Seoul   Singapore   Sydney   Toronto

The **McGraw·Hill** Companies

1 2 3 4 5 6 7 8 9 10   QFR/QFR   1 6 5 4 3 2 1

ISBN   978-0-07-177011-8
MHID 0-07-177011-9

e-ISBN   978-0-07-177012-5
e-MHID 0-07-177012-7

This publication is designed to provide accurate and authoritative information in regard to the subject matter covered. It is sold with the understanding that neither the author nor the publisher is engaged in rendering legal, accounting, securities trading, or other professional services. If legal advice or other expert assistance is required, the services of a competent professional person should be sought.

> —*From a Declaration of Principles Jointly Adopted by*
> *a Committee of the American Bar Association and*
> *a Committee of Publishers and Associations*

Trademarks: McGraw-Hill, the McGraw-Hill Publishing logo, All About, and related trade dress are trademarks or registered trademarks of The McGraw-Hill Companies and/or its affiliates in the United States and other countries and may not be used without written permission. All other trademarks are the property of their respective owners. The McGraw-Hill Companies is not associated with any product or vendor mentioned in this book.

McGraw-Hill books are available at special quantity discounts to use as premiums and sales promotions or for use in corporate training programs. To contact a representative, please e-mail us at bulksales@mcgraw-hill.com.

This book is printed on acid-free paper.

To my daughter, Gabriella, and son, Ryan

CONTENTS

PART 2: TYPES OF EXCHANGE-TRADED FUNDS

PART 3: USE OF EXCHANGE-TRADED FUNDS

Chapter 18

Chapter 19

INTRODUCTION

There is no doubt that one of the most significant changes sweeping the investing marketplace is the rapid development, popularity, and use of exchange-traded funds (ETFs). This incredible trend has literally gone from evolution to revolution in only a dozen or so short years. The future of ETFs will be even brighter than it is today, and that's saying something considering the present buzz swirling around ETFs.

All About Exchange-Traded Funds is written to arm you with the information and tools that you will need to invest in ETFs with success. Perhaps you are less interested in investing in ETFs and instead are looking to gain knowledge of ETFs out of intellectual curiosity or for your job or class. Irrespective of the reason, this book will deliver exactly what you need to know about ETFs from *A* to *Z*. The level of information in this book is written with those investors in mind who have a basic or general understanding of investing, but who also have the intellect and appetite for a solid grounding in the fundamentals of ETFs. Accordingly, my guiding principle is not to insult anyone's intelligence, but instead to constructively build upon and hone it.

As you will read throughout the book, the use of the label *exchange-traded funds* is not completely accurate and appropriate to describe all *exchange-traded portfolios (ETPs)*, which is a more suitable label from a hierarchical perspective. Nonetheless, given the widespread acceptance and generic use of the label *ETFs*, when there is no practical reason to distinguish the two, this book will also defer to ETFs rather than ETPs wherever feasible. In addition, this book will emphasize passively managed ETFs, but does provide detailed information on actively managed ETFs when comparisons and contrasts are appropriately needed.

BEFORE GETTING STARTED

Time and time again I encourage people to manage their portfolio before it manages them. Managing your portfolio always begins with you—never give up control and oversight carte blanche to someone else even if you are working with a trusted and capable investment professional. When it comes to your investments, you really have two options—accomplish those tasks that will help you manage your portfolio with success, or simply forgo them and let your portfolio manage you, for better or worse. Since you are already reading this book, you have demonstrated your ability and willingness to be proactive with managing your portfolio. Consider this book an invaluable tool to help you with this endeavor.

SELF-ASSESSMENT

Before embarking on your objective of using ETFs in your investing, I highly encourage you to complete a top-down self-assessment of your investment management capabilities. Since investing is a personalized process and will change over time as your situation changes, understand as much as you can about what your current financial position is, what you want to accomplish, and how best to bridge the gap. Different investors have not only different financial goals and obligations, but also varying underlying financial circumstances and preferences. As a result, individual investors need to exercise care, skill, and patience to reap the benefits of employing ETFs.

HOW TO GET THE MOST FROM THIS BOOK

All About Exchange-Traded Funds is divided into three parts whereby chapters in each part are similar in subject matter, with no one part—or chapters—of greater importance than the others. Consequently, reading this book from the opening chapter to the last appendix is your best path for understanding the important material. The book is structured to provide maximum benefit, ease of learning, and quick and simple referencing. Furthermore, a significant amount of effort was given to creating visually stimulating charts and graphs that will clarify and enhance the learning process. As such, Part 1 begins with a discussion of the important basics of ETFs and is followed in Part 2 by a detailed discussion of the different types of ETFs available in the marketplace. Part 3 concentrates on how best to employ ETFs in managing your portfolio in addition to presenting peripheral topics relating to ETFs such as investing risk and return and asset allocation principles.

WHAT YOU WILL NOT FIND IN THIS BOOK

All About Exchange-Traded Funds presents ETFs in an easy-to-understand fashion using a very specific format whereby you will first learn the basics and then learn how to apply that knowledge by investing in ETFs. This book will not teach you about the highly complex mathematics of ETFs nor drill down so deep into a topic that you lose sight of the big picture. Although some highly complex information was deliberately toned down or excluded from this book, you will still encounter all the technical information needed to learn and grasp the big picture of ETFs. If after reading this book you still want to immerse yourself in the highly complex aspects of ETFs, I encourage you to investigate some of the more sophisticated books written specifically for investment professionals. Doing so is not necessary for the majority of people, however.

A REVIEW OF THE CHAPTERS

All About Exchange-Traded Funds is divided into three parts to help you find and learn what you want quickly and easily. Included in these three parts are 19 chapters covering all things ETFs from the basics to the peripheral issues. The chapter structure of this book is as follows.

Part 1: Basics of Exchange-Traded Funds

The first chapter of *All About Exchange-Traded Funds* presents a basic tutorial on ETFs, including their defining attributes and the current state of the ETF marketplace. Chapter 2 provides background on ETFs including developments and important milestone events. The next chapter offers a detailed discussion on how ETFs are so different—and advantageous—compared with both mutual funds and common stocks. Chapter 4 examines the core that defines ETFs—the underlying indexes along with profiles on the top index sponsors. The following chapter drills down below the surface to uncover the technical aspects of ETFs. These are the advanced topics that underscore how ETFs work and function within the investing framework. Chapter 6 builds on the information from the previous chapter by introducing the reader to the necessary and complex issues involved with taking an ETF from concept to listed market product. The final chapter in Part 1 examines the main players and participants engaged somewhere within the ETF marketplace.

Part 2: Types of Exchange-Traded Funds

The second part of *All About Exchange-Traded Funds* focuses on the different types of ETFs available for investment by retail and institutional investors alike. The initial chapter lays the groundwork with a discussion of the broad-based ETFs such as those tracking both the S&P 500 and the Dow Jones Industrial Average. The next chapter digs somewhat deeper by analyzing the sectors and industry groups that—when added together—represent the broad-based market. Chapter 10 presents a solid take on why and how fixed-income investing is vitally important, especially for conservative or income-oriented investors. The next chapter targets ETFs from the perspective of both international and global investments. Chapter 12 is divided into three important, but related, real asset markets—commodities, currencies, and real estate. The last chapter in Part 2 focuses on specialty ETFs with significant emphasis on the funds that are all the rage—leveraged and inverse ETFs.

Part 3: Use of Exchange-Traded Funds

The third and final part of *All About Exchange-Traded Funds* takes you inside how you can incorporate ETFs into your investing program as well as what special peripheral topics should be understood and considered before investing in ETFs. The first chapter of

Part 3 presents a look inside investing risk and return—a sort of fundamentals of investing 101 class in abbreviation. This is followed up by an overview of asset allocation and an explanation of why this strategy is so vitally important to safeguard and grow a portfolio. The next chapter uncovers and dismisses the leading misconceptions of ETFs that many casual investors hold. The next two chapters present sample ETF portfolios based on traditional life-cycle investing together with risk profile and specialized portfolios based principally on investor sentiment on the health and direction of the market. The last chapter rounding out the book looks at what the future of ETF investing might hold. Multiple appendixes provide valuable resources and historical data as well as a questionnaire to help you identify your optimal asset allocation.

## PART 1

Basics of Exchange-Traded Funds

CHAPTER 1

Getting Started: A Primer on Exchange- Traded Funds

Exchange-traded funds (ETFs) have grown by over 1,000 percent during the 10-year period of 2001 to 2010. At the beginning of 2001, ETFs had combined assets under management (AuM) of approximately $70 billion with nearly 90 funds available in the U.S. marketplace. Fast-forward 10 years to the end of 2010 and AuM have ballooned to over $1 trillion with nearly 1,100 ETFs available in the marketplace. This is extraordinary growth that few ever predicted when the first ETFs were envisioned and launched only decades earlier. (See Figure 1-1 for a list of the 10 most actively traded U.S. ETFs.)

ETFs are a relatively recent innovation, but have become increasingly popular with casual, sophisticated, and institutional investors alike. ETFs offer shareholders, including those of moderate means, an opportunity to invest in a highly diversified, tax-efficient, and cost-effective basket of securities, such as common stocks, preferred stocks, bonds, real estate investment trusts (REITs), and commodities.

ETFs are not investment strategies; they are the basic structure, wrapper, or basket that contains the underlying securities. It is how the securities are managed that dictates an investment strategy or strategies. The same can be said for mutual funds and hedge funds, for that matter. However, each of the aforementioned investment structures offers unique features and characteristics not avail-

FIGURE 1-1

Most Actively Traded U.S. ETFs

Rank	ETF	Symbol	Volume*
1	SPDR S&P 500	SPY	156,408,828
2	Financial Select Sector SPDR	XLF	68,696,102
3	iShares MSCI Emerging Markets Index	EEM	62,767,602
4	PowerShares QQQ	QQQ	60,317,012
5	iShares Russell 2000 Index	IWM	52,889,184
6	iShares MSCI Japan Index	EWJ	40,517,426
7	iShares Silver Trust	SLV	32,069,658
8	ProShares UltraShort S&P500	SDS	24,325,984
9	Direxion Daily Financial Bull 3X Shares	FAS	24,055,219
10	Vanguard MSCI Emerging Markets ETF	VWO	19,729,682

*100-day average volume.

Source: Frush Financial Group, April 2011

able—either partially or fully—in the other investment structures. To use an analogy, think of ETFs as a car in which the driver is the ETF provider, the passengers are the shareholders, the engine is the underlying securities, and the road map is the tracking index. A car only drives to where the driver steers it (i.e., the strategy). Cars do not drive themselves. However, not all cars are created the same. Some are faster than others, some are safer than others, some come with more conveniences, some hold more passengers, and some are considered more prestigious. Consequently, some types of investment structures (e.g., ETFs, mutual funds, hedge funds) make more sense for one strategy or shareholder but not for others.

When ETFs were initially created, they were designed to track market indexes much like the index mutual funds of the day. However, since 2008 when the first actively managed ETF was launched, most of the new ETFs have been designed to follow proprietary customized indexes. This essentially means that these ETFs are tossing aside the traditional index philosophy and incorporating active-management methodologies, all with the intent to outperform the market rather than generate market returns. Many ETF providers that emphasize active management claim their strategies—and therefore their ETFs—are better than all other ETFs in the marketplace. Perhaps the providers will even boast stellar performance to justify their claim. Smart investors know there is no Holy Grail of investing. Most money managers do not outperform their respective benchmarks in any given year, and those that do cannot outperform consistently over time. There will always be money managers who outperform and those who underperform. It's simple mathematics and the law of large numbers. However, where ETFs do add to the bottom line is in their unique structure that affords them favorable cost savings—namely, taxes, expenses, and trading efficiencies. These factors alone give ETFs built-in advantages and shareholders financial benefits and incentives.

WHAT IS AN ETF?

An ETF is an investment company organized under either the Securities Act of 1933 or the Investment Company Act of 1940 that offers shareholders a proportionate share in a portfolio of stocks, bonds, commodities, or other securities. From one perspective, ETFs can be considered a cross between common stocks and mutual funds whereby an ETF trades intraday on a stock exchange at continuously market-determined prices like common stocks and holds a diversified portfolio of securities like a traditional mutual fund. Mutual funds are "forward priced," meaning they can only be purchased and sold at the end of the trading session, whereas ETFs can be traded at any time the market is open for business. Additionally, ETFs offer stocklike tradability features such as selling short, purchasing via margin, and executing trades using market, limit, stop loss, and other discretionary order types.

One of the most important differences between ETFs and mutual funds is the price at which a shareholder can purchase or sell the fund. Mutual funds are transacted at marked-to-market net asset value (NAV), while ETFs are transacted at market-determined prices, which can differ from NAV. Although the market price for an ETF reflects the market values of the underlying securities, the market price on the fund level is also dictated by simple shareholder supply and demand. Thus, premiums or discounts to NAV can occur. Closed-end funds are much like ETFs in that closed-end funds trade on exchanges and hold pools of securities. However, closed-end funds trade with sometimes significant premiums or more typically discounts to NAV—sometimes as high as 30 percent.

Two features of an ETF's structure ensure that market prices approximate NAV. The first is transparency of holdings. When market participants know an ETF's holdings, they are far less likely to buy or sell at prices that deviate from the aggregate market value—called intraday indicative value (IIV)—associated with the holdings. Second, large institutional investors called authorized participants (APs) are contractually involved to buy or sell ETF shares in a continuous risk-free arbitragelike manner until the spread between the market price and NAV is negligible. Shareholders benefit from this arrangement as the ETF share price is aligned with its NAV, and APs benefit by making a small profit in the process.

As previously mentioned, ETFs are designed to track either market indexes or proprietary custom indexes. The decision about which index to track is up to the ETF provider. Before an ETF can be listed on an organized stock exchange, such as the NYSE Arca (which we will simply refer to as NYSE throughout this book), an ETF provider must receive approval from an appropriate legal entity. In the United States, approximately 90 percent of ETFs are approved and regulated by the Securities and Exchange Commission (SEC) and the remaining 10 percent by the Commodities Futures Trading Commission (CFTC). (See Figure 1-2 for a list of the 15 largest U.S. ETFs.)

How ETFs Operate

ETFs originate with ETF providers, such as Vanguard or PowerShares, which select an ETF's tracking index, establish the basket of securities underlying the ETF, and decide how many shares to offer to the investing marketplace. For instance, when an ETF provider selects an appropriate tracking index, that provider

FIGURE 1-2

Largest U.S. ETFs

ETF	Symbol	Assets ($B)
SPDR S&P 500	SPY	91.9
SPDR Gold Shares	GLD	59.7
Vanguard MSCI Emerging Markets	VWO	49.4
iShares MSCI Emerging Markets	EEM	41.6
iShares MSCI EAFE Index	EFA	40.6
iShares S&P 500 Index	IVV	28.4
PowerShares QQQ	QQQ	25.5
iShares Barclays TIPS Bond	TIP	20.3
Vanguard Total Stock Market ETF	VTI	20.3
iShares Russell 2000 Index	IWM	18.2
iShares Silver Trust	SLV	16.4
iShares Russell 1000 Growth Index	IWF	13.8
iShares iBoxx $ Inv Grade Corp Bond	LQD	13.2
iShares MSCI Brazil Index	EWZ	13.2
iShares Russell 1000 Value Index	IWD	12

Source: Morningstar, 2011

contracts with an AP to obtain the predetermined holdings that make up the basket of securities and to deposit them with the provider. In turn, the provider delivers to the AP what is called a "creation unit" typically representing between 50,000 and 100,000 ETF shares. APs can either hold the ETF shares or sell all or part of them on the open market, which are then purchased by you and me. Chapter 5 provides greater detail of this creation and redemption process.

As a result of the creation and redemption process, shareholders technically do not transact directly with an ETF provider—which is in contrast to mutual funds—and instead transact with APs. The SEC has mandated that ETF providers disclose this material fact in all their prospectuses and other client-approved written materials, such as advertisements.

Major Categories of ETFs

There are six major categories of ETFs available for shareholders to purchase and sell. These ETFs track a number of traditional market indexes in the United States and abroad as well as custom indexes created by ETF providers to employ proprietary investing strategies. The six major categories of ETFs include the following:

1. **Broad-Based ETFs:** These ETFs track indexes based on both size (large caps, mid caps, and small caps) and style (growth, value, and blend). Examples of these include the SPDR (Spider) S&P 500 ETF and the PowerShares QQQ, which tracks the Nasdaq-100 Index.
2. **Sector and Industry ETFs:** These ETFs track indexes that target economic or industry groups such as energy, health care, technology, and home builders. Examples of these include the Financial Select Sector SPDR ETF and the Vanguard Information Technology ETF.
3. **Global ETFs:** These ETFs track indexes that target various countries, geographic regions, and major divisions, such as developing and emerging markets. Examples of these include the Vanguard MSCI Emerging Markets ETF and the iShares MSCI Brazil Index ETF.

4. **Real Asset ETFs:** These ETFs track indexes associated with alternative investments such as REITs, commodities, and currencies. Examples of these include the PowerShares DB Commodity Index Tracking ETF and the Vanguard REIT Index ETF.

5. **Fixed-Income ETFs:** These ETFs track the expansive bond market including Treasuries, municipals, agencies, and corporates. Examples of these include the Vanguard Total Bond Market ETF and the iShares iBoxx Investment Grade Corporate Bond ETF.

6. **Specialty ETFs:** These ETFs track indexes associated with less traditional investment approaches such as leveraged and inverse strategies. Examples of these include the ProShares Ultra Financials ETF and the Direxion Daily Financial Bear 3X Shares ETF.

ETF Expenses

ETFs that follow a strict passive-management strategy typically have very low management fees—generally less than 30 basis points, or the equivalent of 0.3 percent. For ETFs that employ a more active management strategy, expenses will be higher, oftentimes around 60 basis points or more. In addition to management fees, shareholders will need to transact these shares on an exchange, and that means trading commissions will be incurred for both purchases and sales. As a result, be mindful and consider the expenses of these funds prior to building a portfolio of them. (Other minor costs associated with ETFs are detailed in Chapter 5.)

Undivided Interest in ETFs

When a shareholder purchases shares of an ETF, that shareholder owns an undivided and proportional interest in each of the underlying securities. All outstanding shareholders do not divvy up each underlying security whereby each takes a few shares of one or two stocks. Shareholders are owners of each and every security held in the ETF. Consider an analogy of three people going into business with one another and buying a car dealership in equal proportion.

Each of the three business owners will own an undivided interest in the tools in the shop, the buildings on the property, and the cars for sale on the lot. One person will not get the tools, another person the building, and the last person the cars on the lot. Each owns an undivided interest in all of these and the other assets. The same goes for ETF shareholders.

DEFINING ATTRIBUTES

Very specific and definable attributes underlie any investing concept or strategy. ETFs are no different. As Figure 1-3 shows, ETFs can be easily defined by a number of different attributes that present them in a unique light. Although we will discuss each one of these attributes in varying degrees in this book, this section will present the most essential attributes to showcase their importance and compelling benefits. This is a key section for someone who wants to understand why he or she should invest with ETFs since this is the section that will outline the specific reasons for doing so. Note that there are other attributes—such as having high intraday liquidity and having no minimum initial purchase requirements—but these are considered not as important as the following defining attributes, which are presented in no particular order.

FIGURE 1-3

Defining Attributes of ETFs

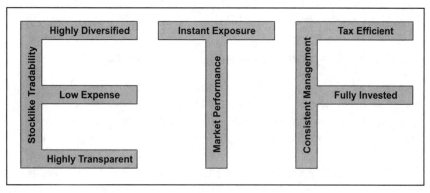

Source: Frush Financial Group

ETFs Are Highly Diversified

Although ETFs look like stocks, they resemble mutual funds in many more ways. ETFs, like mutual funds, have a large number of underlying securities and thus provide built-in diversification. Diversification is appealing since it helps safeguard a portfolio against the severe negative impact on returns from any one security. ETFs adhere to the "don't put all your eggs in one basket" methodology.

ETFs Offer Instant Exposure

Given the substantial number of securities underlying any ETF and the index the ETF is attempting to track, ETFs provide shareholders with instant built-in exposure to the asset class or market segment that the ETF tracks. With one quick and easy purchase, a shareholder can begin reaping the benefits and return potential of the direct exposure he or she desires.

ETFs Offer Stocklike Tradability

One of the first advantages that casual investors recognize is the stocklike tradability offered by ETFs. Although mutual funds are rather constrained by how a shareholder can transact, the same is not true with ETFs. The original blueprint for ETFs called for a significant emphasis on stocklike tradability in order to go head-to-head with stocks and attract new AuM and new revenues for both ETF providers and stock exchanges. Stocklike tradability affords shareholders the ability to execute any number of discretionary order types long reserved for stock investors. These order types include market orders, limit orders, stop-loss orders, buying on margin, and selling short. Individual brokerage firms expand on this list with their own proprietary order types.

ETFs Are Low Expense

One of the most important defining attributes underlying ETFs is their favorable cost structure, especially in comparison with mutual funds. ETFs typically have much lower expense ratios than comparable mutual funds as well as no up-front or back-end sales loads nor any subsidy trading costs. Not having any subsidy costs, or cost of flow, provides protection to shareholders over and above anything available with mutual funds. Low expenses are critical since small annual differences add up to substantial savings over many years.

ETFs Are Highly Transparent

Transparency of fund holdings and applicable costs is essential to evaluating and investing in the most appropriate ETF. In addition to mutual funds not providing a satisfactory level of transparency, their fund-level disclosures are nowhere on the same level as that of ETFs. Shareholders have the ability to investigate the holdings of an ETF on a daily basis. Furthermore, they also have the knowledge of the expenses of the ETF on both the fund level and portfolio level and the confidence that knowledge brings. Shareholders demand to get what they pay for, and full transparency ensures they achieve that aim.

ETFs Are Tax Efficient

Mutual funds are notorious for passing through capital gains tax liabilities that derive from partial or complete liquidations of underlying securities with embedded unrealized gains. ETF shareholders are not exposed to this irritating and financially unfavorable drawback due to the highly innovative and beneficial creation and redemption process. ETF shareholders are confronted with capital gains tax liabilities when they sell shares of their funds with capital gains, but at least that is a controllable decision left to the discretion of the shareholder and not the portfolio manager working for the mutual fund company.

ETFs Are Fully Invested

Many shareholders may not be aware of the fact that most mutual funds are not fully invested and therefore hold a modest to significant cash position. This not only is necessary to satisfy mutual fund shareholder liquidations, but also is necessary for tactical asset allocation purposes. Higher-than-expected investment inflows can also lead to abnormally high cash balances. Irrespective of the reason why, holding cash on the fund level translates to an unintended asset mix that overweights fixed income at the expense of equities—thus giving control over asset allocation policy to an outside party. Since ETFs do not have to satisfy shareholder liquidations and because shareholder cash inflows do not directly flow into ETFs, ETF providers can choose to be fully invested without the need to consider the ramifications a mutual fund would face in the same situation. An ETF that is fully invested takes advantage of rising markets rather than having cash sit idle and not participate in stock market rallies.

ETFs Deliver Market Performance

One of the most striking disadvantages of mutual funds and other actively managed investments is their historical underperformance against appropriate benchmarks. Research has clearly demonstrated that most actively managed investments do not outperform their relative benchmarks in any given year, and when they do outperform, the likelihood of them repeating this achievement is much lower. All active managers outperforming their relative benchmark want you and other shareholders to believe they have truly special investing skills and judgment. From a mathematical perspective, someone is always going to outperform—and some with consistency year after year. In contrast, ETFs do not worry about generating alpha, or outperformance, since many ETFs focus on generating beta, or market returns (see Figure 1-4). This may seem somewhat boring, but when you consider the higher costs and less favorable tax efficiency that you get with mutual funds, then accepting market performance isn't so bad after all.

ETFs Offer Consistent Management

No investors or shareholders want to get involved in a situation where the investment they purchased no longer follows the objective originally desired. When a portfolio manager strays from his

FIGURE 1-4

Investment Management Styles

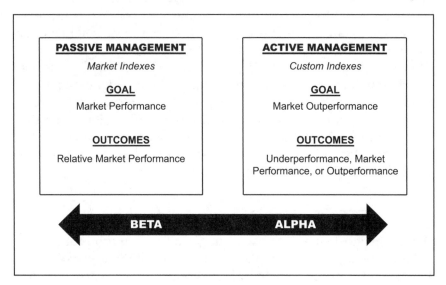

Source: Frush Financial Group

or her intended objective, then that fund is said to exhibit style drift. It's an unfortunate situation since changes in investment objective should only be made by shareholders and not by portfolio managers—especially those you have never spoken to or met with before. Passively managed ETFs and index mutual funds do not fall prey to this pitfall since they are not run by portfolio managers and supporting casts. Rather, passively managed ETFs are run by sophisticated computers that do not make ad hoc decisions detrimental to shareholders. Again, what you see is what you get with ETFs.

STATE OF THE ETF MARKETPLACE

The pace of expansion in both the number and associated AuM in the ETF marketplace is truly astounding. This pace has expanded, and sometimes exponentially, over the last several years, and the trend should only get stronger over time. Since the year 2000, U.S. ETF AuM have grown by approximately 32 percent on average each year. At this pace, ETFs may boast nearly $2 trillion in AuM in only a few short years. Strong markets help the cause, of course. Within a decade or two, it's very possible that ETFs will even overtake mutual funds both in AuM and in number of funds available in the marketplace.

Number of ETFs

Increasingly higher demand for ETFs has led many ETF providers to rapidly increase the number of ETFs they make available in the investing marketplace. Until 2008, few ETFs were closed, but the financial crisis and market crash caused some providers to liquidate their ETFs due to lack of investor interest and, more important, to insufficient AuM, the lifeblood of any ETF. Nearly 100 ETFs were liquidated in 2008 and 2009 combined, 10 times more than the preceding eight years put together.

The number of U.S. ETFs available in the marketplace has never declined year over year. At the end of 2000, there were 89 ETFs in existence—which sounds bizarre today, given their popularity and incredible reach. However, at the end of 2010, there were approximately 1,100 ETFs in existence—an 11-fold increase (see Figure 1-5). Although the number of ETFs has slowly been increasing each year, it was the mid-2000s when the number really took off. By the end of 2005, there were about 219 ETFs, and two years later the number had risen to 672, more than tripling the number available in the marketplace. Even the abnormal number of closings in 2008 and 2009 were not enough to stem the tide of new issues when over 200 ETFs were launched during this two-year period. Once the financial crisis had peaked and began receding, ETF providers began flooding the market with new funds; the year 2010 alone saw an increase of over 20 percent in the number of available options. One would think this rate of increase cannot continue, but we may be in for a sustainable growth for the foreseeable future as presently more than 800 ETFs are somewhere in the registration process with the SEC.

FIGURE 1-5

U.S. ETF AuM and Number by Year

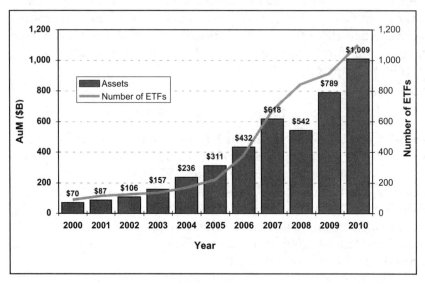

Source: BlackRock, Factset, and Bloomberg

AuM

At the end of the twentieth century, U.S. ETF AuM stood at about $70 billion and two years later only increased to a little over $100 billion. From this point on, inflows of assets began to gain traction, and total AuM hit $600 billion during 2007 just before the beginning of the financial crisis. Although 2008 did see AuM fall from the prior year, the level of assets rebounded by the end of 2009 and closed above their 2007 peak. By the end of 2010, total AuM were well over $1 trillion, with material gains in the first quarter of 2011.

Annual Inflows and Outflows

Throughout the 2000s, inflows of assets into U.S. ETFs were always positive, even during 2008 when market values caused total assets to fall year over year (see Figure 1-6). Coincidently, 2008 witnessed the biggest year for ETF inflows at nearly $180 billion, the same year asset inflows into ETFs surpassed inflows into mutual funds

FIGURE 1-6

ETF Annual Inflows

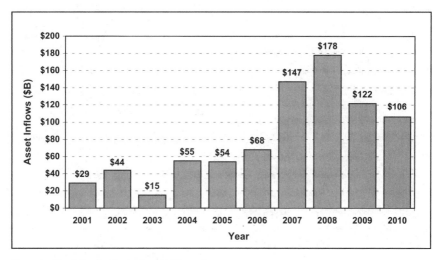

Source: BlackRock, Factset, and Bloomberg

for the first time on an annual basis. The year with the second highest asset inflows was 2007 when nearly $150 billion was invested into ETFs by shareholders. The year with the smallest inflow of assets into ETFs was 2003 at just over $15 billion.

Demand for ETFs

There is no question that the demand for ETFs has increased steadily since their introduction. To meet the increasing demand, ETF providers have launched more funds that have a greater variety of investment objectives and that track lesser-known indexes. During the mid-1990s, ETF providers began launching international equity ETFs, with significant traction gained in these funds in the early to mid-2000s. Toward the end of the past decade, emerging markets led the way with nearly 15 percent of all AuM invested in this category, making it the second largest category of ETFs behind large-cap domestic ETFs (see Figure 1-7). The third most popular category is bond and hybrid ETFs, with devel-

FIGURE 1-7

Top 10 ETFs with Highest Full-Year 2010 Inflows

Rank	ETF	Symbol	Inflows ($B)	% of Total
1	Vanguard MSCI Emerging Markets	VWO	19.3	15.7
2	SPDR Gold Trust	GLD	5.8	4.7
3	SPDR S&P Dividend	SDY	3.5	2.8
4	iShares S&P U.S. Preferred Stock	PFF	2.8	2.3
5	SPDR Barclays Capital High Yield Bond	JNK	2.8	2.3
6	Vanguard Total Bond Market	BND	2.7	2.2
7	Vanguard MSCI Total Stock Market	VTI	2.6	2.1
8	iShares iBoxx $ High Yield Corporate Bond	HYG	2.6	2.1
9	iPath S&P 500 VIX Short-Term Futures	VXX	2.4	1.9
10	Vanguard Dividend Appreciation	VIG	2.3	1.9

Source: Bloomberg and BlackRock

oped international ETFs not too far behind. One of the fastest-growing segments is commodities and commodity-related ETFs. Approximately two-thirds of commodity ETF assets track precious metals via both the spot and futures markets. Consumer and utility ETFs have two of the lowest AuM out of all commodity and sector funds.

Finally, there are more than 20 ETF funds of funds—ETFs that hold and invest primarily in shares of other ETFs—with approximately $1 billion of AuM. This category should continue to grow exponentially as ETFs migrate into 401(k) and 403(b) retirement plan platforms.

Characteristics of Retail ETF Shareholders

According to the Investment Company Institute, an estimated 3.3 million U.S. households owned ETFs in 2010. In addition, of the households that owned mutual funds, 5 percent owned at least one ETF. Of the households that own ETFs, 97 percent owned stocks, stock mutual funds, or variable annuities with stock holdings.

Additionally, 66 percent of ETF-owning households also owned bonds, bond mutual funds, or fixed annuities. Finally, 39 percent of ETF shareholders also owned real estate for investment purposes. For the most part, ETF shareholders are wealthier, have higher incomes, and are more experienced with investing than the national average (see Figure 1-8).

FIGURE 1 - 8

Characteristics of ETF Shareholders

Characteristic	All U.S. Households	ETF-Owning Households	Stock-Owning Households
Average Annual Household Income	$49,000	$130,000	$85,000
Average Household Financial Assets	$75,000	$300,000	$225,000
Four-Year College Degree or Higher	31%	84%	50%
Employed	60%	80%	67%
Hold an IRA	41%	85%	68%

Source: Investment Company Institute, 2011

ETF PLAYERS AND PARTICIPANTS

Although Chapter 7 of this book is dedicated exclusively to key players and participants involved in the ETF marketplace, this section will provide a cursory understanding of each, since you will see these terms mentioned in the early chapters.

- **ETF Providers:** The investment companies that design, introduce, and oversee each ETF in existence today. Examples include Vanguard, BlackRock (iShares), State Street Global Advisors (SPDRs), and Invesco (PowerShares).
- **Index Sponsors:** The companies that create the market indexes, such as the S&P 500, that ETFs attempt to track.

Some examples are Standard & Poor's, Dow Jones Indexes, Morningstar, and Wilshire Associates.

- **Government Regulators:** Federal, state, industry, and international entities that make and enforce rules to ensure the viability and efficiency of the financial markets, including the ETF marketplace. Some examples include the SEC, the Federal Reserve, the U.S. Treasury Department, and the CFTC.

- **Stock Exchanges:** The companies that provide the electronic trading framework, liquidity, and price discovery where the buying and selling of stocks and ETFs is accomplished. Examples include the NYSE, the Nasdaq, and the Toronto Stock Exchange.

- **APs:** Typically, large institutional investors, specialists, market makers, or lead market makers (LMMs) that have signed participant agreements with specific ETF providers to transact directly with providers in a process for share creations and redemptions. Some examples are Deutsche Bank, Goldman Sachs, LaBranche Structured Products, and Société Générale.

- **LMMs:** Formerly known as specialists, the companies that are contracted liquidity providers on an exchange with obligations to maintain continuous ETF quotes, provide price discovery, and drive the inside quote a certain percentage of time throughout the day.

- **Distributors:** The companies that not only act as a liaison between the ETF custodian and the APs but also help to facilitate the sale of ETFs to both retail and institutional investors. Some ETFs take on this role themselves through a subsidiary, while others work with an external partner.

- **Custodians:** Specialized financial organizations that are responsible for physically holding and safeguarding financial assets—namely, the underlying securities of an ETF—and serve the traditional role of transfer agent and fund administrator. Some examples include Bank of New York Mellon, BNP Paribas, and Wells Fargo Bank.

- **Broker-Dealers:** Either the full-service or discount brokerage houses that execute ETF buy and sell orders from everyday shareholders. Examples include TD Ameritrade, Scottrade, Charles Schwab, Merrill Lynch, UBS, and Wells Fargo Advisors.

- **News and Research Sources:** The companies involved in disseminating news, research, and analysis on ETFs. Some examples are Morningstar, IndexUniverse.com (including its *Journal of Indexes*), Value Line, ETFGuide.com, ETFTrends.com, and SeekingAlpha.com.
- **Investment Professionals:** Both the portfolio managers and investment advisors that either help manage a portfolio of ETFs or provide advice and other financial support to clients and shareholders. Examples of titles include Certified Financial Planner, Chartered Financial Analyst, and Certified Fund Specialist.
- **Shareholders:** The end users of ETFs and final links in the ETF chain. Examples of these include casual retail investors, experienced trading speculators, and institutions of all sizes.

INSTITUTIONAL INTEREST IN ETFs

Individual retail investors and institutional investors employ ETFs in somewhat different ways and use different strategies. The following are seven of the most prominent reasons why institutions employ ETFs to some degree in their portfolio management programs.

1. **Core Position:** Here institutional and individual shareholders have the same objective—to construct an optimal portfolio with exposures to multiple asset classes. These can include various styles, sizes, economic sectors, bond market segments, and international markets. The aim is to build a low-expense and tax-efficient portfolio—areas where ETFs excel.
2. **Portfolio Optimization:** When an institution desires specific exposure to a small market segment, wants to fill gaps in asset allocation, or wants to overweight certain asset classes, then ETFs are often used because they provide instant exposure and built-in diversification.

Employing ETFs is a more efficient way to gain the exposure institutions seek.

3. **Unique Exposure:** When an institution wants to add a unique position to its portfolio, such as physical gold or an inverse position without the risk of selling short, then it can turn to ETFs. The growing popularity of ETFs has helped fuel innovations that are unavailable elsewhere in the investing marketplace.

4. **Trading Instrument:** From time to time, institutions identify opportunities they wish to take advantage of quickly and easily. Given their favorable stocklike tradability, ETFs offer a low-cost and highly liquid investment that can be purchased and sold during open trading sessions. Institutions highly covet the ability to sell short ETFs, particularly sector funds.

5. **Tax Management:** When an institution is subject to a capital gains tax liability—the natural result of selling a security with an unrealized gain—it can use ETFs to retain the market exposure it desires without triggering a wash-sale violation. The wash-sale rule prevents the purchase of the same or a "substantially similar" security within 30 days of the sale, or else deduction of the loss is disallowed. ETFs typically do not fit the description of substantially similar, even when tracking the same index.

6. **Hedging Tool:** Many institutions employ ETFs to provide a measure of protection from losses in their underlying securities. The two most popular uses include selling short an ETF to protect on the downside and using options. Buying put options provides a degree of insurance against declining stock prices, while writing covered call options generates extra cash and provides for incremental returns.

7. **Cash Management:** When an institution has abnormally high cash balances, it can use the excess cash to buy ETFs. Because institutions have benchmark goals, putting excess cash to work is very desirable to keep up with the Joneses. This is done typically only for a brief period until the institution decides how it wants to invest the excess cash in accordance with its own policies and under its own proprietary investing strategy.

## CHAPTER 2

History and Milestones: The ABCs of the ETF Revolution

"Let's make some money by trading something different and new." This was the brainchild of Nathan Most of the American Stock Exchange (AMEX) in the late 1980s to early 1990s in response to mounting financial pressures, a lack of resources, and a desire to increase revenues at the AMEX. As a result, exchange-traded funds (ETFs) were born, and the innovation has become an incredible success story ever since. What was the inspiration behind the innovation, and how were ETFs first designed? The story is long and varied, with the beginnings grounded in the 1970s. Figure 2-1 highlights the milestones.

FLASHBACK TO THE 1970s: IN THE BEGINNING FOR ETFs

The very first index mutual fund was established in 1971 at Samsonite (later Wells Fargo and today called Barclays Global Investors) by Nobel Prize winner William Sharpe and Bill Fouse. The index fund was available only to large institutional investors and was of little resemblance to today's mutual funds. Five years later in 1976, John Bogle and Burton Malkeil of Princeton University got together and created the first index fund for retail

FIGURE 2-1

Top Milestones in ETF History

Year	Milestone Event
1989	CIPs and IPSs become the first exchange-traded portfolios introduced.
1989	TIPS, the first ETF, is launched by the Toronto Stock Exchange.
1990	The SEC issues Release No. 17809 permitting a "SuperTrust."
1993	SPDRs S&P 500 (SPY) becomes the first U.S.-based ETF.
1995	Rydex introduces the first currency ETF, the Euro Currency Trust.
1996	WEBS become the first ETFs based on a single-country basket.
1996	WEBS become the first ETFs to use the investment company structure.
1996	Country Baskets become the first ETFs to close.
1996	Deutsche Bank launches the first commodity ETF—DB Commodity Index Fund
2000	First mass launch of ETFs, with 90 new funds launched in the U.S. in one year.
2008	Bear Stearns launches the first actively managed ETF but closes it the same year.
2010	The number of U.S. ETFs crosses the 1,000 mark.
2010	Various brokerage firms begin offering zero trading commissions on select ETFs.
2010	U.S. ETF assets surpass $1 trillion on December 16.

Source: Frush Financial Group

investors—the Vanguard 500 Index Fund. Bogle has been setting the tone for low-expense, tax-efficient investing since this time.

Most investors were happy with the new index fund, where returns consistently outpaced actively managed peer funds. Shareholder inflows turned the Vanguard Group into the largest mutual fund company in the world with over $100 billion in assets under management (AuM). However, soon investors began to call for index funds that traded like stocks on exchanges. It did not take long for the voices to be heard by leading investment participants.

At the same time as index mutual funds were gaining in popularity in the 1970s, so too was what has come to be known as portfolio trading or program trading. Under this trading method, an

entire portfolio of stocks could be created with a single-order structure. For example, in the United States a portfolio of all S&P 500
stocks would be created with a single order executed with a major
brokerage firm. Other indexes in the United States and around the
world were available for the same kind of trading. This is perhaps
the earliest and first step in the development of ETFs. But, of
course, it was only the tip of the iceberg, as history proves out.

In 1976 Professor Nils Hakansson published a paper titled "The
Purchasing Power Fund: A New Kind of Financial Intermediary" in
the November/December issue of *Financial Analysts Journal*. In the
article, Hakansson envisioned a new financial instrument consisting
of "Supershares," where the performance payoff equated to a pre-
specified level of market return. The underlying assets of the
Purchasing Power Fund promulgated in the article were index
funds—but clearly signaled an early-stage ETF design.

FLASHBACK TO THE 1980s: FOUNDATION OF ETFs IS BUILT

In the late 1980s, a company called Leland O'Brien Rubinstein
Associates (LOR), primarily known for developing portfolio insurance products, saw the writing on the wall for a simplified version
of the Purchasing Power Fund. After lining up large institutional
investors—such as the IBM pension fund—LOR designed what it
named a "SuperTrust" based on Hakansson's Supershares vision.
The design called for a basket of S&P 500 stocks available in one
trade—primarily to serve the needs of institutional investors.
LOR's innovation required a product where the underlying index
investment could (1) be listed and traded on a stock exchange (like
a closed-end fund) and (2) continuously offer and redeem shares
(like a mutual fund). Previous to this time, the Securities and
Exchange Commission (SEC) had authorized securities that could
be either open-ended or exchange-listed, but the SEC had never
granted permission for securities that could do both. This was an
obvious hurdle that needed to be resolved. The design called for
the fund to trade on an exchange similar to the way a closed-end
fund did, but without troubling premiums and discounts. To
resolve the issue, the plans directed large institutional investors to

arbitrage any market pricing divergences to net asset value. Problem solved—or at least on paper.

By the early 1980s, it was commonplace for large institutions to trade and own baskets of stocks that tracked indexes and to then turn around and trade futures contracts in those indexes. In the United States, the first officially recognized exchange-traded portfolio (ETP) was the Cash Index Participations (CIPs), an S&P 500 synthetic proxy launched in 1989 that traded on the Philadelphia Stock Exchange. The AMEX quickly thereafter launched a similar ETP called Index Participation Shares (IPSs). CIPs and IPSs traded based on a price that was a ratio of the underlying index. Although both products were very popular, they traded much like futures contracts; and before long, the powers-to-be took notice. Unfortunately, both ETPs were ordered shut down after a brief period of trading by a federal court in Chicago in response to a lawsuit filed by the Chicago Board of Trade (CBOT) that claimed the products were futures contracts and therefore must trade on a commodities exchange and not a stock exchange.

The end of the decade saw the first successful and sustainable launch of an ETP—in Canada. The Toronto Stock Exchange (TSE) established the Toronto Index Participation Shares (TIPS) to track the TSE-35, thus becoming the first stand-alone ETP tied to underlying securities and not derivatives. For this reason, TIPS is considered the first ETF in history. Much like ETFs of today, the underlying holdings of TIPS were actual shares of the index, or in this case the 35 companies constituting the TSE-35 Index. The fund became highly popular from the beginning for its favorable expense ratio and the ability of the trustee to loan out underlying stocks in the portfolio. HIPS (Toronto-100 Index Participations) was subsequently established by the TSE, which, in March 2000, merged the funds into a single, highly liquid TSE-60 fund (XIU) managed by Barclays Global Investors. Soon thereafter, the Toronto Stock Exchange exited the business, while State Street Global Advisors separately introduced its own ETF based on the Dow Jones Canada-40 index.

The popularity of these funds was noticed by the AMEX, which was developing its own ETF version that would satisfy SEC regulations. At the same time, LOR petitioned the SEC to grant the creation of an ETF as the underlying security for its SuperTrust. It was a difficult and expensive endeavor with no real insight into the outcome. As for the SuperTrust, LOR settled on the S&P 500 Index as the structure with the name "Index Trust SuperUnit."

FLASHBACK TO THE 1990s: ETFs GET NOTICED IN A BIG WAY

In 1990, the SEC issued the Investment Company Act Release No. 17809, the "SuperTrust Order," which granted LOR the right to create and file for an ETF—using specific exemptions from the Investment Company Act of 1940—thus enabling LOR to move forward with its plans. The release granted LOR exemptions from the rules regulating unit investment trusts (UITs) and exemptions to the SEC's rules and regulations governing investment companies, specifically how securities must be sold and exchanged. LOR filed for registration in 1990 and received regulatory approval nearly two years later—a long time to wait to launch its new innovation.

By the time the ETF from LOR was ready to launch, Nathan Most and Steven Bloom, executives with PDR Services, a subsidiary of the AMEX, were already at work petitioning the SEC to issue their own index-based ETF (benchmarked to the S&P 500). The application was approved as a UIT that same year (1992) by the SEC, paving the way for the January 1993 launch of the S&P Depository Receipts Trust Series 1, otherwise known as SDPRs or "Spiders" (symbol SPY) managed by State Street Global Advisors (SSgA). (Figure 2-2 lists approval dates for select ETFs, beginning with SPDRs.) In contrast to the Index Trust SuperUnit, the SPDR became very popular and soon enough became the first commercially successful ETF, with assets reaching $500 million within its first year of trading. For this reason, SPY is considered the first U.S.-listed ETF. AuM and trading volumes continued to increase significantly throughout the 1990s and gained substantial traction in the late 1990s. In fact, the S&P 500 SPDR, with net AuM of over $90 billion, has become the largest single share class equity or balanced portfolio product registered with the SEC.

The success of the SPDR S&P 500 ETF is attributed to a lower expense ratio than that of the Vanguard 500 Index mutual fund, a

FIGURE 2-2

SEC Approval Dates for Select ETFs

ETF	Order Granted
S&P Depository Receipts (SPDRs)	10/26/92
MidCap SPDRs	1/18/94
Country Baskets	3/5/96
WEBS	3/5/96
DIAMONDS	12/30/97
Select Sector SPDRs	11/13/98
QQQ	2/22/99
iShares	5/12/00
VIPERs	12/12/00

Source: Frush Financial Group

growing popularity of tax-efficient instruments, and an efficient market maker in regard to share creation and redemption. However, an often overlooked reason for its popularity is attributed to investment advisors who recommended the ETF as a way to stem the outflow of assets transferring to the Vanguard 500 Index mutual fund.

The idea for trading ETFs on the AMEX was promulgated as a way to bring new business and much needed new capital to the financially strapped AMEX. However, the process for launching the ETF was fraught with incredible regulatory pitfalls and hurdles. Nonetheless, the ETF was launched with terrific success and exposure—an accomplishment of both State Street Global Advisors and the AMEX. Due to their ease and flexibility, the first ETFs were structured as UITs. This structure was appealing, as it was less expensive, had no requirement to establish a pricey board of directors, possessed no cash drag, and finally provided the ability to loan out underlying stocks.

After resolving regulatory delays, LOR launched the SuperTrust and the Index Trust SuperUnit in 1993. Both funds offered advantages over other investment products, but the funds were too costly, had unreasonably high minimum investment requirements, and were too complex (they combined a trust and mutual fund structure together) for the vast majority of investors. As a result, LOR did not get the financial backing it had expected and the funds never traded actively. The trust was liquidated in 1996.

That same year, Morgan Stanley was experimenting on its own and launched an ETP lineup that it branded Optimized Portfolios As Listed Securities (OPALS). These ETPs were initially listed on the Luxembourg Stock Exchange in a move to capitalize on that country's less restrictive regulatory environment for issuing securities. OPALS were designed to reflect the different Morgan Stanley Capital International (MSCI) indexes—including the traditional S&P 500, FTSE 100, and Nikkei 225. Marketed primarily to institutional investors whose governments approve the offering, OPALS are a relatively obscure and little known ETP in the United States. OPALS resemble securities more than actual funds, thus the "ETP" reference.

In 1995, the SEC granted permission—again to the AMEX—to list an ETF very similar to the trailblazing S&P 500 ETF. The new Mid Cap SPDR ETF was thus launched to track the S&P Mid Cap 400 Index with management by Bank of New York. Unfortunately the new ETF debuted with an unforeseen design flaw that caused additional tax distributions to shareholders. It was not until 1999 that the flaw was finally fixed.

In the mid-1990s, Barclays Global Investors, then a subsidiary of Barclays PLC, and Morgan Stanley joined forces to design ETFs similar to OPALS intended for American investors to track international markets. Their industry-altering invention was the World Equity Benchmark Shares, or WEBS, subsequently renamed iShares MSCI Index Fund Shares. WEBS were designed to track MSCI country indexes—then numbering 17.

WEBS were highly unusual and revolutionary for three important reasons. First, WEBS gave casual investors a way to invest in foreign securities through a regulated stock exchange— the AMEX in this case—located in the United States and regulated under U.S. laws. Second, WEBS were innovative in their design whereby potential tax liabilities of shareholders were greatly reduced. SPDRs jumped on the innovation bandwagon as well and subsequently changed their structure to capitalize on the favorable tax design. Third, unlike SPDRs, which were organized as UITs,

WEBS were established as regulated investment companies (RICs), the first of their kind, under the Investment Company Act of 1940. The RIC structure provided a means to create multiple ETFs under the same umbrella, or series, thus reducing total costs for an entire family of ETFs. At the same time, the RIC structure gave ETF providers flexibility to modify their holdings to replicate an index, whereas a unit investment structure requires an ETF to purchase all stocks of an index and in the appropriate weights. This change in design was a deliberate decision by Morgan Stanley to leverage its experience with OPALS. Finally, WEBS also became the first fund permitted by the SEC to use the terms *index fund* and *ETF* together in the same marketing literature.

To compete with WEBS, the New York Stock Exchange, in partnership with Deutsche Bank, launched Country Baskets, with the aim of giving investors access to foreign securities with a single trade. Country Baskets covered nine countries (Australia, France, Germany, Hong Kong, Italy, Japan, South Africa, the United Kingdom, and the United States) while employing Financial Times (now FTSE) indexes. Due to various design flaws and a lack of commitment from newly hired top executives, Country Baskets failed in the marketplace, and the trust was liquidated in 1996. Country Baskets is considered the first ETF failure, thus earning it the nickname "Country Caskets." A list of closed ETFs can be found in Appendix C of this book.

The following two years saw the introduction of two widely successful ETFs. In 1997, the SEC approved the launch of the Dow Jones Industrial Average Index—popularly known as the Diamonds ETF—managed by State Street Global Advisors. Although the Diamonds ETF (symbol DIA) was structured as a UIT, the fund was designed to incorporate the tax benefits of the WEBS regulated investment company structure. The Diamonds ETF was subsequently launched in 1998 and became an instant hit with retail investors due partly to its strong name recognition and ease of tracking since every newspaper listed the price for the ETF daily. State Street Global Advisors was not done, and later that year it introduced the Select Sector SPDRs, which represent the nine economic sectors as recognized by Standard & Poor's. All nine of the new ETFs are benchmarked to the nine S&P 500 sectors and therefore comprise only stocks appearing in the S&P 500 Index. The nine sectors include consumer discretionary, consumer staples, energy, financial, health care, industrials, materials, technology, and utilities. Merrill Lynch provided product support to State Street in the development of the SPDRs, thus helping to expand the marketing force behind the ETFs. Select Sector SPDRs became the first successful ETFs with domestic stocks using a RIC structure.

In 1999, the SEC issued an order approving the Nasdaq-100 Trust, nicknamed "Cubes," using the rising popularity of the RIC structure. This ETF (symbol QQQ, originally QQQQ) was designed to replicate the movement of the Nasdaq-100 Index. Although the Cubes ETF is similar to the Diamonds ETF in structure, the Cubes ETF incorporates a modified capitalization-weighted index. This was done for policy reasons to ensure that the Cubes ETF itself is indirectly managed in a limited, but significant, way. The Cubes ETF gained quick acceptance in the marketplace and is now one of the most heavily traded securities—if not the top-traded one—in the world on a daily basis. In 2007, the fund was renamed PowerShares QQQ (along with the symbol change) after its provider.

Before the end of the decade, Barclays applied to the SEC for approval of nearly 50 ETFs, calling them "Exchange-Traded Funds." Using the RIC structure, Barclays petitioned the SEC to permit significant discretion in regard to managing the ETFs while still being able to call them index-based investments. The ETFs offered global exposure including that to the United States. All 50 ETFs were launched in one single day under the iShares brand. In consequence, this day marked a trend of blanketing the ETF marketplace with quantity instead of focusing on quality. Creating and capturing market share was now the overriding aim of ETF providers. Not to be outdone, Rydex filed for nearly 100 ETFs in one day and in the process set a new quantity record.

FLASHBACK TO THE 2000s: THE ETF REVOLUTION ENSUES

In 2000, Barclays Global Investors ratcheted up its emphasis on ETFs through a strong push on education and distribution to retail investors. As a result of this initiative, Barclays rolled out its iShares ETF product—officially launched in early 2000. Within five years iShare ETFs had amassed a substantial amount of AuM, thus surpassing the assets of any other ETF competitor in the world.

The year 2001 witnessed the launch of the Euro STOXX 50 market ETF. By the end of the following year, there were 246 domestic and foreign ETFs across the globe. The leading market was Europe with 106 ETFs (referred to as trackers), followed by the United States with 102. Asia (including Japan) and Canada boasted 24 and 14 ETFs, respectively. The year 2001 was also a significant year in that Vanguard entered the ETF marketplace with the introduction of its first ETF—the Vanguard Index Participation Equity Receipts (VIPERs), which is linked to its existing Total Stock Market Index Fund. The launch of the Vanguard ETF marked the first time in practice that an ETF and open-end fund (index mutual fund) were linked—an innovation that Vanguard even patented. The increased competition from Vanguard and its low-cost claim to fame helped push down expenses for many existing and newly issued ETFs.

Over the next several years Vanguard continued to introduce new ETFs linked to its index mutual funds. In 2002 it introduced its second ETF, the Vanguard Extended Market VIPERs, which tracks the performance of the Wilshire 4500 index. In 2006 Vanguard dropped the VIPERs name in preparation for the 2007 launch of fixed-income ETFs, which obviously cannot use "Equity Receipt" in their names.

In 2002, a former executive from Nuveen Investments, Bruce Bond, founded PowerShares. His goal was to introduce ETFs using custom quantitative indexes with the hope of generating superior performance, not just market returns. The market liked the new ETFs and plowed more than $1 billion in new assets into its ETFs by 2006, the year PowerShares, then the fifth largest ETF provider, was acquired by London-based mutual fund giant Amvescap. PowerShares retained its name and continues to be a major force in the ETF marketplace.

The first currency ETF was introduced in 2005 by Rydex Investments (now Rydex-SGI) under the name Euro Currency Trust, part of the CurrencyShares lineup. Additional currency ETFs under the CurrencyShares name were launched over the subsequent two years. In 2006, Deutsche Bank introduced the first commodities ETF, called the Deutsche Bank Commodity Index Tracking Fund. The fund isn't technically a true ETF because it is structured as a commodity pool rather than as a RIC or UIT. This ETF was unique in that it was the first time an ETF-like product employed derivatives to provide the needed exposure to commodities—namely, crude oil, heating oil, gold, aluminum, corn, and wheat.

Without much fanfare, the first actively managed ETF, Current Yield Fund (symbol YYY), was introduced by Bear Stearns in March 2008. Due to competition from the subsequent launch of the second actively managed ETF, Active Low Duration Fund (symbol PLK), by PowerShares, and the acquisition of Bear Stearns later that year, the Current Yield Fund never got off the ground and closed in October 2008. Nonetheless, 2008 was the birth of actively managed ETFs.

At the end of 2008, there were 747 U.S. ETFs with combined AuM of approximately $535 billion. The top three ETF providers—Barclays, Vanguard, and State Street Global Advisors—controlled an estimated 86 percent of the total assets combined. During 2008 there were 164 ETFs launched with 46 closings—both record numbers in their own right. Some providers, like Northern Trust, exited the ETF marketplace altogether in 2008 in the wake of the financial crisis. The year 2009 saw Barclays Global Investors sold to BlackRock.

2010 TO PRESENT: THE DECADE OF THE ACTIVELY MANAGED ETF BEGINS

According to the Investment Company Institute, at the end of 2010, there were 1,099 ETFs (technically exchange-traded products) in the United States with a combined $1 trillion in assets, which includes an asset inflow of $123 billion in 2010 alone.

ETFs GONE WILD: A LOOK AT NOTABLE CLOSINGS

With all the ETFs issued each year, there will be times when an ETF provider issues an ETF with a flaw, or has bad timing, or overestimates investor demand. Irrespective of the catalyst, we have seen numerous ETFs go down in flames, especially in the late 2000s. The following is a list of the most prominent failures to date in no particular order:

1. **Country Baskets:** Otherwise known as Country Caskets, this linkup of ETFs failed in 1996 due to lack of executive commitment and unforeseen design flaws. The fall of Country Baskets became the first official ETF closure.
2. **Current Yield Fund:** Launched by Bear Stearns, this ETF had no real chance given the eventual collapse and acquisition of Bear Stearns and significant competition from the second actively managed ETF issued shortly thereafter by PowerShares.
3. **HealthShares:** In March 2007, a firm called XShares launched a lineup of 19 ETFs targeting very specific niches in the health-care field. These ETFs ranged from HealthShares Orthopedic Repair to HealthShares Autoimmune-Inflammation. In August of the same year, XShares closed 15 of the ETFs and the remaining 4 by December 2008.
4. **NETS:** NETS was the brainchild of Northern Trust bank based in Chicago. NETS stands for Northern Exchange Traded Shares, a clever name in my opinion. A lineup of 17 ETFs was launched in 2008 to track international, single-country benchmarks but was closed the following year due to the "inability of the funds to attract significant market interest since their innovation." In 2011, Northern Trust filed a petition with the SEC "to create and operate an actively-managed series of the Trust . . . that offers exchange-traded shares." NETS has perhaps returned from the dead.
5. **Adelante Shares:** Launched by XShares in September 2007, these ETFs were designed to track specific segments of the U.S. real estate market. It was bad timing on XShares' part as real estate valuations, and REITs in general, were in the midst of a severe valuation decline. The seven ETFs failed to gain even modest amounts of assets—with only $4.5 million in the largest fund—and were therefore commercially unfeasible. The ETFs were closed in July 2008.
6. **SPA ETFs:** In 2007, SPA ETF Plc based in London introduced six ETFs that tracked the MarketGrader family of indexes. Unlike other custom indexes that were difficult

to track for shareholders, the MarketGrader indexes were widely followed and boasted an impressive history of outperformance. Nonetheless, the company closed all six of the ETFs in March 2009, citing that "current market conditions were unsuitable" for its long-term investment strategy. By the way, the stock market ironically bottomed in the same month the ETFs were closed.

7. **AmeriStock ETFs:** In June 2007, AmeriStock introduced five Treasury bond ETFs. Given stiff competition from the likes of Vanguard, iShares, and PIMCO, all five of the ETFs were closed in July 2008, marking the first major closure of U.S.-listed bond ETFs.

8. **Lehman Opta ETNs:** Launched in February 2008, the Opta lineup of exchange-traded notes featured both commodity and private equity funds. However, as we all know, in late 2008 Lehman became insolvent as a result of a freeze in credit lending and subsequently collapsed— and thereby helping to make the financial crisis even worse. The ETNs were delisted in October 2008, with Barclays declining to absorb the lineup when it acquired much of Lehman's assets during bankruptcy.

9. **FocusShares ETFs:** In December 2007, FocusShares launched four ETFs with each tracking various segments, such as home builders and homeland security. With only $17 million in new assets within nine months after the introductions, FocusShares terminated its lineup. In early 2011, FocusShares rejoined the ETF marketplace and launched 15 ETFs focused on various sectors and styles in the U.S. equity universe, including the Focus Morningstar U.S. Market Index ETF (symbol FMU) with a 0.05 percent expense ratio, cheaper than both comparable Vanguard and Schwab ETFs.

10. **Rydex ETFs:** In 2010, Rydex-SGI closed a dozen leveraged and inverse ETFs as a result of minimal assets under management. The most probable explanation was the stiff competition from other ETF providers of leveraged and inverse funds, namely ProFunds and Direxion, the latter of which closed two ETFs itself in 2010.

## CHAPTER 3

Advantages and Drawbacks: Making the Case for ETFs

Understanding the differences between exchange-traded funds (ETFs) and their chief competitors is essential to understanding why investing in ETFs is so beneficial. This chapter will build on the defining attributes discussed in Chapter 1 by providing both the advantages and drawbacks of ETFs. A true discussion on making comparisons needs to showcase the drawbacks—which are few but noteworthy nonetheless. The chapter is divided into five major areas—shown in Figure 3-1—with each comprising multiple characteristics.

PORTFOLIO MANAGEMENT

In this section we will compare and contrast key characteristics related to portfolio management, specifically built-in diversification, built-in market exposure, degree of turnover, existence of tracking error, performance objective, consistency of management, size drag risk, dividend drag, potential conflicts of interest, and being fully invested.

FIGURE 3-1

Comparisons of Characteristics

| Characteristics | Priority | ETFs | | Mutual Funds | | Stocks |
		Passive	Active	Passive	Active	Portfolio
▶ *Portfolio Management*						
Built-In Diversification	High	Yes	Yes	Yes	Yes	Maybe
Built-In Market Exposure	High	Yes	Maybe	Yes	Maybe	No
Degree of Turnover	High	Low	Medium	Low	Medium	Depends
Existence of Tracking Error	High	Yes	No	Yes	No	No
Performance Objective	High	Beta	Alpha	Beta	Alpha	Alpha
Consistency of Management	High	Yes	Maybe	Yes	Maybe	Maybe
Size Drag Risk	High	Low	Medium	Low	High	Low
Dividend Drag	Medium	Maybe	Maybe	No	No	No
Potential Conflicts of Interest	Medium	Low	Medium	Low	High	Medium
Fully Invested	Medium	Yes	Yes	No	No	Maybe
▶ *Transparency*						
Disclosure of Holdings	High	Favorable	Favorable	Favorable	Unfavorable	Favorable
Disclosure of Costs	High	Favorable	Adequate	Favorable	Adequate	Favorable
Disclosure of Trades	High	Unfavorable	Favorable	Unfavorable	Favorable	Favorable
▶ *Cost-Effectiveness*						
Expense Ratios	High	Very Low	Low	Low	High	Depends
Purchase and Sale Loads	High	No	No	No	Depends	No
Capital Gains Distributions	High	Very Low	Low	Low	High	None

Bid-Ask Spread Costs	High	Yes	Yes	No	No	Yes
Subsidy Trading Costs	High	No	No	Yes	Yes	No
Trading Commissions	Medium	Yes	Yes	Typically None	Typically None	Yes
Early Redemption Fees	Medium	No	No	Maybe	Maybe	No
▶ *Shareholder Interests*						
No. of Choices Available	Medium	Moderate	Low	High	High	High
Call and Put Options Availability	Medium	Yes	Yes	No	No	Yes
Ease of Rebalancing	Medium	Yes	Yes	Yes	Yes	No
Tax-Loss Management	Medium	Yes	Yes	No	No	Yes
Trade Settlement	Medium	3 Days	3 Days	1 Day	1 Day	3 Days
Systematic Investments	Medium	OK	OK	Favorable	Favorable	OK
Minimum Investment	Low	No	No	Yes	No	No
Availability of Prospectus	Low	Yes	Yes	Yes	No	No
Transaction Method	Low	Broker	Broker	Broker or Fund	Broker or Fund	Broker
▶ *Trading Flexibility*						
Intraday Pricing	High	Yes	Yes	No	No	Yes
Intraday Trade Executions	High	Yes	Yes	No	No	Yes
Order-Type Discretion	Medium	Yes	Yes	No	No	Yes
Availability of Margin	Low	Yes	Yes	No	No	Yes
Ability to Sell Short	Low	Yes	Yes	No	No	Yes

Source: Frush Financial Group

Built-In Diversification

ETFs may trade like stocks, but they resemble mutual funds in many more ways than they do stocks. The most important resemblance is their highly diversified nature. By combining dozens or even hundreds of stocks into one investment (the Vanguard Small-Cap ETF has over 1,700 underlying stocks, for example), an ETF provides an incredibly diversified investment within its particular market segment. As a result, an ETF minimizes investment-specific risk associated with a single stock held in the fund. This advantage is important since it safeguards your portfolio from significant losses attributed to investment-specific events—such as mismanagement by a company's CEO (e.g., Enron), at-fault environmental disasters (e.g., BP), or default in a municipal bond from a single municipality. (Figure 3-2 shows the benefits of portfolio diversification.)

Research clearly demonstrates that diversification benefits begin to occur when a portfolio holds 15 to 20 stocks. However, for best results, the stocks need to be of similar nature and within a

FIGURE 3-2

Benefits of Portfolio Diversification

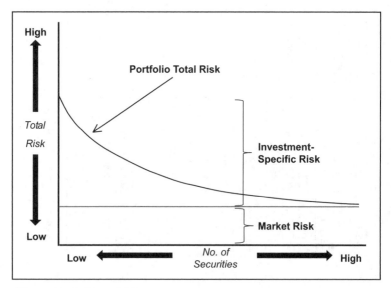

Source: Frush Financial Group

similar market segment. Holding stocks in different industries does not provide the same level of benefit as does holding multiple stocks in the same industry. ETFs by nature follow this approach. Holding stocks in the same industry should not be a concern at this level if proper asset allocation is followed. Asset allocation and diversification are not the same thing—both strategies should be pursued for maximum results.

Built-In Market Exposure

As with mutual funds, ETFs provide investors with a means to gain instant exposure to a desired asset class or market segment. By simply purchasing one ETF, an investor is able to gain proportional ownership in each one of the underlying holdings, which can be in the hundreds to thousands of stocks. If you were to build a portfolio of individual stocks, it would take multiple stocks—and the time it takes to purchase them—to gain material exposure to a particular market segment. For example, purchasing IBM and Google does not assure you of appropriate exposure to the technology sector. However, an ETF that comprises both IBM and Google, as well as dozens of additional technology stocks, will provide the exposure you desire.

Many portfolio managers who build portfolios with individual stocks use ETFs to gain exposure quickly and easily to specific market segments. For example, if a certain portfolio manager believes the Wednesday crude oil inventory report will show much lower inventories than expected, then she can purchase the XLE (Energy Select Sector SPDR) in the hope of generating incremental gains without needing to research and purchase various individual energy-related stocks.

Degree of Turnover

Turnover measures how often the composition or underlying investments in a fund are purchased and sold during the year. Turnover creates capital gains tax liabilities when investments with built-up unrealized gains are sold and passed through to shareholders. Thus, high-turnover funds will typically sock you with a capital gains tax bill versus a fund with low turnover. Low turnover does not mean you will earn a higher return on your investment; it simply means that—all else being equal—it is generally more advantageous to invest in a fund with low turnover than a fund with high turnover to avoid the tax man. Passively managed ETFs and index mutual funds have much lower turnover than actively managed ETFs and like-minded mutual funds. Thus, for investors looking to avoid capital gains taxes via pass-through distributions, actively managed funds are not the ideal fit.

Existence of Tracking Error

Tracking error is defined as the difference in returns between a fund and the index the fund is attempting to track. Any such divergence between the two is quantified and reported as tracking error. The best funds have low tracking error, while high tracking error is considered a potential performance penalty. When shareholders invest in a fund, they should get what they pay for. If the fund the investors purchased has unusually large tracking error, then the investors are not exactly getting what they thought they would. Stock portfolios do not have tracking error since they do not attempt to replicate an index, but index mutual funds and passively managed ETFs will have tracking error. Thus, before investing in either fund, investigate the tracking error and compare and contrast with both its peer funds and other funds you are considering. The difference in tracking error from ETF to ETF and from ETF to mutual fund is typically quite small. There are bigger fish to fry (e.g., expense ratios), so to speak.

Performance Objective

When you pay higher costs to a portfolio manager to generate alpha (outperformance), you expect to get what you pay for—or at least most of the time. However, when less than half of portfolio managers beat their benchmark, it makes you wonder what you are paying for. Not to fear, as ETFs earn their respective market return (beta)—and at a much lower cost. When a benchmark is known and can be easily replicated (e.g., S&P 500), then by definition an S&P 500 ETF should generate the same return. Any difference between the underlying index and the ETF is a result of tracking error. As previously mentioned, the preferred ETFs have the smallest margin of tracking error.

When you invest in a passively managed ETF, you are essentially saying that you want to earn the benchmark return, nothing more and nothing less. Yes, you could have the opportunity to earn a higher return in an actively managed mutual fund, but there are no certainties that outperformance would happen (see Figure 3-3). The only certainties you have with mutual funds are higher costs, less favorable tax treatment, less transparency, less than full investment, etc. Of course, outperformance can help you forget the bad stuff, but the odds are not in your favor that outperformance will happen and will happen consistently over time.

FIGURE 3-3

Active versus Passive Performance

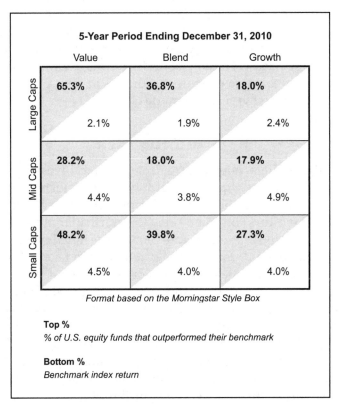

5-Year Period Ending December 31, 2010		
Value	Blend	Growth
65.3%	**36.8%**	**18.0%**
2.1%	1.9%	2.4%
28.2%	**18.0%**	**17.9%**
4.4%	3.8%	4.9%
48.2%	**39.8%**	**27.3%**
4.5%	4.0%	4.0%

Large Caps / Mid Caps / Small Caps

Format based on the Morningstar Style Box

Top %
% of U.S. equity funds that outperformed their benchmark

Bottom %
Benchmark index return

Source: Standard & Poor's Index Versus Active (SPIVA), 2011

Consistency of Management

Have you ever heard the term *style drift* before? It refers to the tendency of a portfolio manager to deviate from his or her fund's specific strategy or objective. For example, a portfolio manager running a large-cap mutual fund might include some mid-cap stocks. I trust this is done with the best intentions—to make shareholders money—but decisions to alter an objective should be done on the individual portfolio level by investors and not on the fund level by portfolio managers. Investors are best able to design and rebalance their portfolios to meet their needs and objectives rather than defer this work to someone they have never seen, talked to, or perhaps even heard of before.

Style drift is more common than you might think. No, it doesn't happen all the time, nor does it happen to a significant degree when it does happen. ETFs, on the other hand, offer a steadfast management style. This is because ETFs do not have portfolio managers that can make ad hoc decisions; instead ETFs track known indexes using computers. When building a portfolio of multiple asset classes, having confidence that your investments are what they say they are provides assurance in your portfolio and its ability to achieve the results you desire.

Size Drag Risk

One of the primary nonexpense drawbacks to investing in mutual funds is the potential problem of having too much money in the fund and not being able to invest it properly. Over time, as more and more investors commit money to a particular mutual fund, the fund becomes too big to generate the returns it had produced when it was smaller and more nimble and could take advantage of investable opportunities with greater ease. One of the best examples of this dilemma is the Magellan Fund from Fidelity Investments. Managed by legendary money manager Peter Lynch, this fund generated strong performance when fund assets were at a manageable level. Once investors began to recognize the strong returns the fund was generating, they began to invest in Magellan at increasing rates to get in on the action. Many financial experts say these capital inflows were too much for the fund to handle, and the returns the investors were accustomed to earning were no longer being generated.

Why does this occur? The funds get too large and cannot put the money to work in the same manner or under the same strategy they had traditionally done. That is not to say that the opportunities themselves disappeared completely, just that the opportunities are only so large and even a modest investment from a titanic fund will exploit that opportunity fully. Actively managed ETFs can run into the same issue if they too become too large for their own good. Passively managed ETFs and index mutual funds are much less susceptible to this inherent flaw.

Dividend Drag

Dividend drag refers to the implicit cost some ETFs incur as a result of the Securities and Exchange Commission (SEC) rules stipulating that certain ETFs cannot immediately reinvest back into the portfolio the dividends paid by companies held in the fund. Instead, some ETFs must accumulate the dividends in a cash reserve account and pay them to shareholders at periodic intervals—typically quarterly. This requirement differs for mutual funds, as they can reinvest dividends immediately. When the market is doing well, dividends are better served being reinvested rather than held back until paid out on specific dates. This creates a penalty for ETFs that cannot reinvest dividends and ultimately leads to a drag on performance that otherwise would not have occurred had dividends been reinvested at the time of payment.

Potential Conflicts of Interest

Passively managed ETFs and index mutual funds by definition track known market indexes. As a result, no portfolio manager calls the shots about how the assets in a fund should be managed. This alone ensures very low chances of conflicts of interest occurring. The same cannot be said for actively managed ETFs and mutual funds, as they are run by a team of portfolio managers and research analysts—together with a support staff. This mere difference opens actively managed funds to greater chances of conflicts of interest.

For instance, if a mutual fund family is owned by a much larger asset management firm that also has its own investment banking group, then there is the potential to leverage assets in the mutual fund to support the activities—such as launching initial public offerings (IPOs) or voting in favor of mergers—of the investment banking group. Another conflict of interest includes taking chances on high-risk and high-return potential stocks intra quarter in the hope of enhancing returns without needing to report the securities as holdings since they were purchased and sold between quarterly reporting periods. This is commonly known as window dressing and is quite prevalent in the asset management field.

Fully Invested

If you were to build a portfolio of 60 percent equities and 40 percent fixed income and later discovered that many of your equity mutual funds hold 10 percent cash, you might not be too happy since that means that your actual portfolio allocation is closer to 54/46 percent equities to fixed income, respectively. Due to the need for cash to satisfy shareholder liquidations, mutual funds must allocate part of their holdings to cash. Portfolio managers do not like having to liquidate underlying holdings to satisfy shareholder redemptions. In addition, mutual funds hold cash either because portfolio managers choose to do so for tactical investment reasons or because the fund recently experienced a higher inflow of shareholder capital that has not been invested as of yet. Irrespective of the reason why, mutual funds will always have a portion of their assets invested in cash and cash equivalents.

So why is having more cash not exactly ideal for investors? There are two reasons—one relevant to the fund level and one to the portfolio level. First, mutual funds with cash inherently create a proportionate "cash drag" on performance. When a fund is fully invested, the entire fund will change in proportion to the change in value of the underlying securities—whether up or down. However, if a fund holds 10 percent cash, then only 90 percent of the fund will benefit if the underlying securities rise in value. The second reason why holding more cash is a negative is that it impacts your asset allocation. As previously mentioned, when you build a portfolio, you want your holdings to adhere to your design. If your holdings do vary, then your actual portfolio allocation will differ from your designed allocation. This will result in underweighting equities and overweighting fixed income. The consequence, of course, is lower expected returns over time.

ETFs are different in that they do not have, nor need, to hold a cash position. Cash is not needed to satisfy shareholder redemptions, and cash is not needed to track an underlying index, given that indexes by definition comprise all equities, all bonds, all REITs, all commodities, etc. Indexes do not have a pure cash position. As a result, ETFs are fully invested by nature—and that's a very good thing for investors. If you want to hold more cash, then rebalance your asset mix. Don't let a mutual fund dictate the decision for you.

TRANSPARENCY

In this section we will compare and contrast key characteristics related to transparency, specifically the disclosure of underlying holdings, disclosure of costs, and disclosure of trades executed.

Disclosure of Holdings

What you see is what you get. When you invest in an ETF, you know what you are getting (i.e., the underlying holdings). Take the Vanguard Small-Cap ETF. This fund holds over 1,700 individual common stocks. If you want to know the names of each company, you can find this information; it's not hidden in some black box. ETFs publish their holdings on a daily basis, whereas most mutual funds only need to disclose the same information on a quarterly basis—and with a 60-day lag (used to hide trading strategies until they have been executed). Furthermore, if a revision is made to the underlying tracking index, then you know a change to the ETF will be made. This level of information is not available with mutual funds. Another nice benefit is that the high level of transparency discourages dishonesty on the part of ETF providers and index mutual fund companies. I'm not so naive to think that knowing the holdings of an ETF will improve its performance (sometimes it actually hurts performance), but it sure does provide comfort in knowing that you are getting what you want.

Disclosure of Costs

Understanding the full costs associated with an investment is vital when comparing and contrasting ETFs, mutual funds, and stocks for possible investment in your portfolio. By far, stocks are the most cost effective since there are little ancillary costs with building a portfolio comprising all stocks—assuming trading commissions are comparable. Of course, an investment management fee similar to an expense ratio is typically charged by investment firms to design, build, and manage such a portfolio, and so differences in cost structure will emerge. Mutual funds and ETFs have additional fees, arising from their pooling of securities and related activities. For the most part, mutual funds and ETFs report costs that are fairly the same. Actively managed funds will have additional costs that are at times not easily identified, such as soft-dollar costs. As such, actively managed funds are given an adequate rating, whereas passively managed funds and stocks are given a favorable rating.

Disclosure of Trades

Trading transparency usually results in higher costs for shareholders of passively managed funds. Portfolios comprising all stocks typically have no expense associated with trading transparency, given the inherent nature of nonstandardized stock portfolios. However, passively managed ETFs and index mutual funds are exposed to higher costs as a result of the transparency of the underlying indexes they track. When an index sponsor preannounces composition changes to a market index, then scalpers can front-run any rebalancing conducted by an ETF or index mutual fund by purchasing the security being added to the index and selling the security being removed to take advantage of any predictable changes in security prices. These front-running transactions will drive up costs for passively managed funds that need to make changes to track the underlying market index. These arbitragelike profits come at the expense of shareholders. Actively managed

ETFs and mutual funds do not track well-known market indexes and therefore do not have the same issue. This implicit expense is unique to passively managed funds.

COST-EFFECTIVENESS

In this section we will compare and contrast key characteristics related to cost-effectiveness of an investment, specifically the expense ratios (or investment management fees), purchase and sale loads, capital gains distributions, bid-ask spread costs, subsidy trading costs, trading commissions, and early redemption fees.

Expense Ratios

Compared with mutual funds, ETFs are significantly more cost effective—especially as measured by the expense ratio. This expense is assessed on a pro rata basis each trading day and is used to pay for fund-level expenses such as operating costs and index sponsor royalty fees. Even though the difference in expense ratio between a mutual fund and a comparable ETF may seem trivial, always keep in mind that small annual differences in expenses can add up to big money over many years (see Figure 3-4).

Why the difference in expense ratios between mutual funds and ETFs? Most mutual funds are actively managed—meaning a portfolio manager and back-office team of professionals run the fund and make buy and sell decisions as they see fit. Having a staff and related research budget is not cheap. As a result, mutual funds must charge higher fees to ensure they cover their underlying operating and marketing costs. With most ETFs, there are neither high-priced portfolio managers nor research analysts. The stock or bond holdings are tied to known indexes that can be easily replicated by sophisticated computers. In doing so, the underlying holdings are adjusted when there are revisions to the index, which is infrequent. Less frequent buying and selling means corresponding lower trading costs.

In the early 2000s, a research study of equity mutual funds by Morningstar concluded that lower-expense funds outperformed higher-expense funds for the five-year period ending December 31,

FIGURE 3-4

Impact of 1 Percent Extra Costs on Portfolio Value

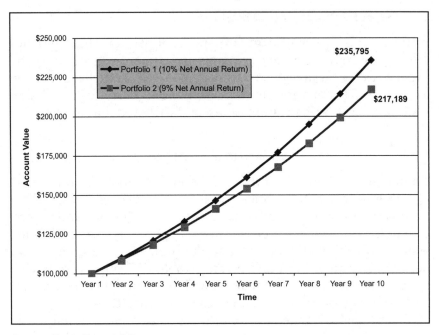

Source: Frush Financial Group

2001. Lower expenses and better performance sound good to this investor. In addition, lower expenses with ETFs create a ripple effect (a good thing in this case) with other investment products (specifically index and actively managed mutual funds), thus helping to drive down internal expenses across the board.

Low expense is a common theme for ETFs that track market indexes. (Figure 3-5 lists a dozen ETFs with very low expense ratios.) However, ETFs that track custom indexes tend to charge higher expenses, but still less than what a comparable actively managed mutual fund typically charges. Index mutual funds do charge lower expense ratios than actively managed mutual funds, but are still higher than comparable ETFs.

FIGURE 3-5

ETFs with Very Low Expense Ratios

ETF	Symbol	Expense Ratio	Category
Vanguard S&P 500 ETF	VOO	0.06%	Large-Cap Blend Equities
Schwab U.S. Broad Market ETF	SCHB	0.06%	All Cap Equities
Vanguard Total Stock Market ETF	VTI	0.07%	All Cap Equities
Schwab U.S. Large-Cap ETF	SCHX	0.08%	Large-Cap Blend Equities
SPDR S&P 500	SPY	0.09%	Large-Cap Blend Equities
iShares S&P 500 Index Fund	IVV	0.09%	Large-Cap Blend Equities
PIMCO 1-3 Year US Treasury Index Fund	TUZ	0.09%	Government Bonds
Intermediate-Term U.S. Treasury ETF	SCHR	0.12%	Government Bonds
SPDR Barclays Shrt Trm Corp Bond ETF	SCPB	0.12%	Corporate Bonds
Wilshire 5000 Total Market ETF	WFVK	0.12%	All Cap Equities
Russell 1000 ETF	VONE	0.12%	Large-Cap Blend Equities
Vanguard Total Bond Market ETF	BND	0.12%	Total Bond Market

Source: Frush Financial Group

Purchase and Sale Loads

In regard to fees and expenses, mutual funds can be divided into two camps—load funds and no-load funds. When shareholders purchase shares of a load mutual fund, they will incur a large up-front sales commission somewhere in the range of 2 to 5 percent of the initial investment. Load commissions are charged for the sole reason of compensating investment professionals for selling the mutual fund. In contrast, no-load mutual funds charge no up-front sales commissions and thus are far more cost effective for share-holders from this perspective. Furthermore, most no-load mutual funds even charge lower expense ratios than comparable loaded mutual funds.

Investors are not exposed to loads when purchasing ETFs or stocks. Although typical trading commissions are incurred, the loads charged by some mutual funds are avoided with ETFs. As a result, ETFs and stocks have an advantage over loaded mutual funds, all else being equal.

Capital Gains Distributions

Another significant advantage ETFs have over mutual funds is their highly favorable tax treatment. Taxes on realized capital gains can have a significant impact on a shareholder's portfolio and resulting performance. All else being equal, it is better to defer taxes to future years instead of paying them in today's dollars for the following two reasons:

1. The present value of $1 is worth more than the future value of $1 due to inflation.
2. There is a compounding effect on returns based on money otherwise not paid in taxes.

Mutual funds are notorious for their poor tax efficiency. Mutual fund shareholders are exposed to capital gains in one of two ways. First, when a shareholder sells either all or a portion of her full mutual fund position—and at a gain—then she is responsible for capital gains on the difference between the sales price and the cost basis. Thus, if you sell a position for $125,000 with a cost basis of $90,000, you will be required to pay taxes on the gain of $35,000. This kind of exposure is the same for ETF shareholders, but the second way is not.

The second way shareholders of mutual funds are exposed to capital gains occurs when the mutual funds pass through fund-level capital gains to their shareholders at the end of the year. During the course of the year, mutual funds purchase and sell securities in their funds. If a mutual fund sells a position with an unrealized gain, then capital gains must be distributed to the shareholders.

Mutual funds are required to make distributions of capital gains and losses since mutual funds are considered pass-through pooled investments. If a mutual fund were not to distribute capital gains, then the mutual fund itself would be responsible for footing the tax bill. Mutual funds make these distributions at the end of the year—typically in December—to shareholders of record as of a certain date prior to the distribution date. At tax time, shareholders will have to pay taxes to Uncle Sam, thus reducing their investment performance.

Nearly all mutual funds attempt to minimize capital gains distributions by either offsetting capital gains against capital losses or transferring securities with unrealized gains to another mutual fund within the same fund family rather than selling it outright. Transferring accomplishes the goal of eliminating the position from the mutual fund without selling it and incurring a capital gains tax liability. When shareholders receive capital gains distributions, they receive them in cash—much like a stock dividend—and have the option to reinvest in the fund. The price for the mutual fund adjusts for the cash distributed; thus there is no arbitrage opportunity for shareholders to purchase the fund simply to obtain the cash distribution and then turn around and sell the fund.

Building up capital gains and then distributing them to shareholders rarely happens with ETFs, given their tax-friendly structure. Tax deferral with an ETF is a natural result of Subchapter M of the Internal Revenue Code, which permits fund redemptions in kind without triggering a taxable event inside the fund. During the redemption process, an authorized participant (AP) will receive the lowest-cost lots of a security, while the higher-cost lots are retained by the ETF. Therefore, the distribution of capital gains to shareholders is very uncommon.

In addition to the negative consequence of recognizing capital gains, built-up unrealized capital gains on the fund level can also pose a serious problem, specifically its influence on the behavior of mutual fund portfolio managers. This problem can create a situation that adversely impacts tax-exempt investors and puts them at a disadvantage compared with taxable investors. For instance, if a mutual fund has a sizable built-up unrealized gain, then the portfolio manager may decide not to sell a security to avoid recognizing capital gains even though the security is considered fairly valued and deserving of being liquidated and the proceeds reinvested elsewhere.

Bid-Ask Spread Costs

Bid-ask spreads represent the difference between the purchase price (ask) and the selling price (bid or offer). Given their tradability on stock exchanges, all ETFs by nature trade with bid-ask spreads. As a result, one-half of the bid-ask spread is a cost to the buyer when an ETF is purchased, and one-half of the bid-ask spread is a cost to the seller when an ETF is sold. The same goes for stocks, as they also trade on exchanges. For the most part, bid-ask spreads are quite small, and they are completely transparent. Nonetheless, they are considered a trading cost that mutual fund shareholders do not pay when they purchase or sell shares of a fund at the net asset value (NAV). This is a distinct, but somewhat limited, benefit of mutual funds over ETFs.

Subsidy Trading Costs

When a shareholder purchases or sells shares in a mutual fund, then that shareholder expects to pay a fair share of the transaction costs. However, most shareholders in mutual funds do not just pay for themselves; they also pay for the transactions of other shareholders. Yes, that is correct. Existing shareholders compensate others out of their own pockets for the trades of others. In practice, this cost is referred to as flow cost, but we will refer to it as subsidy trading cost since it is more descriptive.

When an ETF shareholder sells his or her shares, then that shareholder picks up the trading tab. However, when a mutual fund shareholder sells his or her shares, the trade is executed at the NAV for the day without regard for the costs to sell underlying holdings to generate the cash proceeds. Depending on the situation, the mutual fund will execute the needed transactions the following day—together with those to satisfy other liquidating shareholders—thus assessing trading fees on all but the shareholder that just liquidated his or her position. When a shareholder transacts shares of an ETF, that shareholder only pays his or her own cost of entry or exit—the shareholder is insulated from events generated by other shareholders in the fund. In contrast, a shareholder of a mutual fund will pay a pro rata share of the entry and exit costs of all fund buyers and sellers for as long as he or she is invested in that mutual fund.

In 2007, a study by Roger Edelen, Richard Evans, and Gregory Kadlec found that subsidy trading costs amounted to approximately 0.75 percent annually. Furthermore, the same researchers determined that fund-level transaction costs for a mutual fund equal or exceed the expense ratio of the fund itself. They also found a stronger negative correlation between a mutual fund's trading costs and its performance than between the fund's expense ratio and performance.

When mutual fund shareholders redeem shares, the proceeds of their fund liquidations are paid directly by the mutual fund company. If the fund company must raise cash to satisfy shareholder redemptions, cash will be generated by the sale of underlying securities. If the mutual fund company realizes a capital gain on these sales, the capital gain is passed through to the shareholders. Thus, the actions of other shareholders may result in your tax liability.

Under normal circumstances, it's the AP who picks up the tab for trading and passes those costs on a pro rata basis to individual shareholders when the shares are traded. Through the in-kind creation and redemption process of ETF shares, most ETFs eliminate subsidy trading costs completely for existing shareholders. Not having to pay subsidy trading costs is a protection for shareholders and one of the top advantages of ETFs over mutual funds.

Because ETF shareholders do not have to pay subsidy trading costs for other shareholders, the performance realized by an ETF shareholder should, over time, be significantly higher than the performance realized by a shareholder in an otherwise comparable mutual fund, whether actively or passively managed. Additionally, one of the indirect benefits of not having subsidy trading costs is a fully invested ETF.

Finally, given that ETF shareholders do not pay subsidy trading costs—and contrary to popular misconception—ETFs (both passively managed and actively managed) are much better suited for shareholders who want to invest for the long term and do not want to trade and market-time their investments. This is true even though ETFs possess stocklike tradability, which tricks people into thinking ETFs make better sense for traders rather than investors. In contrast, mutual funds are better matched for those shareholders who like to time their investments.

Trading Commissions

When an investor purchases or sells shares of stock or when a shareholder purchases or sells shares of an ETF, a trading commission is typically charged by the executing brokerage firm. Commissions can range from a few dollars to many hundreds of dollars, depending on the firm that executed the trade. Some discount brokerage firms now offer commission-free trades on select ETFs, and so this cost can be minimized or eliminated altogether. When mutual fund transactions are executed with the associated mutual fund family, there are no trading commissions. However, many brokerage firms now charge commissions on mutual fund trades. I have witnessed one firm charge $25 per trade for the liquidation of a loaded mutual fund and $125 for the purchase or sale of a no-load mutual fund. As a result, be selective about where you place your orders. Nonetheless, mutual funds boast an advantage over ETFs and stocks with regard to trading commissions.

Early Redemption Fees

Depending on the mutual fund, a shareholder may be exposed to fees if he or she sells a mutual fund prior to a certain date. The most common situation is associated with Class B mutual funds. The typical Class B mutual fund uses a five-year surrender schedule whereby if a shareholder liquidates shares (either partially or fully), then he or she will incur early redemption fees or commissions. Fortunately, Class B mutual funds are on their way out, a consequence of the intense scrutiny by the SEC. Nonetheless, some brokerage firms still allow the purchase of Class B funds, and so the elimination will take a little more time.

In addition to Class B shares, most Class C mutual funds also charge early redemption fees if a shareholder liquidates within the first year. Also, some specialized mutual funds that hold less liquid securities assess early redemption fees if a shareholder liquidates within the first 30 days. ETFs and stocks do not charge early redemption fees.

SHAREHOLDER INTERESTS

In this section we will compare and contrast key characteristics related to shareholder (investor) interests, specifically the number of choices available for certain investments, call and put options availability, ease of rebalancing, tax-loss management, trade settlement, systematic investments, minimum investment amount, availability of a prospectus, and transaction method.

Number of Choices Available

Stocks and mutual funds have been around far longer than ETFs. As a result, the number of available investing options is significantly larger with mutual funds and stocks—a benefit to these shareholders. ETFs have only been around for a couple of decades, with most of the popularity gained in the last 12 years or so. Nonetheless, more than 1,100 ETFs are available to shareholders, with more than 800 in registration with the SEC. Many of the ETFs in registration will never become listed products, but the sheer number of ETFs in registration signals a growing list of ETFs over the next few years. In the year 2010 alone, more than 100 new ETFs hit the market.

Call and Put Options Availability

Calls and puts provide investors with the means to either produce incremental revenue or safeguard a portfolio against declining market prices and thus falling portfolio values. For example, writing (selling) covered call options provides the seller with incremental income in the form of premiums collected. Using a strike price above the current market price of an ETF will provide for not only the income collected on premiums, but also gains from the appreciation of the ETF up to the strike price. Additionally, purchasing a put option provides insurance against the market price of the ETF falling below the put strike price. ETFs and stocks typically have call and put options assigned to them, whereas mutual funds never do. Most investors do not get involved with options, but having the opportunity is always better than not.

Ease of Rebalancing

Identifying an ideal asset allocation and selecting the appropriate investments to build out the asset mix is only half the battle. The other half—arguably more important—is rebalancing and reallocating the asset allocation in response to changes in underlying investment values over time. ETFs are by far the most investor-friendly for rebalancing a portfolio. With a few simple trades, an entire portfolio can be rebalanced quickly and easily. Mutual funds require more effort since investors do not know with confidence what they will purchase and sell their funds for at the end of the day. A mutual fund shareholder can get close, but an ETF shareholder can get even closer with his or her calculation. Stock investors go through the same process as ETF shareholders, but the process is extremely cumbersome because of the significant number of stocks needed in a portfolio to achieve suitable diversification.

Tax-Loss Management

This characteristic refers to the discretion investors have in managing unrealized gains and losses in a portfolio to deliver an optimal tax result. For example, if an investor has a capital gains tax liability in his or her portfolio, then that investor could sell one or more investments with capital losses to offset and perhaps eliminate the capital gains tax liability. Shareholders of ETFs and investors of stocks have much greater flexibility than mutual fund shareholders do in making tax-loss management decisions. Mutual fund shareholders do have the ability to manage their holdings in this regard as well, but the clear advantage goes to ETFs and stocks for their ability to be executed intraday with knowledge of appropriate prior execution price.

Trade Settlement

Trade settlement refers to the process by which securities or interests in securities are delivered—typically against payment—to fulfill contractual obligations arising under securities trades. In layperson lingo, trade settlement is the number of days before full payment for a purchase is required to be made or the time before the full proceeds of a securities sale are delivered to the selling investor. With ETFs and stocks, the settlement period is three business days after the trade date. In practice this is called T+3 to represent the trade date and the subsequent three business days to settlement. When I started in this business in the early 1990s, settlement was referred to as T+7, meaning trades took a crazy seven business days to settle. In contrast, mutual funds employ a T+1 settlement period. Thus, a shareholder can have access to his or her funds in only one day rather than waiting three days with stocks and ETFs. This, of course, favors mutual funds.

Systematic Investments

The term *systematic investments* (also called dollar cost averaging and systematic purchase agreements) refers to programs established by investment firms to allow shareholders the ability to make periodic investments into a held fund or funds from a bank or related account. Systematic investing is popular with investors—particularly mutual fund shareholders—whereby a certain amount of money is electronically withdrawn from a shareholder's checking account and invested in more shares of an existing mutual fund or funds. However, it is difficult (and potentially expensive) to establish a systematic purchase agreement into an ETF or stock portfolio, as each security purchase is potentially subject to brokerage trading commissions, thus making the investment economically unfeasible. This characteristic clearly benefits mutual funds over ETFs and stocks.

Minimum Investment

From an investment product perspective, ETFs and stocks do not have initial purchase requirements. However, some brokerage firms do impose minimums irrespective of the security or product an investor desires to purchase. Furthermore, some securities indirectly impose initial minimums as a result of their market price. For instance, when Apple common stock is trading in the $300-per-share range, an investor must spend at least that amount to purchase one share.

In contrast to stocks and ETFs, most mutual funds do impose initial purchase requirements starting at $1,000, with some reaching $5,000. Institutional share classes require even more. Many mutual funds require minimums because each shareholder, regardless of the amount invested, adds new costs to the mutual fund, such as monthly statements and postage to mail prospectuses. Just because someone invests $1 million in a mutual fund does not mean that the costs to service that shareholder are 10 times higher than a shareholder who invests $100,000. As a result, mutual funds establish minimum investments to ensure that each shareholder invests enough to cover his or her variable expenses. For many shareholders, these minimums pose no real issue, but for others the minimums are prohibitive. Compounding the difficulty with meeting minimums is the fact that a shareholder who barely makes the minimum will probably only invest in one mutual fund, and that leads to a nondiversified portfolio. ETFs and stocks have clear advantages over mutual funds with this characteristic.

Availability of Prospectus

A prospectus is a legal document that financial institutions use to describe the securities they are offering to participants and buyers. A prospectus typically provides investors with material information about the securities in question, such as, but not limited to, a description of the company's business, the company's financial statements, biographies of officers and directors, any litigation occurring, and a list of material properties. Investment firms are required to deliver prospectuses to shareholders of mutual funds and ETFs, but not stocks post-IPOs. In doing so, shareholders possess additional information about the fund they have purchased to help make them more informed investors. However, from my experience very few people ever read the prospectus and therefore do not take advantage of this useful resource.

Transaction Method

There are essentially two places investors can execute transactions to purchase or sell ETFs, stocks, and mutual funds. With ETFs and stocks, transactions can only be executed through a brokerage firm. However, mutual fund transactions can be executed through two different distribution channels: indirectly through brokerage firms and directly from the fund company itself. Some brokerage firms—typically the full-service firms—may not permit trading in all mutual funds, just approved funds. In these cases, a brokerage firm will tell its clients that it only permits trading in certain mutual funds since those funds provide extra services that the other mutual fund families do not. As an insider, I can tell you with strong conviction that this is simply not true. Many mutual fund families do not pay platform fees to brokerage firms (and banks for that matter) and therefore are shut out from being added to the approved mutual fund list. Although mutual funds can be purchased from two sources rather than just one, the advantage offered mutual funds in this case is not especially important.

TRADING FLEXIBILITY

In this section we will compare and contrast key characteristics related to trading flexibility, specifically intraday pricing, intraday trade executions, order type discretion, availability of using margin, and ability to sell short.

Intraday Pricing

One of the biggest knocks against mutual funds is their inherent limited market price transparency. In other words, investors do not know with confidence what price they will receive when they purchase or sell shares since prices are not established until the market is closed and valuation work is performed. ETF investors do not face this same challenge since market prices are known throughout the day as a result of being listed and traded on organized exchanges. This means that when you decide to execute a transaction, you will have greater confidence in knowing what you will pay or what you will receive in the transaction.

Intraday Trade Executions

As mentioned previously, ETFs permit shareholders the opportunity to place trades anytime during trading hours. This advantage is attributed to the exchange-traded feature built into ETFs. Purchase and sale trades for mutual funds can be entered during the day, but they only will be executed at the end of trading—referred to as for-

ward pricing—once a mutual fund's marked-to-market NAV is calculated. Executing trades anytime the market is open allows shareholders the ability to define when and how a trade should be
executed to best meet their needs. This is a significant advantage for
ETFs and stocks over mutual funds. However, stocklike tradability
also has the drawback of influencing an otherwise sound long-term
investor into making short-term focused trades. It is for this reason
that John Bogle of Vanguard recommends index mutual funds over
passively managed ETFs to retail investors.

Order-Type Discretion

With mutual funds, you can place either a purchase or sale order. It
does not get any more complex than that. With ETFs, you can place
many different types of orders (see Figure 3-6), just as you can with
stocks. For instance, if you want to place a limit order, a stop order,
or good-till-canceled order, you can do just that. For more sophisticated investors, if you like placing stop-limit orders, then you can
do that with ETFs. What does this mean to investors? It means that
you have more options for getting the best execution for your purchase or sale order—and that can result in incremental gains or better safeguarding of your investments.

Availability of Margin

For investors looking to purchase more of a certain ETF without
investing more of their own money, purchasing on margin provides an alternative. When you purchase on margin (a practice also
known as leveraging), you are borrowing money from your brokerage firm and using that money to buy more shares of the ETF.
As long as the rate of return on the ETF is higher than the interest
rate charged on the borrowed money, then you will benefit.
However, if the ETF falls in value or does not generate a return at
least as high as your borrowing costs, then you will lose money.
The stakes go up when you purchase on margin, but so too does
the potential reward. Since ETFs and individual stocks trade on
stock exchanges, shareholders have the ability to trade on margin.
This option is not available with mutual funds.

F I G U R E   3 - 6

FIGURE 3-6

Summary of Primary Order Types

Order	Profile	Positive	Negative
Market	An order to buy or sell an ETF at the current best available price	Typically ensures immediate execution	In fast-moving markets the order may get filled at different prices and times
Limit	An order to buy or sell an ETF with a restriction on the maximum price to be paid or the minimum price to be received	If executed, the order will only be filled at the specified limit price or better	No assurance of order execution
Stop	An order to buy or sell an ETF at the market price if the ETF trades at or through the limit price	An automatic buy or sell trigger once a certain price level has been satisfied	In fast-moving markets the order may get filled at a much higher or lower price than the stop
Stop Limit	An order to buy or sell an ETF at a limit price if the ETF trades at or through the limit price	Once triggered, the order will only be executed at a desired limit price or better	No assurance of order execution
Sell Short	An order to sell an ETF not owned and buy back the borrowed shares at a lower price	Gains from the decline in the price of the borrowed ETF shares	Losses from the appreciation of the borrowed shares

Source: Frush Financial Group

Ability to Sell Short

The final stocklike tradability characteristic that benefits ETF shareholders and stock investors is the ability to sell short. As with all other stocklike tradability characteristics, mutual funds are unable to sell short their investment. For most investors, selling short is not appropriate, as it takes extra insight and the risk tolerance to accept an unlimited loss. Why? Because if an investor were to sell short an investment and that investment increases in price rather than declines in price, the investor will lose money. If the investment continues to rise in price, the losses will build up. Theoretically speaking, the most an investor can lose when buying (going long) an investment is the capital invested. However, the most an investor can lose by selling short is unlimited since stocks can continue to rise in value and never look back. Although this is a benefit to ETF shareholders and stock investors, the importance is actually quite low in the overall scheme of investing.

Figure 3-7 provides a "report card" grading the characteristics of ETFs.

FIGURE 3-7

The ETF Report Card

College for Investment Education			Semester: Spring 2011
Subject	**Credits**	**Grade**	**Professor's Notes**
Diversification	5	A	Top of class
Intraday Liquidity	3	A	Always prepared
Cost-Effectiveness	5	A+	Highly competitive
Tax Efficiency	5	A+	Very innovative approach
Trading Flexibility	3	A	Jack-of-all-trades
Portfolio Transparency	3	A	What you see is what you get
Cost Transparency	3	B+	Good, but speak up even more
Fully Invested/Cash Drag	3	A-	Much better than your peers
Management Consistency	1	A	Very focused, as expected
No. of Selections Available	1	B	Young, but brimming with talent
Trading Transparency	3	F	Others know your next move
Portfolio Turnover	3	B+	Nice job with the restraint
Dividend Drag	3	B-	Could improve things a bit
Built-In Market Exposure	5	A	Quick with the correct answer

CREDITS		
5 = Most Important	3 = Important	1 = Least Important

Source: Professor Scott Paul Frush

## CHAPTER 4

Underlying Indexes: The Benchmarks and Strategies That ETFs Track

The focal point of any exchange-traded fund (ETF) is the underlying index the ETF tracks. The index serves as a road map for the ETF, and without it, an ETF will not reach its intended destination. Moreover, ETFs are benchmarked to an ever-growing universe of indexes—some older and some recently established. These indexes range from fundamental passive benchmarks (e.g., the S&P 500) to custom indexes employing sophisticated quantitative strategies and alternative weighting methods. As a result, understanding the difference among indexes, their intended purpose, and the way they are created is essential to building an ideal ETF portfolio. Not having at least a cursory understanding of the underlying indexes can cause individuals to sabotage their financial plan and doom their portfolio. I liken this scenario to the expression *garbage in, garbage out.*

Indexes can be classified by general purpose and underlying specific strategy. The investment profession recognizes two basic types of indexes—market indexes and custom indexes. A market index is a traditional and fundamental nuts-and-bolts measure of market value using passive security selection and weightings based on current market capitalization, which is the value of a company's outstanding stock calculated by multiplying the market price for a share of stock by the number of common stock shares outstanding. Since they reflect good cross sections of a market, market indexes are tools used to measure and analyze changes in a market segment given changes in each of the underlying holdings. Conversely, a custom index is best described as a strategy, no less and no more. A custom or strategy index is a method for investment selection rather than a tool to measure and analyze overall changes. Since a market index tracks a specific market segment, it represents that particular market and by definition provides beta, or the market return—less tracking error—and market risk as measured by volatility. In contrast, custom indexes do not track a particular or well-defined market segment and thus by definition attempt to generate outperformance, or alpha—but this time without the need for tracking error.

The vast majority of newly issued ETFs are based on custom indexes. These indexes are strictly strategy based and provide little to no meaningful insights into the pulse of the market. Custom indexes cannot be used to compare against other indexes, nor can they be used to guide asset allocation policy decisions. Custom indexes provide no relevance for evaluating levels of changes in economic progress and resulting investor confidence. Only market indexes can serve this important role. Custom indexes are designed subjectively, with security selection and security weighting—according to specific rules-based methodologies—of utmost importance.

Comparing custom indexes is similar to comparing apples and oranges. There is simply no viable connection between them for most indexes. Consequently, there has been only modest research into the benefit that custom indexes bring to investment management. To compound the issue, the Securities and Exchange Commission does not define what indexes should look like or how they should be structured or constructed. This lack of overall direction means investors can sometimes lose sight of what true indexing and passive management are all about. To take advantage of the environment, many providers of actively managed ETFs have aggressively pushed their claim that their indexing methodology is far superior to that of others—especially ETFs using market indexes—and therefore you should invest in their ETFs. The days of relying on tried-and-true market indexes based on capitalization weights and market representation are now in trouble. The growth of custom index ETFs is gaining far more momentum than the growth in ETFs using market indexes.

Believe it or not, one of the largest custom index sponsors is actually Standard & Poor's, the manager of the exceptionally well-known and quoted S&P 500 stock index. Custom index sponsors view indexes through a money-generating looking glass, whereas indexes are created using rules-based methodologies and then licensed to ETF providers that create corresponding ETFs and pay continuing royalty fees to the index sponsor. ETF providers will then stake claims that their strategy—based on a custom index—is far superior to "old-fashioned" market indexes. Make no mistake, the investing business is big, big money, and any edge is exploited with extreme effort.

PURPOSES OF INDEXES

Indexes serve three primary roles. The first and most important is that of a *benchmark,* whereby a comparison of performance as an asset class can be made against other asset classes, such as the S&P 500 and real estate investment trusts. Here market indexes are used as yardsticks. The second purpose of an index is that of *indicator,* whereby changes in the index will offer an indication of how well or poorly a particular market segment is doing. Economic research is often conducted using indexes as indicators. The third purpose of an index is that of an *investable instrument,* whereby investors can gain exposure through the purchase of an ETF (or perhaps mutual fund) that tracks the index. This final purpose is the basis for asset allocation decisions. Be aware that not all indexes have ETFs or index mutual funds that track them—thereby rendering them noninvestable.

Being investable is one of the seven characteristics of ideal indexes you should consider when evaluating an ETF and its underlying index for investment. The seven investor-centric characteristics of what identifies ideal indexes include the following:

1. **Specified in Advance:** The index should be known at the time of portfolio design.
2. **Investable:** The index itself can be purchased with ease.

3. **Measurable:** The return of the index can be calculated on a reasonably frequent basis.
4. **Appropriate:** The index style is aligned with the aim of an investor.
5. **Composition Known:** The securities that compose the index are known.
6. **Uniform:** The index's time horizon, liquidity, tax management considerations, or other inherent characteristics are similar and appropriate for the investor.
7. **Unambiguous:** The securities and their weightings within the index are representative of the market segment tracked.

In addition to the aforementioned characteristics of ideal indexes, the CFA Institute, arguably the top industry organization for investment management, provides guidelines on what attributes it believes define best-of-breed indexes. These characteristics include the following:

1. **Comprehensive:** Indexes should incorporate all opportunities that are realistically available for investment by all market participants under normal market conditions.
2. **Expenses:** The index should not charge excessive costs, and all expenses should be understood by market participants.
3. **Low Barriers to Entry:** The markets or market segments tracked by an index should not contain significant barriers to entry.
4. **Relevance:** The index should be relevant and of interest to market participants for investing purposes.
5. **Replicability:** The total returns for an index should be replicable by and readily available to all market participants.
6. **Simple and Objective Selection Criteria:** Indexes should be created, forecasted, and modified according to clear sets of rules governing the inclusion of securities or markets.

7. **Stability:** The index should not change composition frequently, and when changes are needed, they should be easily understood and highly predictable.

INDEX CREATION

Custom indexes are tailored to a specific strategy an ETF provider wants to employ and advertise to investors. The ETF provider may target a particular asset class or sector, but may keep the parameters quite broad. The ETF provider may include leverage or design an ETF that moves inversely to a predetermined index. The options are vast and varied. Market indexes, on the other hand, tend to be passively selected, either incorporating all the securities in a particular market segment or selecting securities using a cross-section sample of the market. The intent is not to design a strategy that will outperform a specific market segment, but instead to design an index that captures and replicates the performance of a specific market segment.

Market Capitalization Weighting

When prices for the securities underlying an index change, the index value itself will change. But this calculation is not as straightforward as it might appear. Why? Some companies in an index have larger market capitalizations—meaning they are bigger than some of the others. So the important question is how to weight the companies to provide the best measure of price change on the index level. Market indexes have taken the position that the companies should be capitalization weighted, meaning that larger market capitalization companies exhibit greater influence on the index than do small market capitalization companies. This is not a material issue for indexes that track specific market capitalization segments, such as small caps and mid caps, but it is for indexes that do not segment by size.

There are times when small price movements in large-capitalization securities will influence the index far more than large price movements in small-capitalization securities. As a result, the use of market capitalization–weighted indexes has come under fire from some people, who claim this indexing method is trend following and therefore creates an inefficient risk and return trade-off profile. Irrespective of the claims, market capitalization more closely tracks a market, because in reality companies are of various sizes.

Market capitalization can be divided into four types—full cap, free float, capped, and liquidity. Full cap uses the traditional calculation of market capitalization, whereas the free-float type uses a market capitalization based on the amount of shares available for trading to the public. This is an important distinction since many companies have meaningful amounts of stock that are restrictive—such as those tied up by corporate employees. Capped is used to control the impact from one or more companies that dominate the index based on market capitalization. Under this type, the weighting for any one security may be capped at a specific percentage—such as 10 percent. The liquidity type essentially takes the free float to a more stringent level. Here, only the normal trading volume in a particular security is used in the calculation. This helps to alleviate a situation where a security has a much lower trading volume than other securities with comparable free floats.

The market capitalization–weighted method is not the only method available. A newer methodology, referred to as fundamentally weighted, is making modest inroads with index sponsors. This method selects securities based on company fundamentals such as revenue, dividend rates, earnings, and book value.

Another popular methodology is called equal-weight capitalization, which is primarily used by ETF providers that focus on custom indexes. As the name implies, each security in such an index is weighted the same under this method. The benefit of this method is that each security has a proportional influence on the index and eliminates any significant influence from much larger capitalization securities and therefore the market as a whole. The obvious drawback is that these indexes are not truly representative of changes in the underlying securities. For example, an equal capitalization–weighted index comprising only Microsoft (over $200 billion market cap) and JDS Uniphase ($5 billion market cap) will show a 2 percent return if Microsoft were to gain 1 percent and JDS

Uniphase 3 percent in a single trading day. As you can see, the smaller company—JDS Uniphase—influenced the index as much as the substantially larger Microsoft did. Nonetheless, the market capitalization–weighting and equal capitalization–weighting methods are popular with particular ETF providers and thus will be around for the foreseeable future.

INDEXES BY MARKET SEGMENT

In addition to broad-market indexes, there are other indexes that track more defined styles, sectors, and fixed-income segments. Examples include large-cap value, large-cap growth, small-cap value, and small-cap growth. Sectors include, but are not limited to, financials, health care, utilities, and technology. Fixed-income segments can be composed of corporate bonds, municipal bonds, mortgage-related bonds, and Treasuries. There are also international and real assets.

This differentiation is important since broad indexes are essentially the sum of their parts. Market indexes stake claim to this key characteristic; custom indexes cannot make the same claim, as they are strategies with no regard to their constituent parts. An example of how constituent indexes sum to form a broad-market index is the Russell 3000 Index, which represents nearly 98 percent of the investable U.S. equity market. By drilling down, you can divide the Russell 3000 Index into the Russell 1000 Index, which represents 1,000 large-cap stocks, and the Russell 2000 Index, which represents 2,000 small-cap stocks.

MAJOR INDEX SPONSORS

Although there are dozens of index sponsors—particularly on the custom index side—seven major market index sponsors dominate the marketplace. These include Standard & Poor's, Dow Jones Indexes (DJI), Morgan Stanley Capital International (MSCI), Russell Investments, Barclays Global Investors, Wilshire Associates, and Morningstar Associates (see Figure 4-1). We'll examine each on the following pages.

FIGURE 4-1

U.S. Market Capitalization Representation by Index Sponsor

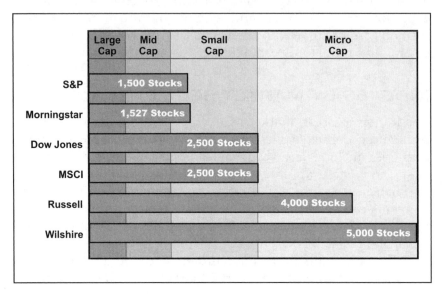

Source: S&P, Morningstar, Dow Jones, MSCI, Russell, and Wilshire

Standard & Poor's

Standard & Poor's is a U.S-based financial services company and a division of the McGraw-Hill Companies, publisher of this book. Along with Moody's Investor Service and Fitch, Standard & Poor's is one of the Big Three credit rating agencies in the world. The company publishes a large number of stock market indexes, covering every region of the world, market capitalization level, and type of investment. More specifically, Standard & Poor's covers approximately 30 global markets constituting approximately 70 percent of total global market capitalization.

According to Standard & Poor's, about $1.1 trillion of investment assets is directly tied to S&P indexes, while more than $3.5 trillion is benchmarked to the S&P 500 Index—representing more assets benchmarked to an index than any other index in the world today. The State Street SPDR S&P 500 ETF is so mammoth in size that it boasts more assets under management than many ETF providers manage in all their ETFs combined. Although most of the companies in the S&P 500 Index are large and are leaders in their respective fields, the index does contain some mid-cap companies as well.

In addition to the dominating S&P 500 Index, other widely recognizable indexes include—but are not limited to—the following:

- S&P Mid Cap 400 Index (including blend, growth, and value versions)
- S&P Small Cap 600 Index (including blend, growth, and value versions)
- S&P 1500 Index (a supercomposite comprising the S&P 500, Mid Cap 400, and Small Cap 600 Indexes)
- S&P 100 Index
- S&P GSCI (formerly the Goldman Sachs Commodity Index)
- S&P Global 100 Stock Index

DJI

The DJI was established in 1997 as an entity within its parent Dow Jones & Company. However, Dow Jones sold a 90 percent stake in its index business for approximately $600 million to the Chicago-based CME Group in February 2010. Accordingly, the company became known as Dow Jones Indexes, a CME Group Company.

With employees in 14 cities worldwide, DJI produces, maintains, licenses, and markets indexes as benchmarks and as the basis of investable products. DJI has created more than 3,000 proprietary U.S. and international indexes. Its most recognizable index is the Dow Jones Industrial Average (DJIA), created in 1896. Its oldest index—and, in fact, the oldest index in use today—is the Dow Jones Transportation Index, created in 1882 by Charles Dow, founder of the *Wall Street Journal*. In addition to the aforementioned two indexes, other widely recognizable indexes in the Dow Jones family include the Dow Jones Utility Average, Dow Jones Composite Average, Dow Jones Total Stock Market Index, Dow Jones-UBS Commodity Index, and Dow Jones U.S. Total Market Index (represents the top 95 percent of the free-float value of the total U.S. equity market).

The DJIA is a price-weighted average comprising 30 of the most well-known and largest megacorporations in the United States. The use of the word *Industrial* in the name is largely historical, given that many of the current components have little or nothing to do with traditional heavy industry. The market value of the 30 stocks represents over one-fifth of the total market value of all U.S. stocks. As of early 2011, the 30 stocks and the years each was added to the index include the following:

1. General Electric, 1907
2. ExxonMobil, 1928
3. Procter & Gamble, 1932
4. DuPont, 1935
5. United Technologies, 1939
6. Alcoa, 1959
7. 3M, 1976
8. IBM, 1979
9. Merck, 1979
10. American Express, 1982
11. McDonald's, 1985
12. Boeing, 1987
13. Coca-Cola, 1987
14. Caterpillar, 1991
15. JPMorgan Chase, 1991
16. Walt Disney, 1991
17. Hewlett-Packard, 1997
18. Johnson & Johnson, 1997
19. Wal-Mart, 1997
20. AT&T, 1999
21. The Home Depot, 1999
22. Intel, 1999
23. Microsoft, 1999
24. Pfizer, 2004
25. Verizon Communications, 2004
26. Bank of America, 2008
27. Chevron Corporation, 2008
28. Kraft Foods, 2008
29. Cisco Systems, 2009
30. Travelers, 2009

MSCI

The MSCI global equity indexes have been calculated since the late 1960s, with the U.S. equity indexes created much later in 2003 together with the assistance of Vanguard. MSCI's most recognizable indexes include the MSCI Emerging Markets and MSCI EAFE Index—EAFE stands for Europe, Australasia, and Far East. MSCI indexes are widely used as the benchmarks for global equity portfolios. Morgan Stanley is responsible for sponsoring the first iShares ETFs, initially known as WEBS, which are designed to track various MSCI indexes. MSCI also provides U.S. equity indexes based on three market capitalization segments: large, mid, and small, as well as value and growth style indexes.

In 2007, parent company Morgan Stanley spun off part of MSCI through an initial public offering of a minority of stock in November. The full divestiture was completed in 2009.

In addition to the aforementioned two indexes, other MSCI indexes include the following:

- MSCI All Country World Index
- MSCI Europe Index
- MSCI BRIC Index
- MSCI Asia Pacific Index
- MSCI Brazil Index
- MSCI Japan Index
- MSCI China Index

Russell Investments

Acquired in 1999 by Northwestern Mutual (but retaining the name), Frank Russell & Company of Tacoma, Washington, launched its family of U.S. indexes in 1984 to measure U.S. market segments and track the performance of investment managers. The outcome created the broad-market Russell 3000 Index and sub-components such as the small-cap Russell 2000 Index, the company's most popular index. Using a rules-based methodology, Russell structures its indexes by listing all companies in descending order by market capitalization adjusted for float (actual number of shares available for trading). The Russell 3000 Index consists of stocks of the top 3,000 largest companies domiciled in the United States and its territories and thus representing nearly 98 percent of the investable U.S. equity market. Of those 3,000, the top 1,000 are used to create the large-cap Russell 1000 Index, with the bottom 2,000 constituting the small-cap Russell 2000 Index. Finally, Russell also sponsors constituent value and growth versions of each U.S. index. All indexes are reconstituted annually using market values from May 31 of each year.

According to Russell, there are more investable assets ($4 trillion) benchmarked to its indexes than all other U.S. equity indexes combined. Furthermore, Russell indexes accounted for 63.3 percent of assets benchmarked by institutional investors as of 2008. Russell's most recognizable indexes include the following:

- **Russell 3000 Index:** The large-cap index of the top 3,000 largest companies domiciled in the United States and its territories
- **Russell 2000 Index:** The small-cap benchmark index of the bottom 2,000 stocks in the Russell 3000 Index
- **Russell Microcap Index:** The micro-cap index of the 1,000 smallest companies in the Russell 2000 Index plus the next 1,000 smallest stocks
- **Russell 1000 Index:** The large-cap index of the top 1,000 stocks in the Russell 3000 Index
- **Russell Top 200 Index:** The mega-cap index of the largest 200 stocks in the Russell 3000 Index

Barclays Global Investors

Prior to the financial meltdown of 2008 and 2009, Lehman Brothers sponsored and maintained a number of fixed-income indexes. As we all know, Lehman did not survive the crisis and had much of its assets purchased by Barclays PLC, the large international bank based in London. Upon the acquisition, Barclays said good-bye to Lehman and included the venerable Lehman fixed-income indexes under a new Barclays brand name—Barclays Capital. The transition was rather seamless since Barclays already sponsored a number of indexes prior to the acquisition.

According to Barclays, its flagship indexes include the aggregate, inflation-linked bond, high-yield, emerging markets, municipal, floating-rate, government/treasury, universal, and swaps (nominal and inflation) index families, which include both global-multicurrency macro benchmarks and single-currency versions.

Due to mounting financial concerns and the need to raise capital, Barclays PLC sold its iShares ETF asset management business to BlackRock in 2009, with Barclays holding a 20 percent economic interest in BlackRock.

Wilshire Associates

Wilshire Associates is an independent and privately owned investment management firm based in Santa Monica, California, offering many types of investment consulting services and analytical products. Wilshire manages more than $8 trillion of capital for more than 600 institutional investors. Wilshire is known for its Wilshire 5000 stock index established in 1974 and more recently the Wilshire 4500 stock index—which includes all stocks in the Wilshire 5000 except for the most part those companies in the S&P 500. The Wilshire 4500 tracks the performance of small and mid-cap stocks within the Wilshire 5000. Wilshire also provides style and size indexes derived from the Wilshire 5000 index, including large, mid, small, and micro caps, and then subdivides those into growth and value styles.

Morningstar Associates

Based in Chicago, Morningstar is a leading provider of independent investment research in North America, Europe, Australia, and Asia, with operations in over 26 countries across the globe. Morningstar's research provides data and insight on nearly 400,000 stocks, mutual funds, and ETFs. The Morningstar Style Index family comprises 16 indexes that track the U.S. equity market by size and style using the company's popular rules-based 10-factor methodology. These 16 indexes cover more than 97 percent of the free-float U.S. equity market and are rebalanced quarterly and reconstituted annually.

The 16 indexes cover the nine asset classes that make up the Morningstar Style Boxes, plus one index for each of the aggregate sizes (small caps, mid caps, and large caps), one index for each of the aggregate styles (growth, value, blend), and one index that comprises all the other 15 indexes. Large caps represent the largest 70 percent of investable market cap, mid cap the next 20 percent, small cap the next 7 percent, and finally micro cap with the final 3 percent. Micro caps are not represented in the Morningstar Style Boxes, however.

## CHAPTER 5

Internal Workings: The Technical Features of ETFs

Thus far we have discussed the basics of exchange-traded funds (ETFs) and highlighted the important defining attributes that make the case for investing in ETFs. Many of the concepts and characteristics only scratch the surface of ETFs and the associated marketplace. This chapter will drill down below the surface and present the more technical aspects and topics of ETFs, including the critical and defining creation and redemption process, important moving parts, the true costs of investing and holding an ETF, and, finally, the valuation metrics underlying ETFs.

CREATIONS AND REDEMPTIONS

The key to what makes ETFs so different from any other investment—especially mutual funds—is the creation and redemption process. This process is so vitally important that without it, ETFs would not resemble anything like they do today and instead would closely resemble closed-end funds. The creation and redemption process affords ETFs the ability to be less expensive, more transparent, traded without premiums and discounts, fully invested, and more tax efficient than nearly all other investments in the marketplace today. But what exactly is the creation and redemption process, and why is it so unique and important?

Background

Previous to ETFs, all exchange-traded portfolios traded with a premium or discount to their mark-to-market net asset value (NAV). To avoid this inherent flaw under then-existing models, ETF providers envisioned a process in which no premiums and discounts would exist since they would be arbitraged away quickly and easily by independent third-party money managers. Why third party? ETF providers realized that any involvement in the trading of underlying securities could create conflicts of interest—whether fictional or factual—and thus derail any innovation that relied on the creation and redemption process. Consequently, the plan was to rely on outside third-party money managers—such as Merrill Lynch, Goldman Sachs, and Morgan Stanley—to decide when new ETF shares would be issued and when existing ETF shares would be redeemed in accordance with an ETF framework. In due time, these outside third-party money managers became known as authorized participants (APs).

Although their role is exceedingly important, from an inside perspective their role is nearly free of risk—something we refer to as arbitrage. In their designed role, APs buy and sell shares to ensure there are no premiums or discounts. The original designers of ETFs were not stupid—they realized that involving the work of multiple competing APs was essential to the competitiveness and credibility of the process. Therefore, there are times when both Morgan Stanley and Goldman Sachs will each execute arbitrage transactions in the same ETF, thus reducing the potential for conflicts of interest, providing for greater transparency, and ultimately leading to reasonable arbitrage profits. *Reasonable* is the catchword here since it makes no sense to create an investment where the bulk of the profits go to a firm rather than the shareholders. Government watchdogs oversee all aspects of the creation and redemption process and would not be pleased otherwise.

The Process

When ETFs are created, APs are involved with either buying or borrowing the appropriate basket of securities underlying an ETF and exchanging them with the ETF provider for what are called *creation units* (see Figure 5-1). The creation units comprise large blocks of tens of thousands of ETF shares and must be equal to the mark-to-market NAV published holdings from the previous market close. In doing so, the ETF provider is prevented from indirectly profiting from the share creation and redemption process since the closing NAV is a known quantity. This safeguard satisfies the Securities and Exchange Commission (SEC) concern for potential abuse within the process.

FIGURE 5-1

Simplified Creation Process

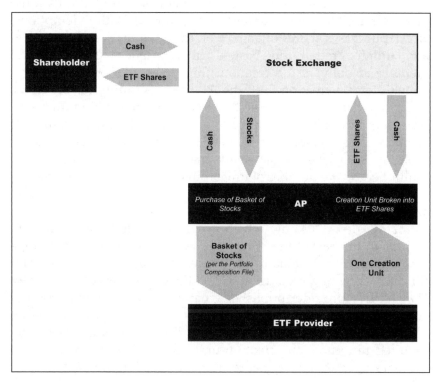

Source: Frush Financial Group

When an AP delivers a basket of underlying securities and related cash to the ETF provider (through the custodian bank), the AP in turn receives one creation unit issued by the provider through the designated custodian. These creation units are typically large blocks of ETF shares—usually up to 50,000—but can be as high as 600,000 and as low as 20,000. Upon receiving creation units, an AP has the option of holding the units or selling some or all outright in the open market—perhaps to another AP. The AP may even go the route of breaking up creation units into individual ETF shares underlying the fund and selling them to shareholders throughout the day on a stock exchange. ETFs may permit an AP to substitute cash for some or all of the securities underlying a creation unit when the securities are difficult to obtain or not held by certain types of investors.

When a shareholder sells shares of his or her ETF or when there is a divergence between the market price and NAV, then the process goes into reverse order (see Figure 5-2). With redemptions, an AP purchases shares of an ETF on the open market, forms a creation unit (or "redemption basket") in accordance with the requirements, and delivers the creation unit to the ETF provider. Upon delivery of the creation unit, the AP receives individual securities and related cash equal to the exact NAV of the creation unit. ETF providers typically assess a fee to an AP based on the quantity of creation units created or redeemed. The amount is rather low—typically $1,000 per 50,000-share transaction—but enough when multiplied by the number of units transacted to give ETF providers incremental revenues to pay for work involved with the creation and redemption process.

How do APs know which securities underlying an ETF to include in the basket they turn over to ETF providers in exchange for creation units? Actually, the process is much more refined and fluid than one might envision. Upon the close of each trading session, an ETF provider publishes what is called a portfolio composition file, or PCF for short. The data tell an AP what securities—including the quantity—and what amount of cash are required to receive one creation unit. The timing and accuracy of the data is essential to ensure that the creation and redemption process runs smoothly.

FIGURE 5-2

Simplified Redemption Process

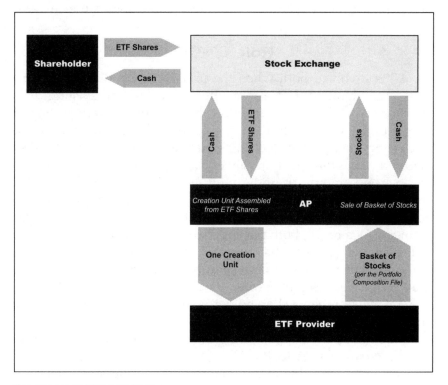

Source: Frush Financial Group

A third-party organization called the National Securities Clearing Corporation is charged with the responsibility of accepting, processing, and disseminating all PCFs to interested APs prior to the opening of the market on the following trading session. Any changes in the composition of the market index being tracked can be accommodated between an ETF provider and AP through PCFs. For instance, when the underlying securities in an ETF are revised—and thus the creation unit altered—an AP will deliver the newly added security to the ETF provider and receive in return the security that was removed—all via the custodian bank.

Technically speaking, it is not the ETF provider that is selling the shares, but rather it is the AP that takes on this function. As a result, shareholders have no direct relationship with the provider itself. This difference is trivial in nature, but one worth mentioning nonetheless.

Role of APs

An AP is involved both when the new ETFs are starting up and when the demand for transacting shares of an existing ETF increases. An AP's job is to facilitate the creation and redemption of shares underlying an ETF. The in-kind exchange of a basket of stock comprising the underlying securities and creation units takes place on a one-for-one, fair-value basis. Specifically, the AP delivers a certain amount of underlying securities, or basket of stocks, and receives the exact same value in ETF shares—based on the NAV and not the market value of the ETF at that particular moment. As a result, both parties benefit from the transaction. The ETF provider receives the securities it needs to track the index, while the AP receives a corresponding number of ETF creation units to hold or resell for profit.

Likewise, when a shareholder is selling his or her investment, an AP removes ETF shares from the open market by purchasing an equivalent amount of shares to form a creation unit and then delivers the creation unit to the ETF provider. In exchange, the AP receives the same value in the underlying securities of the ETF.

How do APs profit from the creation and redemption process—what gives them the financial incentive to be involved? The primary way is to gain from the arbitrage transactions needed to eliminate the premiums and discounts on the fund level and make risk-free profits in the process. For instance, when an ETF is selling at a premium to its underlying NAV, then an AP—perhaps multiple APs—will step in and sell shares of the ETF on the open market and simultaneously buy shares of the underlying securities. The AP continues this process until the market price for the ETF is in line with the NAV of the ETF. Thereafter the AP will exchange with the ETF provider the recently purchased underlying shares of securities for creation units. Although this process may appear cumbersome and time consuming, the opposite is closer to reality. Sophisticated computers facilitate the purchases and sales using detailed and explicit models, making for a quick and easy process. The ultimate result is a properly aligned ETF with risk-free profits to the AP.

Importance of the Creation and Redemption Process

The creation and redemption process is vitally important with regards to ETFs for three key reasons. These reasons are provided below with detailed explanations following the numbered summaries:

1. Eliminates trading premiums and discounts by keeping all ETF market prices and their corresponding NAVs in line with each other
2. Eliminates transaction costs (both subsidy and AP) paid by existing shareholders for transactions of others
3. Eliminates financial conflicts of interest (specifically abusive trading practices and unacceptable arbitrage profits) because of the involvement of APs

First, the creation and redemption process ensures that the ETF share price trades in line with the underlying NAV. Without this advantage, an ETF would trade much like a glorified closed-end fund with either a premium or discount. Since an ETF has stocklike tradability, the price for an ETF fluctuates during trading sessions—due to supply-and-demand fundamentals. As such, when an ETF becomes more expensive than the sum of its underlying securities, an AP can sell shares of the ETF and purchase and deliver underlying shares to the ETF provider—thus receiving a creation unit—and exchange that creation unit outright or sell the ETF shares on the open market. This process returns the market price for an ETF back to its NAV. Likewise, if the underlying securities become more expensive than the ETF market value, then the AP can purchase shares of the ETF equivalent to the value of a creation unit and redeem them for the underlying securities—which can be sold in the open market. The ultimate result of the arbitrage creation and redemption process is an ETF market price that trades in line with its underlying NAV.

Second, the creation and redemption process ensures that current shareholders do not pay for transactions executed by either market-timing investors or APs in conjunction with their arbitrage role. As a result, ETFs are an extraordinarily efficient and fair way for all involved participants. In contrast, when mutual fund shareholders invest new money, the fund company must take that money and purchase underlying securities in the open market. This unfortunately translates into higher costs for all shareholders. And as we all know, higher costs ultimately harm returns. The same process occurs when shareholders withdraw their money from a mutual fund.

Fortunately, ETFs are much different, as APs do much of the buying and selling and incur the bulk of the trading costs, whether explicit or implicit. APs typically pay all the trading costs and fees—including additional fees to the ETF provider for the "paperwork" involved in processing all the creations and redemptions. As a result, the ETF system shifts the burden of underlying trading costs associated with shareholder transactions to the AP and away from the ETF. This is not true for mutual funds, where the fund and therefore existing shareholders pay costs—subsidy trading costs—when other shareholders sell their positions. The mutual fund in this case bears the trading cost without regard for a specific shareholder. Nonetheless, ETFs are responsible for picking up the tab for nonshareholder transactions such as an index change where a constituent security is being replaced by another and the ETF is required to make related revisions.

Third, the creation and redemption process ensures that financial conflicts of interest are eliminated since all underlying securities and their weightings are known by way of the portfolio composition file. In addition, since multiple APs are contracted, there is greater competition among APs to ensure the process operates as needed. As we all know from economics 101, greater competition typically equates to lower returns—or in this case mutually acceptable arbitrage profits. If an ETF provider only engaged one AP, the opportunity to capture unacceptability high arbitrage profits—at the expense of shareholders—and having greater discretion over when and to what degree to buy or sell the underlying securities would be otherwise more common.

ETF MOVING PARTS

This section is dedicated to those topics that relate to the internal moving parts, or anatomy, of an ETF. The four most important considerations include market price, NAV, tracking error, and liquidity, which is oftentimes misunderstood by investors. We start off by investigating the intricacies of market price.

Market Price

Market price refers to the last price at which an ETF was transacted, which can be the bid price, ask price (also known as the offer price), or somewhere in between. Bid and ask prices provide the pricing level at which 100 shares or more of an ETF are available for transaction—at least 100 shares at the bid or selling price and 100 at the ask or purchase price. The difference between the two is called the bid-ask spread or trading spread. The market price reflects the best known price for an ETF and is therefore used in many valuation calculations such as NAV and market capitalization.

Some ETFs trade with relatively narrow spreads, whereas others trade with wide spreads. Although investor demand and supply does play a minor role in determining the trading spread, the leading determinant of ETF trading spreads arises from the spreads of the underlying securities. As a result, ETFs that hold highly liquid securities with narrow spreads on average will tend to exhibit narrow spreads themselves, all else being equal. ETFs tracking blue chip companies, such as the Dow Jones Industrial Average, will enjoy this advantage. Other ETFs, especially those that track emerging markets, will find their own spreads to be wider than others.

One of the significant benefits of ETFs is the involvement of APs to arbitrage and bring the spread in line with the spreads of the underlying stocks. Without this risk-free trading, the ETF spreads would deviate from the underlying spreads—and that could mean wider spreads on the fund level and thus higher trading costs.

Finally, ETF spreads are not static—they are constantly moving in response to how the market is behaving and how trading is impacting the spreads of the underlying securities. When there is added risk in the market resulting from geopolitical events, spreads typically widen. Conversely, a calm and benign few days in the market can cause spreads to narrow.

NAV

NAV, or *net asset value*, is a term used to describe the accounting value for an ETF on a per-share basis. The calculation for NAV is quite simple: the fund's assets less liabilities are divided by the number of shares outstanding. The result is expressed in dollar terms. Mutual funds use NAV as well and calculate the value in the same manner as ETFs.

Calculating NAV is the work of a fund accounting group, sometimes called portfolio accounting. The computer systems used by fund accounting groups are rather sophisticated and are used to account for investment inflows and outflows, purchases and sales of the underlying securities, fund operating expenses, and any security-specific income, gains, and losses. Once the valuation process is complete and all accounting entries are posted, then the accounting books are considered "closed," thus enabling the NAV per share to be calculated and disseminated to the marketplace. Although both ETFs and mutual funds employ this same system, ETFs also provide an intraday real-time estimate of current valuation appropriately called intraday indicative value (IIV). This value per share is published every 15 seconds for investors and APs alike to view. This value is essential given that ETFs trade continuously throughout the day and are not transacted at the close of trading at a fund's NAV price like mutual funds.

Tracking Error

Tracking error is a ratio expressed as a percentage which measures the unplanned deviation of return generated by an ETF compared with the return of an index benchmark over a fixed period of time. The greater the use of passive management, the smaller the tracking error tends to be over time. Tracking error is expressed as either a positive number for outperformance of the ETF or a negative number representing underperformance. Deviations between the returns are generally very small and thus expressed in basis points rather than full percentage points.

Analyzing ETFs using tracking error was not done to a significant degree many years ago because of the low number of indexes tracked. However, as ETFs began to track greater and greater numbers of indexes, the need to analyze, evaluate, and compare ETFs became much more important. Although there are several different methods for calculating tracking error, the most widely accepted method is the difference between the marked-to-market NAV return of the ETF and the return of the index being tracked. Since ETF market values converge to the NAV over time, any differences between NAV return and ETF return are insignificant.

One of the final pieces to the puzzle for calculating tracking error is whether or not to include expense ratio costs. From the perspective of some within the ETF marketplace, expense ratios are outside the management of an ETF and thus not a true factor in explaining any difference in net returns. In consequence, expense ratios should be added back to arrive at a more investment-centric measure. However, from the perspective of ETF shareholders, the expense ratio cost is an actual cost that must be paid in order to invest in ETFs and furthermore helps to better compare ETFs. Therefore, ETF investors are better served by keeping the cost in the calculation. Low-cost ETF providers prefer the cost included as well since it helps their cause by showing lower tracking error than their peers' tracking error—all else being equal.

Some ETFs produce small tracking error, while others produce larger tracking error. When tracking error is abnormally large for the index tracked, it is generally attributed to one or more of the following three reasons:

1. Difficulty in tracking an index due to illiquid index constituents
2. Difficulty in tracking an index due to sampling and optimization snags—particularly small-cap stocks—given indexes with unusually large numbers of index constituents
3. Cash drag arising from ETF providers that, for various reasons, decide not to fully invest the cash within an ETF

Liquidity

ETFs were originally viewed as being more liquid than traditional mutual funds due to their stocklike tradability. Although this is true in aggregate, it is not necessarily true in all cases. Why is greater liquidity more favorable? Lower levels of liquidity can lead to wider ETF bid-ask spreads and wider divergences between an ETF's NAV and the value of its underlying stocks; in addition, lower levels of liquidity can reduce an investor's ability to trade profitably.

The level of liquidity for an ETF is based on four factors. First and most important, ETF liquidity is influenced by the liquidity of the underlying securities. Large blue chip names will provide excellent liquidity, whereas emerging market stocks and REITs provide much less liquidity. Where securities are listed—exchange and country—also impacts underlying securities and their related liquidity.

Second, ETF liquidity is influenced by the trading volume of the underlying securities. Securities with higher trading volumes will enable quick and easy transactions, ultimately translating into greater liquidity. Stocks with lower trading volumes have wider spreads and provide less favorable opportunities to buy and sell. This all trickles up to the fund level.

Third, ETF liquidity is influenced to a small degree by the trading volume of the ETF itself. The more buying and selling going on with an ETF, the more liquid the ETF tends to be.

Fourth, ETF liquidity is influenced by the perceived investment opportunity for the underlying securities. When crude oil is rising, there are more investors interested in purchasing energy stocks. Likewise, when an economy is believed to be coming out of a recession, there is a shift from consumer staple stocks to consumer discretionary stocks.

THE COSTS OF ETFs

One of the most important differences between ETFs and mutual funds is the total cost a shareholder pays to own the fund. Most shareholders are keenly aware that an ETF is lower cost, if not significantly lower cost, than a comparable mutual fund. However, even though ETFs are cost favorable, that does not mean they are free—there are costs that must be paid. Some of these costs are highly transparent, while others are much less transparent. Furthermore, costs can be grouped according to where they are assessed (fund level or shareholder level) and whether or not the costs impact tracking error (see Figure 5-3). If costs do impact tracking error, then they are appropriately called tracking costs.

FIGURE 5-3

Summary of ETF Costs

Tracking Costs	
Cost	**Assessment**
Expense Ratios	Fund Level
Dividend Drag	Fund Level
Cash Drag	Fund Level
Trading Transparency	Fund Level
Tracking Snags	Fund Level

Nontracking Costs	
Cost	**Assessment**
Commissions	Shareholder Level
Bid-Ask Spreads	Shareholder Level
Premiums	Shareholder Level
Taxes	Shareholder Level

Source: Frush Financial Group

Tracking Costs

The following section highlights internal costs incurred on the fund level that impact how closely an ETF tracks its underlying index. For most ETFs, higher costs means greater tracking error while lower costs mean less tracking error—which of course is the main objective. The primary tracking costs include expense ratios, dividend drag, cash drag, trading transparency, and tracking snags.

Expense Ratios

The most transparent cost you will pay when investing in an ETF is the expense ratio, called MER (management expense ratio) in Europe. An expense ratio is expressed in percentage terms, assessed on the market value of the ETF, and paid by shareholders on a pro rata basis daily. Operating costs are the most significant component of expense ratios, but also included are other costs incurred by an ETF provider such as royalty fees—which are ongoing fees paid to index sponsors to track and market their indexes.

When you compare apples to apples, ETFs have much lower expense ratios than comparable mutual funds. One of the reasons explaining this fact is the existence of expenses called 12b-1 fees (typically 0.25 percent)—assessed by many mutual funds to compensate investment professionals for serving (i.e., keeping) shareholders in their funds. Mutual fund companies refer to this fee as a service or marketing fee. ETFs do not charge 12b-1 fees.

Dividend Drag

Dividend drag refers to the implicit cost some ETFs (unit investment trusts) incur as a result of SEC rules stipulating that ETFs cannot reinvest dividends paid by companies held by the ETF back into the portfolio immediately. Instead, some ETFs must accumulate the dividends in a cash reserve account and pay them to shareholders at periodic intervals—typically quarterly. This requirement differs for mutual funds, as they can reinvest dividends immediately. When the equity market is doing well, dividends are better served being reinvested rather than held back until paid out on specific dates. This drawback with some ETFs creates a performance penalty and ultimately a drag on returns that otherwise would not have occurred had the dividend been reinvested at the time of payment by an underlying stock.

Cash Drag

Cash drag refers to the loss of potential performance as a result of an ETF not being fully invested. The vast majority of ETFs are fully invested since they do not have to satisfy shareholder withdrawal requests—a normal fact of life for mutual funds. Nonetheless, there are times, although infrequent, when ETFs are not fully invested even though nothing was holding the fund back from investing all available cash. As with dividend drag, when markets are rising, cash is better served being invested and not idle making only a fraction of what could be earned in the stock market.

Trading Transparency

Trading transparency refers to the implicit costs that passively managed ETFs incur as a result of needing to rebalance given preannounced index reconstitutions. Once an index sponsor preannounces upcoming changes to a market index, then speculators—known in practice as scalpers—can front-run any ETF provider by purchasing the security being added to an index and selling the security being removed—all before the index is officially reconstituted and ETFs can make their change. These front-running transactions drive up costs for an ETF that needs to make changes to mirror the underlying market index. The cost is embedded in the fund, with little to no knowledge of shareholders.

Tracking Snags

Tracking snags can be very problematic—and costly—for ETFs that track market indexes. This cost—along with the expense ratio cost—is the leading factor explaining tracking error. One of the most common issues arising with ETFs in regard to tracking snags is the difficulty of replicating a market index that contains either illiquid securities or a significant number of securities, particularly small-cap stocks. Illiquid securities can cause transaction timing delays and may mean higher costs to transact. Additionally, when a market index contains an exceptionally large number of securities, then an ETF provider will typically employ a sampling method to replicate the index to reduce custodial and administrative costs. However, since sampling and optimization methods typically underweight small-cap stocks, then the ETF will outperform the index when small caps underperform and underperform when small caps outperform. Irrespective of the catalyst, tracking error attributed to index replication snags is a real cost to ETF shareholders and is incurred on the fund level.

Nontracking Costs

The following section highlights costs incurred on the shareholder level that do not impact how closely an ETF tracks its underlying index. These costs are appropriately called nontracking costs. The primary nontracking costs include commissions, bid-ask (or trading) spreads, premiums (to NAV), and taxes.

Commissions

Unlike mutual funds, ETFs are exclusively purchased and sold via traditional brokerage firms—not through the providers themselves, with the exception of Vanguard. These brokerage firms want to get paid for their efforts and therefore charge trading commissions. ETFs for the most part are subject to these expenses. Buy and sell transactions are typically not assessed commissions with mutual funds, but this is because some funds charge up-front or back-end loads, or commissions, while all mutual funds bake shareholder trading costs into their fund—which ultimately impacts a fund's NAV. Nonetheless, having a transparent expense is always preferable to a hidden and unknown fee.

Additionally, many brokerage firms—namely, Fidelity Investments, TD Ameritrade, Charles Schwab, Scottrade, and Vanguard—now offer commission-free trading on select ETFs to attract more investors and additional assets under management. When a shareholder wants to purchase an ETF, he or she executes a transaction with a brokerage firm. ETFs listed on the New York Stock Exchange have three-letter symbols, while the Nasdaq issues ETF symbols with four letters.

Bid-Ask Spreads

Bid-ask spreads, also referred to as trading spreads, are best defined as the difference between the price at which an investor sells a security and the price at which the counterparty investor purchases the security. Figure 5-4 shows some examples. Given their tradability on stock exchanges, all ETFs by nature trade with bid-ask spreads. There is simply no way around this cost. As a result, one-half of the bid-ask spread is a cost when you purchase an ETF, while the other half is the cost when you sell an ETF.

FIGURE 5-4

Trading Spreads for Select ETFs

ETF	Symbol	$ Spread	% Spread
Market Vectors China	PEK	0.755	1.67
PowerShares Active Low Duration	PLK	0.403	1.61
WisdomTree Dreyfus Euro	EU	0.317	1.37
SPDR S&P International Health Care	IRY	0.322	1.03
Vanguard Mortgaged Backed Securities	VMBS	0.275	0.55
SPDR S&P 500	SPY	0.014	0.01

Source: Frush Financial Group

For the most part, bid-ask spreads are quite small and com-pletely transparent. There is no hiding either bid and ask prices or the corresponding spread in between. The spread between the bid price and ask price is dictated by an ETF's liquidity, which itself is based on the spreads of the underlying stocks. More liquid ETFs trade with narrower spreads (just pennies per share), whereas less liquid ETFs have wider spreads—sometimes reaching over $0.50 per share.

Knowing the spread is very important since it arms you with the ability to cut the spread with a limit order to buy or sell rather than entering a market order and accepting the spread as is. Mutual funds do not have bid-ask spreads on the fund level and therefore present a distinct advantage over ETFs in this regard. This is because mutual funds are not purchased or sold on a stock exchange and instead are transacted at the end-of-day price, which is the NAV. No matter how you slice it, the spread you pay to pur-chase or sell an ETF is a cost that simply cannot be avoided. Consider it your ante with investing.

Premiums

Premiums and discounts are nonexistent with mutual funds since shareholders transact at the NAV. Premiums and discounts are most widely associated with closed-end funds. Consequently, most closed-end funds trade either at discounts to NAV or at premiums to NAV. As for ETFs, premiums and discounts are typically a non-issue given the creation and redemption process via arbitrage trades by APs. Nonetheless, premiums and discounts do exist for some ETFs and sometimes for extended periods of time. Non-Treasury bond ETFs are the most susceptible due to illiquidity of underlying fixed-income securities or to uncontrollable external factors such as the halt of the creation and redemption process attributed to regulatory scrutiny. International ETFs are more susceptible to the occurrence of premiums than U.S. ETFs.

Taxes

The favorable tax treatment afforded ETFs is one of the top two reasons for investing in ETFs over comparable mutual funds. Unlike mutual funds, ETFs have inherent efficiencies due to the creation and redemption process, where little to no capital gains tax liability is incurred. Of course, the tax liability depends on the type of ETF since currency, leveraged or inverse, and, most important, commodities-related holdings have less favorable tax treatment. Most plain vanilla ETFs have never made a capital gain distribution in their existence—a claim very few mutual funds can make. For tax-exempt investors, capital gains are a nonissue since they are reinvested with no outflow of capital to pay taxes. However, fully taxable investors cannot say the same thing. Furthermore, mutual fund portfolio managers can find themselves in tricky situations when they must decide between selling an overvalued underlying security with unrealized gains and holding the security to avoid triggering capital gains taxes.

Leveraged and inverse ETFs have paid out substantial capital gains, and so too have currency-related ETFs. Not knowing this difference between ETFs can get investors in trouble and expose them to unintended taxes. For instance, most investors do not know that investing in precious metals ETFs, such as the massive SPDR Gold Shares (symbol GLD), will mean that capital gains are taxed at a 28 percent rate since precious metals are considered collectibles. Additionally, most investors are not aware of the tax provisions of commodity investing. According to IRS rules, for an ETF in which the underlying securities are commodity futures, gains are taxed as 60 percent long-term gains and 40 percent short-term gains. Complicating the issue is the IRS rule that gains are considered "marked to market," meaning the gains are recognized at the end of the year and thus payable even though the investment was not liquidated.

In addition to capital gains taxes, taxes on dividends and interest are also quite common. This is nothing different from investing in mutual funds, however. When an underlying security pays a dividend or interest payment, the ETF will reinvest or accrue the income and pass through to shareholders on certain dates. Depending on the type of account, income is fully taxable and typically charged against the taxpayer's federal tax rate.

Wash-Sale Rule with ETFs

The wash-sale tax rule was designed by the IRS to prevent an investor from claiming capital loss tax deductions on securities when the same investor turns around and purchases either the same security or one that is "substantially similar" within 30 days before or after the original sale. For investors that have embedded capital losses with an ETF, they may be able to do so and still avoid the wash-sale rule by buying an ETF in the same sector as the liquidated ETF from a different provider.

What is a "substantially similar" security you might ask? According to the IRS, a substantially similar security is either the same security or a security that is convertible to the same security, such as a call option or a convertible preferred stock or bond. As a result, purchasing a different ETF that tracks the same market segment—such as large-cap value stocks—would avoid the wash-sale rule since the ETF is not the same security nor is convertible to the same security. Similarly, investors are able to sell an ETF to take a capital loss and purchase a different ETF based on the same index without violating the wash-sale tax rule. This is something to keep in mind.

ETF VALUATION

In a perfect world, the listed market price for an ETF should equal its true fair value, but this is not always the case. As mentioned previously, market price is based on investor supply and demand for a security—with a little help from APs in the case of ETFs. However, when you drill down below the surface, you will discover a number of metrics or elements that define an ETF's fair value. This section provides details on the six metrics involved in deriving fair value. Each one of these metrics is fully transparent and published at least once every day—and some hundreds of times daily.

NAV

Most ETF providers calculate marked-to-market net NAV at least once per day, typically at the end of trading at 4 p.m. Eastern Time. The calculation of NAV is quite simple: the total liabilities of an ETF are subtracted from the total assets and then divided by the total number of ETF shares outstanding. The resulting number is expressed as a value per share and is used for the following day. Mutual funds also calculate NAV in the same manner.

IIV

Also referred to as intraday value or underlying trading value, this value is calculated and published under a separate symbol every 15 to 60 seconds. IIV is a calculation that determines the most recent real-time market value of an ETF based on the market prices of the underlying securities plus any estimated cash amounts (accrued dividends) associated with the creation unit. This figure is expressed on a per-share basis and is available from most quote data services. This calculation is important since it provides investors with a snapshot value of the holdings, which can then be compared against the current market price of the ETF—all intraday.

Shares Outstanding

Shares outstanding is simply the number of shares an ETF has issued as of the close of the market on the previous trading day. This number, expressed in the 1,000s, is used to calculate NAV. However, given that ETFs are open-ended funds, the number of shares outstanding is not fixed and instead changes intraday due to purchase and sale transactions by shareholders.

Accumulated Dividends

Although only applicable to certain ETFs, accumulated dividends refers to the amount of cash an ETF has received and currently holds before issuing cash dividends to shareholders. The ETF typically, but not always, pays dividends to shareholders on a quarterly basis. During that quarter, the ETF will have received numerous dividends from the underlying stocks since they pay at different times. The amount of accumulated dividends embedded in an ETF is captured in the market price as well as the IIV. Accumulated dividends are expressed in per-share terms and can be determined separately.

Estimated Cash Amount

Estimated cash amount—per creation unit—is designed to provide APs with an idea of approximately how much cash per creation unit will be required to create or redeem ETF shares on a specific trading day. The methodology employed differs from one ETF provider to another provider based on their investment policies and procedures.

Total Cash Required

This value refers to the cash needed—per creation unit—in regard to the creation and redemption process executed the prior day. This value ensures that the creations and redemptions occur at the NAV, thus avoiding any dilution in value of existing ETF shares as a result of the process.

## CHAPTER 6

Regulations and Issuance: Bringing an ETF to Market

Exchange-traded portfolios (ETPs) are regulated by a number of divisions within the Securities and Exchange Commission (SEC) as well as other regulatory entities, such as the CFTC, or Commodity Futures Trading Commission. Within the SEC, the Division of Trading and Markets (formerly known as the SEC Division of Market Regulation) is charged with the responsibility of regulating the "exchange-traded" feature of ETPs—including the regulation of all major stock exchanges in the United States. Additionally, the SEC Division of Investment Management is charged with the responsibility of regulating the "portfolio" feature. There is a clear and distinct separation of enforcement and regulatory duties between divisions and entities within and outside the SEC. For example, the CFTC has jurisdiction over commodity-based ETPs, while the SEC Division of Corporate Finance holds jurisdiction over exchange-traded notes (ETNs). The SEC adheres to and enforces rules and regulations based on a number of acts of Congress.

GOVERNMENT REGULATION

The two most important and applicable legislative acts impacting the registration, issuance, and ongoing oversight of exchange-traded funds (ETFs)—and all other ETPs—are the Securities Act of 1933 and the Investment Company Act of 1940.

Securities Act of 1933

In the aftermath of the stock market crash of 1929, the U.S. Congress enacted the Securities Act of 1933, requiring that any offer or sale of securities using the means and instrumentalities of interstate commerce be registered pursuant to the 1933 act unless an exemption from registration exists under U.S. law.

The enactment of the 1933 act is considered a milestone event in securities legislation because it was the first major piece of federal legislation to regulate the offer and sale of securities—a task primarily given to the states and regulated under state laws, commonly referred to as blue-sky laws. Unless a security qualifies for an exemption, any security offered or sold to the public in the United States must be registered by filing a registration statement—typically along with a prospectus—with the SEC. The SEC then conducts a thorough screening of the proposed security, a process that can take many months or even years.

Investment Company Act of 1940

To again help restore the public's confidence in the stock market after the 1929 crash, Congress passed the Investment Company Act of 1940 on August 22, 1940. The aim was to enhance regulations of investment companies to protect the interests of the public by setting strict standards of conduct. Many provisions of this act were updated by the Dodd-Frank Act of 2010.

Under this act, investment companies were now required to establish regular reporting procedures for each fund, set minimum standards of fund diversification, and introduce new rules for advertising; and the act gave the SEC regulatory oversight. Material facts—including conflicts of interest—were now required to be disclosed to the investing public. Furthermore, the act required investment companies to disclose all material facts concerning their financial health.

Most important, the act strictly defined and divided investment companies into three classifications—face-amount certificate companies, unit investment trusts (UITs), and investment management companies. Before 1940 no standard for what an investment company looked like was yet established. Imagine that.

Exemptive Relief

When the Investment Company Act of 1940 was drafted, Congress could not have envisioned the creation of or demand for ETFs some 50-plus years later. As a result, for ETFs to receive approval from the SEC, they need to be granted exemptive relief from a number of rules and regulations associated with the 1940 act. Let's investigate four of the most pressing needs.

First, ETF providers must be permitted to issue shares redeemable only in large blocks—creation units. Thus, exemptive relief is needed from Section 22d and Rule 22c-1. Second, in-kind purchase and redemption of creation units by authorized participants must be allowed—thus exemptive relief from Sections 17(a) and 17(b) is needed. Third, exemptive relief from Rule 22c-1 is needed to permit trading of shares to occur at prices other than at the net asset value (NAV). Finally, an exemption needs to be granted allowing investment companies to purchase shares of the ETF in excess of the act's fund-of-fund regulations—Section 12(d)(1). Petitioning the SEC to grant the aforementioned exemptions and others is a time-consuming and costly activity. Given the significant growth in ETFs and the need for exemptions, the SEC announced in 2008 a proposal to adopt Rule 6c-11, a regulation change that would automatically grant several exemptions without the need to seek exemptions for each new ETF.

Listing Requirements

In addition to SEC rules and regulations, stock exchanges themselves present their own requirements for listing on their platforms. All ETFs, whether they hold domestic securities or international securities, are required to issue a minimum of 100,000 shares at the time of trading commencement, with a minimum quoting price variation of $0.01 per share. However, stock exchanges have additional requirements for domestic stock ETFs, international stock ETFs, and fixed-income ETFs. Per the *NYSE Listed Company Manual*, domestic stock ETFs are required to meet the following five listing rules:

1. Component stocks that in the aggregate account for at least 90 percent of the weight of the index or portfolio each must have a minimum market value of at least $75 million;

2. Component stocks that in the aggregate account for at least 90 percent of the weight of the index or portfolio each must have a minimum monthly trading volume during each of the last six months of at least 250,000 shares;
3. The most heavily weighted U.S. Component Stock may not exceed 30 percent of the weight of the index or portfolio, and the five most heavily weighted component stocks may not exceed 65 percent of the weight of the index or portfolio;
4. The index or portfolio must include a minimum of 13 component stocks; and
5. All securities in the underlying index or portfolio must be U.S. Component Stocks listed on a national securities exchange and shall be NMS stocks as defined in Rule 600 of Regulation NMS under the Exchange Act.

Per the *NYSE Listed Company Manual*, fixed-income ETFs are required to meet the following six listing rules:

1. The index or portfolio must consist of fixed-income securities;
2. Components that in aggregate account for at least 75% of the weight of the index or portfolio must have a minimum original principal amount outstanding of $100 million or more;
3. A component may be a convertible security; however, once the convertible security component converts to the underlying equity security, the component is removed from the index or portfolio;
4. No component fixed-income security (excluding Treasury Securities or GSE Securities) will represent more than 30% of the weight of the index, and the five highest weighted component fixed-income securities in the index do not in the aggregate account for more than 65% of the weight of the index;
5. An underlying index or portfolio (excluding one consisting entirely of exempted securities) must include a minimum of 13 non-affiliated issuers; and
6. Component securities that in aggregate account for at least 90% of the weight of the index or portfolio must be either a) from issuers that are required to file reports pursuant to Sections 13 and 15(d) of the Exchange Act; b) from issuers that have a worldwide market value of its outstanding common equity held by non-affiliates of $700 million or more; c) from issuers that have outstanding securities that are notes, bonds debentures, or evidence of indebtedness having a total remaining principal

amount of at least $1 billion; d) exempted securities as defined in Section 3(a)(12) of the Exchange Act; or e) from issuers that are a government of a foreign country or a political subdivision of a foreign country.

Exemption to Rule 12(d)(1)

Today, many institutions—including mutual funds—employ ETFs in their portfolios for a number of reasons. These include cash management and ease of gaining exposure to a defined market segment. Some mutual funds hold only ETFs and no stocks. This is typically seen with asset allocation funds or sector rotating funds. Nonetheless, for investment companies registered under the 1940 act to make investments in other companies registered under the same act, an exemption to Section 12(d)(1) of the Investment Company Act of 1940 must be granted by the SEC. The first such exemption was granted in 2003 to Barclays Global Investors and has become commonplace today for most ETF providers.

LEGAL STRUCTURES

For most investors, ETFs represent all funds that are listed and traded on an exchange. Unbeknown to many, ETFs are just one of the many different types of ETPs available. Even the *Wall Street Journal* lists prices for ETFs under the title "Exchange-Traded Portfolios." This is an appropriate move since many special trusts, limited partnerships, and notes have the same look and feel as an ETF, but simply do not have many of the same important characteristics. Nonetheless, the use of the term ETF has become engrained in popular culture and is now the preferred title for all ETPs. As mentioned, many ETPs do not have all—and some none—of the primary characteristics that define ETFs. Some ETPs are not truly low cost, while others are not tax efficient. Consider currency funds, for example, where—by law—gains are taxed as ordinary income, which is typically a higher rate than taxes on capital gains. Still others do not have a creation and redemption process, specifically physical precious metals trusts.

This section provides a brief overview on each legal structure to enable investors to better differentiate each type of ETP.

Closed-End Fund

Closed-end funds, like ETFs, are collective investments where investors pool their money in one fund that invests in an underlying basket of securities. Figure 6-1 outlines some of the prominent similarities and differences.

FIGURE 6-1

Differences Between ETFs and Closed-End Funds

Characteristic	ETFs	Closed-End Funds
Organization Method	Investment Company Act of 1940	Investment Company Act of 1940
Method of Launch	Seeded and Listed	IPO
Exchange Traded	Yes	Yes
Number of Outstanding Shares	Changing	Fixed
Stocklike Tradability	Yes	Yes
Traded at Premiums and Discounts	No	Yes
Can Be Sold Short	Yes	Yes
Purchased on Margin	Yes	Yes
Portfolio Turnover	Low	Low
Source Liquidity from Underlying Holdings	Yes	No

Source: Frush Financial Group

Contrary to misconception, closed-end funds are not closed to new investors. But rather, closed-end funds do not issue new shares of the fund once the initial shares are sold to investors. Once all the initial shares are sold, the only way investors can purchase shares is in the secondary market on a stock exchange. This means that prices for closed-end funds are dictated by supply-and-demand forces, much like that of ETFs. However, closed-end funds do not involve authorized participants (APs) and therefore cannot arbitrage away any trading premiums or discounts to NAV. This disadvantage is actually an advantage to some investors, who only invest in closed-end funds and make purchase and sale decisions based solely on the amount of premium or discount and on how that premium or discount is changing over time. Furthermore, some investors seek out closed-end funds that they believe will experience narrowing in the discount to NAV.

For example, suppose an investor purchases a certain closed-end fund for $20 per share when the NAV is $22. If the discount were to narrow from $2 to $1 per share, then the investor will make $1—even if the value of the underlying securities stayed the same. Most closed-end funds trade with discounts that range from 15 to 25 percent of NAV and, given these sizable discounts, make closed-end funds more price volatile than other ETPs. Regardless of the presence of discounts or premiums, closed-end funds offer an alternative way for people to invest their money. If you want to know more about closed-end funds, the Closed-End Fund Association, a national trade association of approximately two dozen fund managers, can offer help. The association's Web site is www.cefa.com.

UIT

Organized under the Investment Company Act of 1940, the UIT structure was the first legal structure employed to launch ETFs. Today, some of the most well-known ETFs are organized as UITs, including SPDR S&P 500, SPDR Dow Jones Industrial Average "Diamonds," and finally the PowerShares QQQ Trust, which tracks the Nasdaq-100 Index. Unlike the subsequent open-end fund structure, UITs are required to include all securities in an index—no sampling and optimization is permitted. ETF providers do not have the discretion over which securities to include and which to remove—they must include all securities of the tracking index—no less and no more. The only flexibility granted by the SEC is the timing of when to make the fund rebalancing needed to track an index that was recently reconstituted.

Additional restrictions include the following:

- No more than 25 percent of the assets of the fund can be tied to a company that has a weighting of 5 percent or greater.

- No more than 50 percent of the assets of an ETF can be tied to industry sectors or concentrated holdings.
- No more than 10 percent of the voting stock of any one company can be controlled by the fund.

These restrictions are typically not of concern for most broadly diversified UITs but can be problematic for funds that target economic sectors or specific country segments. Finally, even though UITs may receive a dividend from an underlying stock, the trust is not permitted to reinvest the money back into shares of the underlying stocks. Instead, the trust must hold dividends in non-interest-bearing escrow accounts until quarter end when the trust distributes the accumulated cash to shareholders. Because the performance of the tracked index includes the immediate reinvestment of dividends, tracking error will occur. This performance penalty is referred to as dividend drag.

Open-End Fund
(Regulated Investment Company)

Most newly launched ETFs are organized as regulated investment companies (RICs) under the Investment Company Act of 1940. There are five primary reasons for this trend. First and foremost, the RIC structure provides significant flexibility to ETF providers in regard to managing underlying holdings. Gone is the restriction that an ETF must comprise each and every security in the tracking index as with the UIT structure. Instead, a RIC can use sampling and optimization to track an index. RICs can also include futures, options, and fixed-income securities as well as common stocks.

Second, in contrast to UITs, RICs are permitted to reinvest—rather than accrue in escrow accounts—dividends by purchasing additional shares of the paying stocks. This eliminates the performance penalty associated with dividend drag that other ETFs may experience.

Third, ETFs organized as RICs are permitted to invest up to 50 percent of their assets in single concentrated positions and 25 percent in any one security, provided the ETF is registered as a nondiversified fund and controls no more than 10 percent of any one company's voting stock.

Fourth, the RIC structure also provides for an unusual, but very lucrative, activity—the loaning of underlying securities. When a RIC loans underlying securities, the extra revenue earned can be used to offset operating expenses and thus charge reduced expense ratios to shareholders. BlackRock, Vanguard, State Street, and other large ETF providers are highly engaged in this activity for this very reason.

Fifth, ETFs organized as RICs give shareholders the right to vote the shares they own. To some shareholders this is extremely important, and to some it's much less important.

The leading drawback of the RIC structure results from the inherent flexibility that providers have in managing the fund. As a result, poor decisions and policies on behalf of ETF providers lead to tracking error and therefore potential underperformance of the tracking index.

Grantor Trust

An exchange-traded grantor trust is not a RIC nor a UIT and is instead registered under the Securities Act of 1933. Shareholders have voting rights in the underlying companies and can transact shares in round lots of 100. Dividends are not reinvested in the trust and are instead paid immediately to shareholders. The portfolio of stocks under the exchange-traded grantor trust does not change and, as a result, cannot be rebalanced. Over time, this arrangement will ultimately lead to a less diversified portfolio since some of the underlying stocks appreciate in value while others are removed by way of merger, acquisition, or bankruptcy. Some ETPs organized under the grantor trust structure are commodity related. Under this arrangement, actual physical commodities are held by the trust and thus constitute the underlying holdings. Three of the most widely recognized ETPs include CurrencyShares, iShares Gold Trust, and iShares Silver Trust.

Holding Company Depositary Receipts
A type of grantor trust, holding company depositary receipts (HOLDRs), are very much like ETFs from the perspective of invest-

ing in a fund where the underlying securities track a certain index or market segment. However, HOLDRs are not actually funds like ETFs. HOLDRs may resemble ETFs, but there are a several important dissimilarities.

First, HOLDRs represents a pool of only 20 initial stocks that are held in a grantor trust owned by Merrill Lynch, the brainchild behind the product. Over time, the number of stocks in the trust can fall as the companies are acquired or merge with other companies. No replacements are made to the trust when a company is removed. As mentioned, this will ultimately lead to a less diversified fund, much like the Internet Holding HOLDRs (symbol HHH), where more than 50 percent of its fund is invested in Yahoo! and eBay with no allocation to Google since the initial public offering (IPO) was issued after the fund creation date.

Second, unlike UIT structure ETFs, where the voting rights are held by the ETF providers, not the fund shareholders, HOLDRs provide the unique ability for shareholders to receive proxies and vote directly on issues involving the companies held in the trust, such as voting on the board of directors.

Third, shareholders of HOLDRs are entitled to receive dividends directly from the companies held in the trust. Fourth, shareholders do not pay expense ratios and instead are assessed an annual custody fee per share for cash dividends and distributions. Finally, to invest in HOLDRs, a shareholder must purchase and sell shares in blocks of 100, which is in contrast to ETFs where trades can be executed with as little as 1 share. HOLDRs typically cover a narrow market segment, such as the Biotech (symbol BBH) or Broadband (symbol BDH) HOLDRs.

ETNs

First issued in 2006 by Barclays Bank, ETNs are debt instruments that track the return of a single currency, commodity, or index. See Figure 6-2 for a thumbnail comparison of ETFs and ETNs.

In contrast to ETFs, ETNs do not hold or represent a pool of underlying securities. Rather, ETNs are senior, unsecured, unsubordinated direct debt of a leading bank and registered under the Securities Act of 1933. ETNs employ an arbitrage strategy whereby market prices are closely linked to the intrinsic value of the bench-

FIGURE 6-2

Differences Between ETFs and ETNs

Characteristic	ETFs	ETNs
Ability to Sell Short	Yes	Yes
Composition of Instrument	Portfolio of Securities	Issuer Credit
Continuous Pricing and Trading Throughout the Day	Yes	Yes
Distribution of Dividends	Yes	No
Have a Maturity Date	No	Yes
Have an NAV	Yes	No
Marginable	Yes	Yes
Method of Registration and Regulation	Investment Company Act of 1940	Securities Act of 1933
Purchased Through a Traditional Brokerage Account and IRA	Yes	Yes
Quantity Available	Significant	Few
Risks to Investment	Market Risk	Market Risk and Issuer Credit Risk
Tax Treatment	Typically similar to stocks where positions held for longer than one year qualify for long-term capital gains treatment	Similar to stocks where positions held for longer than one year qualify for long-term capital gains treatment

Source: Frush Financial Group

marks each ETN tracks. ETNs are established with 30-year maturities and offer no principal protection. In addition, ETNs do not pay dividends or interest payments, do not offer voting rights to shareholders, and are subject to call provisions at the discretion of the issuer.

The primary drawback or risk of investing in ETNs is the credit risk associated with the issuing bank. If the credit rating of the issuing bank were to be cut, then the value of the ETN may fall even though there is no change to the tracking index. A bankruptcy by the issuer can lead to a completely worthless investment.

The primary advantage of ETNs is their favorable tax treatment—positions held for at least one year are taxed as long-term capital gains and thus receive lower tax rates. This is especially important for those investors who hold taxable portfolios and wish to gain exposure to specific sectors of the commodities market. Secondary advantages include stocklike tradability and the opportunity to invest in defined market segments such as grains, sugar, and livestock.

Investors who hold ETNs have three ways to liquidate their investment:

1. Sell the shares in the secondary market like any other security
2. Sell the shares through a weekly redemption program with the issuing bank for cash (only for large shareholders)
3. Hold the shares to maturity and receive the market value of the position in cash from the issuing bank

Traded Commodity Pool

One of the most recent innovations with ETPs is the exchange-traded commodity pool—typically organized as Delaware limited partnerships. Traded commodity pools are not registered with or regulated by the SEC under the Investment Company Act of 1940. Instead, traded commodity pools are regulated by the CFTC. ETFs that hold physical commodity positions are regulated by the SEC under the Securities Act of 1933, however. About 10 percent of all assets held in ETFs are invested in traded commodity pools.

These partnerships or trusts issue units that may be purchased and sold on the NYSE. Instead of using stocks or physical commodities for the underlying holdings, the partnership uses commodity futures contracts and other commodity-related futures, forwards, and swap contracts to gain the targeted exposure they desire. Shareholders become limited partners when they invest in a traded commodity pool, while the general partners (equivalent to ETF providers) oversee the management of the partnership assets. One of the largest general partners is United States Commodity Funds, LLC, which runs the popular United States Oil Fund (symbol USO) and the United States Natural Gas Fund (symbol UNG). Similar to other ETFs, traded commodity pools attempt to generate a return that tracks specific indexes rather than attempting to outperform them outright.

Traded commodity pools have come under intense scrutiny over the last couple of years, given their inherent drawback when exposed to what is called "contango." Contango is a pricing situation in which futures prices get progressively higher as monthly contract dates get progressively longer. As a result, when a monthly contract is rolled forward, the contract must be purchased at a higher price than that of the previous monthly contract, thus creating negative spreads and hurting performance. Nonetheless, traded commodity pools offer investors an extra option to gain exposure to target commodity classes.

Figure 6-3 presents a summary of the legal structures for the different kinds of ETPs.

LOGISTICS OF LAUNCHING AN ETF

The logistics of launching an ETF and bringing it to market start with the process of creating a blueprint of the planned ETF. But before the ETF can be listed and offered for sale to the general investing public, there are a number of time-consuming and expensive activities that must be accomplished. Figure 6-4 presents a regulatory timeline for some ETFs that shows how long the process can take.

The following is a simplified overview of the process from concept to listed product to give you a better handle on the complexities of launching an ETF.

Product Design

During this initial phase, an ETF provider will design exactly what ETF it wants to establish. Will the ETF provider look to start an ETF that tracks a market index, or will the provider create an ETF that tracks a custom index and thus employ active management. Selecting the appropriate legal structure—including related regulatory, tax, and accounting considerations—is, of course, vital and necessary during the design phase. Other important considerations include how to incorporate issues relating to the underlying securities (e.g., liquidity, transparency of trading and pricing, and clearance and settlement arrangements), how complex to make the fund (e.g., multiclass, master feeder, or fund of funds), how to deal with intellectual property issues (e.g., trademarks and patents), and finally how best to satisfy shareholder demands and preferences.

FIGURE 6-3

Summary of Legal Structures

FEATURE	CLOSED-END FUND	UNIT INVESTMENT TRUST (UIT)	OPEN-END FUND (RIC)	GRANTOR TRUST	EXCHANGE-TRADED NOTE (ETN)	TRADED COMMODITY POOL
Leading ETFs	N/A	Diamonds, SPDRs, and PowerShares QQQ Trust	iShares, Select Sector SPDRs, PowerShares, and Vanguard	CurrencyShares, iShares Gold Trust, and HOLDRs	iPath ETNs, ELEMENTS ETNs	U.S. Oil Fund
Registered Under	Investment Company Act of 1940	Investment Company Act of 1940	Investment Company Act of 1940	Securities Act of 1933	Securities Act of 1933	Securities Act of 1933
Structure	Corporate or Trust	Trust	Corporate or Trust	Trust	Bond or Note	Trust or Limited Partnership
Tracks an Index	No	Yes—Must Fully Replicate	Yes—May Sample and Optimize	No—Custom-Weighted Basket	Varies	Varies
Reinvests Dividends	Yes	No	Yes	No	Implied	Varies
U.S. Tax Reporting Method	Form 1099	Form 1099	Form 1099	Grantor Trust Letter	Interest or Prepaid Contract	Form K-1
Redemption In-Kind Option	No	No	No	No	Yes	No
Concentrated Positions Permitted	No	No	No	Yes	Yes	Yes
Underlying Holdings	Actively Managed	Index	Index or Limited Active Management	Preset Basket of Securities or Physical Commodities	Secured Notes	Index Futures Fund

Source: Frush Financial Group

FIGURE 6-4

Regulatory Timeline for Select ETFs

ETF	Structure	Application Filing Date	Order Granted	Elapsed Time*
QQQ	Unit Investment Trust	8/19/98	2/22/99	6 Months
DIAMONDS	Unit Investment Trust	6/17/97	12/30/97	6 Months
VIPERs	Open-End Fund (RIC)	5/12/00	12/12/00	7 Months
iShares	Open-End Fund (RIC)	4/30/99	5/12/00	13 Months
WEBS	Open-End Fund (RIC)	9/19/94	3/5/96	18 Months
Select Sector SPDRs	Open-End Fund (RIC)	5/13/97	11/13/98	18 Months
Country Baskets	Open-End Fund (RIC)	8/19/94	3/5/96	19 Months
MidCap SPDRs	Unit Investment Trust	5/28/93	1/18/95	20 Months
S&P Dep. Rec. SPDRs	Unit Investment Trust	6/25/90	10/26/92	28 Months

Sorted by shortest to longest elapsed time.

Source: Frush Financial Group

Partnerships

Once the design phase is complete, the ETF provider will select and form partnerships with a number of important intermediaries. These include a listing stock exchange, custodian (i.e., service provider), distributor, specialist firm, and APs. When selecting an exchange, an ETF provider will consider product support, reputation, liquidity, trading volume, and cross-listing arrangements. As for a custodian, an ETF provider will consider reputation and commitment, technology, complete product offerings, and programs in which to participate in the lending of securities to generate incremental revenue. With distributors, an ETF provider will select the best firm to act as liaison between the custodian and the APs. Specialists and APs with reputations for providing liquidity and facilitating a robust creation and redemption process are sought after. Finally, an ETF provider will need to make personnel decisions such as choosing a chief compliance officer and trustees.

Registration

At this point, an ETF provider is now prepared to file a registration statement (including the prospectus and exhibits) for the desired ETF with the SEC. All exemptive relief requests will be made at this time as well. Amendments to the registration statement may need to be filed from time to time before ultimate approval. The SEC is not especially quick in its responses, and the approval process could take many months or even longer.

Marketing

Once the SEC has granted formal approval for the launch of the planned ETF, the marketing machine of the ETF provider goes into high gear. Without the early attention to the upcoming launch, the ETF could fail to attract shareholder interest and subsequent assets.

Seeding (Incubation)

During the seeding phase, an authorized participant will deliver a basket of underlying securities predetermined by the ETF provider for deposit into the ETF's portfolio with the selected custodian. This basket of underlying securities typically includes most—if not all—of the underlying securities that constitute the tracking index. In exchange for delivering the basket of securities, the authorized participant will receive an equivalent value of ETF shares in creation units. From this point forward, the AP can elect to hold the shares in creation units or sell some or all into the secondary market, where they are purchased, sold, and priced throughout the day on a stock exchange.

Listing

Now that the new ETF has received seeding, it is essentially ready to be listed on the selected stock exchange and begin trading. Within a short period of time, the ETF provider will find out if its hard work will be rewarded through shareholder interest and accompanying asset inflows.

## CHAPTER 7

Players and Participants: The Who's Who of All Things ETFs

Have you ever wondered on which stock exchange or exchanges most exchange-traded funds (ETFs) are listed? How about which ETF provider is the biggest and which the least expensive? Perhaps you're interested in who is behind the creation and management of the indexes themselves? This chapter is all about getting to know the key players and participants in the ETF marketplace. As you would expect, there are many different types of players and participants, each fulfilling a unique and important role. Viewing each as links in a chain—beginning with the index sponsors and ending with the shareholders—is a simple but effective analogy.

Knowing the key players and participants will help you to understand the complexities of the ETF marketplace, and that's important when making decisions on where and how to invest your money. To illustrate where they fall from a timing perspective, I have divided the players and participants into three simplified groups—back office, middle office, and front office. There are additional participants not included in this chapter, as they serve only minor roles in the ETF marketplace. These include consultants, tax professionals, and fund supermarkets. Figure 7-1 is a graphical illustration of the ETF ecosystem.

FIGURE 7-1

The ETF Ecosystem

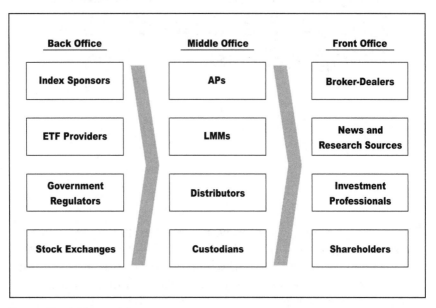

Back Office	Middle Office	Front Office
Index Sponsors	APs	Broker-Dealers
ETF Providers	LMMs	News and Research Sources
Government Regulators	Distributors	Investment Professionals
Stock Exchanges	Custodians	Shareholders

Source: Frush Financial Group

BACK OFFICE: WHERE IT ALL BEGINS

The following section highlights the key players and participants involved in the early stages of bringing an ETF to market. These include index sponsors, ETF providers, government regulators, and stock exchanges.

Index Sponsors

The focal point of any ETF is the index an ETF tracks—a road map of sorts. There are two kinds of indexes—market and custom. Some providers emphasize well-known and traditional market indexes, such as the S&P 500 and the Dow Jones Industrial Average (DJIA), while other providers emphasize custom indexes that they create on their own. Standard & Poor's, most recognized for its credit rating services, is owned by McGraw-Hill, the publisher of this book. Standard & Poor's maintains hundreds of indexes in addition to its most widely recognized index, the S&P 500. There are more ETFs tracking S&P indexes than any other index sponsor in the world. With over 3,000 indexes, Dow Jones Indexes is a formidable competitor, especially when you consider that the DJIA is the most widely recognized index in the world. Other significant players in the index space include Russell Investments, Morgan Stanley Capital International, and Wilshire Associates.

Much of the growth in new ETFs can be attributed to the increase in popularity of proprietary custom indexes. The reason for this is quite simple—the big players have more or less cornered the market on the market indexes, leaving the smaller and newer providers no other option but to create custom indexes. Nonetheless, many smaller and newer ETF providers such as Claymore, First Trust, and Guggenheim have developed interesting ETFs using nontraditional indexes that give investors greater investing options and ways to enhance their portfolios.

ETF Providers

Providers are those investment companies that create, launch, and manage ETFs. There are literally dozens and dozens of providers issuing any number of ETFs—from just a couple to over 100. However, control of ETFs is concentrated in both number and total assets under management in a few big providers—namely, BlackRock (iShares), State Street (SPDRs), Vanguard, Invesco (PowerShares), and ProFunds (ProShares). See Figure 7-2 for the top 10 largest providers.

Most, but not all, of the largest ETF providers were firmly entrenched in their investment management business when ETFs were first developed. As the popularity of ETFs soared, so too did the involvement of the big providers in the ETF space. It was a natural transition for many. However, some of the providers do have to walk a fine line, as they are firmly committed financially and in reputation to active portfolio management. Consider Charles Schwab, for example. Although not a significant ETF provider, Schwab prides itself on managing portfolios and generating out-

FIGURE 7-2

Top 10 Largest ETF Providers

Rank	ETF Provider	Assets ($M)	Assets %	ETFs #	ETFs %
1	BlackRock (iShares)	448,389	44	220	20
2	StateStreet (SPDRs)	234,738	23	93	8
3	Vanguard	147,926	15	63	6
4	Invesco (PowerShares)	54,020	5	142	13
5	ProFunds (ProShares)	23,569	2	112	10
6	Van Eck (Market Vectors)	20,000	2	33	3
7	Bank of New York Mellon	12,211	1	1	1
8	WisdomTree	9,891	1	44	4
9	Barclays (iPath)	8,474	1	50	5
10	Direxion	6,571	1	39	4

Source: Strategic Insight and BlackRock, December 2010

performance (alpha) in many of its mutual funds. To then turn around and offer passively managed ETFs can send a conflicting signal. If active management can be so powerful, then why allocate resources to passively run ETFs?

There are many smaller providers as well that you may not have heard of before—such as AdvisorShares, Deutsche Bank, ETF Securities, FaithShares, First Trust, FocusShares, Global X, Guggenheim, Pax World, Revenue Shares, and ALPS. Most of the smaller to mid-sized providers attempt to carve out a niche rather than issue an ETF that already exists and go head-to-head with the big providers—and their massive marketing budgets and name recognition. The name of the game is to design it better or different. Please see Appendix A at the back of this book for a detailed list of select ETF providers.

Who is the top ETF provider as measured by loyalty from financial advisors? That prize goes to Vanguard—according to a 2010 study by Cogent Research. Vanguard is followed by BlackRock (iShares) at number two, State Street Global Advisors at number three, and Pacific Investment Management Company (PIMCO) at number four—and that's out of dozens of ETF providers.

Government Regulators

As with anything else related to investing, you can't escape big brother. This is exemplified by the memorable line from the movie *The Firm*: "Somewhere, inside, in the dark, the firm is listening." Although ETFs do not have a dedicated regulator such as the Commodity Futures Trading Commission (CFTC) for commodity futures trading, the Securities and Exchange Commission (SEC) and the Financial Industry Regulatory Authority (FINRA) are highly engaged in monitoring and shaping the ETF marketplace. For example, the SEC is responsible for approving new ETFs as well as the rules related to how they are traded—among other dictates. FINRA is a private corporation acting as a self-regulatory organization that performs financial regulation of member broker-dealers and exchange markets. Together they serve to make and enforce rules to ensure the viability and efficiency of the financial markets. Other regulators that have a role to play with ETFs include the Federal Reserve, the U.S. Treasury Department, and the aforementioned CFTC.

Stock Exchanges

Stock exchanges are active hubs where the buying and selling of stocks and ETFs is accomplished. In the past, exchanges were dominated by pits, where traders physically gathered to execute purchase and sale orders through an open-outcry system. Today, ETF trading is handled by electronic systems that enhance the efficiency of the exchange and provide for greater trading volumes. Perhaps dropping the word *stock* from *stock exchange* is now in order. Stock exchanges serve the role of intermediary between the ETF provider and the investing public. Figure 7-3 lists the top 10 largest individual stock exchanges in the world.

The three most important stock exchanges for ETFs, past and present, include the American Stock Exchange, or AMEX (now owned by the New York Stock Exchange, or NYSE), the Nasdaq,

FIGURE 7-3

Top 10 Largest Global Stock Exchanges

Rank	Individual Stock Exchange	Headquarters	Market Cap. ($B)	No. of Listings
1	NYSE	New York, U.S.	13,390	2,317
2	Nasdaq	New York, U.S.	4,931	2,872
3	Tokyo Stock Exchange	Tokyo, Japan	3,827	2,292
4	London Stock Exchange	London, U.K.	3,613	2,966
5	Shanghai Stock Exchange	Shanghai, China	2,717	900
6	Hong Kong Stock Exchange	Hong Kong, China	2,711	1,421
7	Toronto Stock Exchange	Toronto, Canada	2,170	3,741
8	Bombay Stock Exchange	Mumbai, India	1,631	5,034
9	National Stock Exchange of India	Mumbai, India	1,596	1,552
10	BM&F Bovespa	São Paulo, Brazil	1,545	381

Snapshot as of December 2010

Source: Frush Financial Group

and finally the NYSE, the second oldest stock exchange in the United States after the Philadelphia Stock Exchange. Up until 2005, the AMEX was the top exchange for ETFs. However, in 2005 Barclays switched all 75-plus of its ETFs from the AMEX to the NYSE, citing better technology. As a result of the switch, the AMEX and NYSE boasted about half the ETFs in the marketplace listed on their exchanges. After the acquisition of the AMEX by the NYSE, the NYSE now controls more than 90 percent of all ETF listings in the United States. The Nasdaq controls a much smaller number of listings, but does boast the PowerShares QQQ ETF (tracking the Nasdaq-100), which is one of the most highly traded securities in the world.

MIDDLE OFFICE: THE TRANSITION TEAM

The following section highlights the key players and participants involved in the middle stages of bringing an ETF to market. These include authorized participants, lead market makers, distributors, and custodians.

Authorized Participants

Authorized participants (APs), also called creation unit holders, are typically large institutional investors, specialists, market makers, or lead market makers (LMMs) who have signed participant agreements with specific ETF providers to transact directly with providers in a process known as creations and redemptions. The creation process involves obtaining the underlying securities required to create an ETF and then transferring them to a custodian bank for the benefit of the ETF provider. In return, the provider delivers to the AP a creation unit of ETF shares—which are usually 50,000 or a multiple thereof—thus permitting the AP to either retain the ETF shares or sell them on the open market.

In the case of redemptions, an ETF provider will receive a creation unit (redemption basket) from the AP and deliver underlying securities with the lowest cost basis to the AP in order to minimize capital gains taxes for the ETF. As a result, the ETF provider will sell underlying securities with a higher cost basis, thus generating lower capital gains for the fund. The exchange of the underlying securities between the AP and the ETF provider is considered an "in-kind" exchange—meaning no exchange of cash and thereby reducing tax exposure on the fund level.

Some of the leading APs include the following:

- Bluefin Specialists
- Credit Suisse
- Deutsche Bank
- Goldman Sachs
- HSBC
- Jane Street
- JP Morgan Chase
- Knight Equity Markets
- Newedge USA
- LaBranche Structured Products
- Merrill Lynch Professional Clearing
- Nomura International Plc
- Societe Generale
- Susquehanna International Group
- UBS
- Wedbush Morgan Securitie

LMMs

Formerly known as specialists, LMMs are first and foremost contracted liquidity providers on an exchange. In addition, they have obligations to maintain a continuous quote, manage the opening and closing auction, provide price discovery, and drive the inside quote a certain percentage of time throughout the day. The most important difference between the old system of using specialists and the new system of using LMMs is that there is no longer a time and physical location advantage. As a result, LMMs are required to provide electronic liquidity in a specific ETF—the NYSE attempts to tie an LMM to all new products—with no more or better information than the rest of the investing public has. In addition to experience as a market maker, to become an LMM, the NYSE requires adequacy of capital, issuer preference, operational capacity and support personnel, and a willingness to promote the NYSE.

Obviously LMMs will only perform this role for compensation. For satisfying the requirements, LMMs receive a small additional rebate for each product in which they are involved. The more an ETF trades, the more an LMM stands to be compensated. This arrangement aligns the goals of the exchange with the compensation of the LMM. LMMs can also make money through traditional specialist activities such as buying on the bid, selling on the ask, and pocketing the spread. Furthermore, they can receive fees for loaning securities in inventory.

Distributors

When an ETF provider does not want to distribute its own ETFs, it must hire an external distributor. The primary role of the distributor is to act as a liaison between the ETF custodian and the APs when creating or redeeming shares in creation units. In addition, distributors deploy experienced sales teams composed of external and internal wholesalers to market ETFs to institutional asset managers and financial advisors in the broker-dealer and registered investment advisor marketplaces. Distributors also help with product positioning in order to differentiate ETFs from the crowd and to capitalize on platform opportunities to increase asset inflows.

Custodians

Also known as a service provider, a custodian is best described as a specialized financial organization that is responsible for physically holding and safeguarding financial assets—namely, securities for an

ETF. Custodians serve the traditional role of transfer agent and fund administrator and do not engage in traditional commercial or consumer banking activities such as mortgages or personal lending. Rather, custodians process and account for the purchases, sells, and position quantity for each security in an ETF. When there are creations and redemptions in an ETF, the custodian is charged with the task of ensuring that the type and quantity of securities are exactly what they should be. Custodians are compensated much like ETF providers; they earn a fee based on the value of the assets held. Custodians do not exclusively work with ETFs. They are involved with many other securities, such as American Depository Receipts, which are also held and safeguarded by custodians.

The following companies offer custodian banking services:

- Bank of New York Mellon
- BNP Paribas Securities
- Brown Brothers Harriman
- Citibank
- Credit Suisse
- Deutsche Bank
- Fifth Third Bank
- Goldman Sachs
- HSBC
- J.P. Morgan Chase Services
- Japan Trustee Services Bank
- Northern Trust Bank
- The Master Trust Bank of Japan
- UBS
- Wells Fargo Bank

FRONT OFFICE: SERVING THE END USER

The following section highlights the key players and participants involved in either the final stages of bringing an ETF to market or once an ETF is trading in the marketplace. These include broker-dealers, news and research sources, investment professionals, and shareholders.

Broker-Dealers

Broker-dealers refer to those brokerage houses that help facilitate ETF purchases and sales. Broker-dealers not only provide the trading platform to make it possible to trade your account, but also provide much needed information on ETFs and other investments. Broker-dealers can be divided into two types—full service and discount. Full-service broker-dealers include the big-name firms Merrill Lynch, Morgan Stanley, Wells Fargo Advisors, and UBS, to name a few. These firms pride themselves on offering top-notch solutions and services over and above what can be had from a discounter. Of course, you can expect to pay more in commissions and fees with a full-service firm.

On the other hand, discount firms promote their competitive advantage—low commissions and minimal account fees. In 2010, many discount firms began offering unlimited commission-free trading on a select number of ETFs. At present, TD Ameritrade offers the most (100+) ETFs at no commission to buy or sell. In going with discount firms to get more favorable pricing, investors typically give up high-end services and dedicated customer service. Nonetheless, the option is yours on which type of firm makes the most sense.

Five of the top discount firms include the following:

- TD Ameritrade: (800) 454-9272; www.TDAmeritrade.com
- Charles Schwab: (866) 232-9890; www.Schwab.com
- Fidelity Investments: (800) 343-3548; www.Fidelity.com
- Scottrade: (800) 619-7283; www.Scottrade.com
- eTrade: (800) 387-2331; www.eTrade.com

News and Research Sources

Although the number and breadth of companies solely involved in disseminating news and research on ETFs is not as great as with mutual funds, there still exist a few solid companies. IndexUniverse.com (including its *Journal of Indexes*) is an excellent source of information, as is Morningstar, of course mostly known for its mutual fund ratings. IndexInvestor.com, ETFZone.com, ETFGuide.com, ETFTrends.com, and SeekingAlpha.com are five other highly regarded sources. Other mainstream sources provide solid information on ETFs, such as Yahoo! Finance, Bloomberg, and CNBC. I suspect many more sources dedicated exclusively to ETFs will emerge as the popularity and reach of ETFs continue to accelerate.

Mutual funds have individual ratings, so why not ETFs? Actually, there are a number of well-known services that either provide data or rate ETFs. Ratings are not as important for ETFs that track market indexes as they are for ETFs that track custom indexes. Why? Comparing the rating on an S&P 500 ETF with the rating on a DJIA ETF is not especially beneficial, as you basically already know what you are going to get. However, comparing the rating on an ETF that tracks a custom group of high-dividend stocks with another ETF with the same strategy—but with different underlying stocks—obviously yields beneficial information. Making comparisons of expense ratios and tracking error is a quick and easy task shareholders can do without the help of a rating service.

Two of my favorite ETF rating services are Morningstar and Value Line. Morningstar applies the same star ratings to ETFs as it does to mutual funds. This obviously helps investors understand and interpret specific ratings since most people are aware of the mutual fund ratings. Value Line does a similarly superb job by drilling down and providing excellent insight—much like what it does with stocks. According to Value Line, its "user-friendly screening" provides data on asset class, geography of holdings, investment philosophy, primary exchange, and many more. Additionally, Value Line reviews both structural integrity data to measure efficiency and investment metrics to evaluate performance, and it offers global heat maps to quickly locate holdings in specific regions and countries.

Investment Professionals

There are two principal types of investment professionals—portfolio managers and financial advisors that interact with shareholders. Portfolio managers handle more of the behind-the-scenes investment functions, whereas financial advisors are typically the first point of contact for shareholders.

Portfolio managers are considered the top dog in the investment management food chain. The primary responsibility of a portfolio manager is to manage a pool of client money within the rules and guidelines of each portfolio. Some portfolio managers strive to outperform a specific peer index—this is referred to as relative performance—while others simply attempt to generate positive performance with little regard to outperforming a peer group—called absolute returns. Although mutual funds typically come to mind when hearing the title "portfolio manager," ETFs are employed by various other types of money managers. Many private investment advisors and insurance companies employ ETFs in their practice. Still others use ETFs within a stock portfolio when the need for a certain asset class exposure is desired. The use of ETFs is very broad.

Although many investors using ETFs are self-directed, many others are not, and therefore the guidance from a qualified financial professional on portfolio matters can prove to be advantageous. Financial advisors play an important role with ETFs in that they are typically the first ones to expose many investors to the ETFs. Financial advisors often have the trust and confidence of their clients and serve as the natural connection and source of education on ETFs. Financial advisors typically provide excellent means for clients to learn about ETFs and how best to incorporate them into their portfolios. The title "financial advisor" is a generic label that many financial professionals use. Other titles underscoring the same label include "financial planner," "wealth manager," "wealth advisor," and "investment counselor."

Shareholders

You can't have a market without investors and traders. That's pretty obvious stuff. Nonetheless, let's delve below the surface a bit. In basic terms, investors and traders buy and sell with the objective of profiting from the price appreciation or depreciation (selling short) and perhaps earning interest and dividends. But how each goes about the task is typically much different from one another. Investors tend to buy and hold for the long term and seldom make short-term decisions that will impact a long-term financial plan. Furthermore, investors typically have well-diversified and optimally allocated portfolios—they do not concentrate their portfolios to magnify ups and downs. Many individuals and most institutions can be grouped in the investor category.

On the other hand, traders shy away from buy-and-hold strategies and instead make more short-term investments. The hope is that the sum of the short-term returns will be higher than the return on a long-term buy-and-hold strategy over the same time horizon. Traders tend to concentrate their portfolios for maximum benefit and take advantage of selling short and buying on margin. These are generalities, but they hold true in most cases. Both investors and traders bring efficiency into the marketplace.

PART 2

Types of Exchange-Traded Funds

Broad-Based ETFs: Spiders, Diamonds, and Cubes, Oh, My!

Well over 150 million Americans own common stock either directly or indirectly through mutual funds, exchange-traded funds (ETFs), managed accounts, or insurance products. The number of Americans owning equities has ballooned over the last couple of decades, and the trend continues to rise year over year.

Equities are considered the core of any traditional investment portfolio. Broad-based equities can be divided into specific and fundamentally different categories based on size and style (growth or value). Each fundamental difference provides greater investment opportunities and additional ways to enhance a portfolio's inherent risk and return profile.

Although we will be focusing on equities exclusively in this chapter, note that not all equities are the same—there are inherent fundamental differences. During different time periods, some types of equities will perform well, while at other times other equities will perform well. For instance, during economic recessions, consumer staple stocks, or the stocks of those companies that produce products we need (toothpaste, shaving razors, toilet paper) regardless of how well the economy is faring, will outpace consumer nonstaple stocks. This second group—the nonstaple stocks—encompasses companies that sell products or services that are considered more discretionary in nature, such as premium foods, fancy wines, and music albums. However, during economic recovery and expansion, consumer nonstaple (also referred to as consumer discretionary) stocks will outperform the consumer staple stocks. These sector stocks are discussed in greater detail in Chapter 9.

WHAT ARE EQUITIES?

Equity assets represent an ownership interest in a corporation and signify a claim to a corporation's assets. In order to fund business operations, corporations first raise capital by issuing equity securities. Each share of stock owned gives an investor a proportional share of the corporation's profits, which are usually distributed in the form of dividends. In addition, owners of most equity securities are given voting rights. Voting rights allow you, for instance, to vote for a corporation's board of directors, approve or disapprove of employee stock option programs, or vote for or against acquisitions. Many individual investors foolishly do not exercise their right to vote. In response, more power shifts to corporate management and to large institutions and away from retail investors. Corporate management and large institutions each have their own agenda, which typically isn't always what is best for individual retail investors.

FRAMEWORK OF EQUITY ASSETS

Today you can count thousands of publicly traded corporations that trade in the United States, with about half those companies listed on a national stock exchange, such as the New York Stock Exchange (NYSE) or the Nasdaq. The NYSE lists over 2,300 companies, and the Nasdaq lists over 2,800. On a market-value basis, the NYSE comprises about 73 percent of the aggregate U.S. equity market value, with the Nasdaq comprising about 25 percent. It is safe to say that the breadth and depth of investment alternatives are quite extensive.

There are two forms of equity securities—preferred stock and common stock, with common stock being the more widely held security. Do not get caught up in the names of each equity stock since owning preferred stock is not necessarily more desirable than "common" stock. Each offers its own benefits, and each is suitable for different types of investors (see Figure 8-1). We will first explore preferred stock and then common stock.

Preferred Stock

Preferred stock, like common stock, represents ownership of a corporation, but is still slightly different from common stock. Preferred stock shareholders do not have voting rights. In exchange, shareholders receive a higher priority on the assets of the corporation in the event of liquidation due to bankruptcy. Furthermore, it is commonplace for shareholders of preferred stock to receive not only a higher-yielding dividend, but also priority in receiving dividends over that of common stock shareholders. For example, if a corporation is having difficulty in meeting its dividend payments to both preferred and common stock shareholders, then the corporation must make dividend payments to the preferred stock shareholders first. Afterward, providing enough cash remains, common stock shareholders will receive their dividend payments. Cumulative preferred is a type of preferred stock that has priority in receiving dividends over that of common stock. The

FIGURE 8-1

Leading Characteristics of Stocks

Preferred Stock	Common Stock
▶ Greater price stability, but less potential for price appreciation	▶ Greater potential for stock price appreciation
▶ No voting rights	▶ Possess voting rights
▶ Second to last to receive capital in the case of bankruptcy	▶ Last owners to receive capital in the case of bankruptcy
▶ Fixed dividends that must be paid before common shareholders are paid dividends	▶ Directly participates in the success or failure of the business

Source: Frush Financial Group

cumulative provision obligates the corporation to pay all accumulated, but yet unpaid, dividends before dividends can be made to the shareholders of common stock.

Finally, many corporations issue what is called convertible preferred stock. This type of preferred is very similar to nonconvertible preferred stock with one significant difference. Convertible preferred stock gives shareholders the option to convert their preferred shares into (exchange their stock for) a fixed number of common stock shares after a predetermined date. The market value of this type of preferred is more volatile since its value is influenced by the market value of the underlying common stock.

Common Stock

Common stock is the most widely used form of equity ownership across the globe. Common stock shareholders have voting rights and often participate in receiving profits in the form of dividends. However, not all corporations distribute profits in the form of dividends. Rather, some reinvest the dividends back into their companies in order to fund existing operations and planned expenditures.

Two of the most common broad-based groups associated with common stock are style and size equities. Style refers to a certain stock as being growth or value oriented, while size refers to a certain stock as being large cap, mid cap, small cap, or even micro cap. The differences within each asset subclass exhibit their own unique risk and return trade-off profile. Growth stocks are stocks of companies that produce strong long-term earnings growth rates along with solid cash-flow, sales, and book-value growth rates. Value stocks, on the other hand, are stocks of companies with low stock prices in comparison with projected earnings, book value, and sales per share, among other lesser important defining variables. As a result of the differences between style and size stocks, correlations between the two are semifavorable and therefore provide a degree of diversification benefits.

Morningstar employs the following factors and weightings to define and classify stocks as value stocks:

- Stock price to projected earnings: 50 percent
- Stock price to book value per share: 12.5 percent

- Stock price to sales per share: 12.5 percent
- Stock price to cash flow per share: 12.5 percent
- Dividend yield: 12.5 percent

To define and classify stocks as growth stocks, Morningstar uses the following factors and weightings:

- Long-term projected-earnings growth rate: 50 percent
- Historical-earnings growth rate: 12.5 percent
- Sales growth rate: 12.5 percent
- Cash-flow growth rate: 12.5 percent
- Book-value growth rate: 12.5 percent

Depending on the variable for each factor, Morningstar will assign a particular stock as either growth, value, or core. A core stock is essentially a balanced stock that does not exhibit material growth or value tendencies. These aforementioned rankings by Morningstar are the backbone of its stock and mutual fund star ranking system.

Intuitively, one can see how a particular security can be considered a value stock at one time and then a growth stock at a later time as the price of the stock rises. Since growth and value stocks do not move in perfect lockstep with each other, investors have the opportunity to improve the risk-adjusted return of their portfolio by allocating to both asset classes. Low-cost ETFs are excellent ways to accomplish this task.

In the past, companies were exclusively divided into large caps, mid caps, and small caps. However, as companies grew larger and stretched the limits of existing market capitalization cutoffs, the addition of mega caps and micro caps (and sometimes nano caps) became a necessity. Grouping companies into relevant categories is a rather subjective process since there is no official definition of, or full consensus agreement about, the exact cutoff values. Some research companies set cutoffs based on percentiles, whereas others are based in nominal dollars. Complicating the situation is the fact that market capitalizations are not static—they are constantly changing and growing larger over time. As a result, cutoffs for each category have been increased each decade or so to keep in line with present market values. For example, a company with a market capitalization of $1 billion or more was considered a large cap in 1950, but today that same market cap could be categorized as being either small cap or mid cap, but nowhere close to being large cap. Different countries around the globe also recognize different valuations for cutoffs. Again, there are no hard rules for defining companies based on size.

Nonetheless, the following are the most widely accepted current levels for stocks based on market capitalization value:

- **Mega Cap:** Over $100 billion
- **Large Cap:** $10 billion to $100 billion
- **Mid Cap:** $1 billion to $10 billion
- **Small Cap:** $100 million to $1 billion
- **Micro Cap:** $10 million to $100 million
- **Nano Cap:** Below $10 million

Equities: Advantages and Drawbacks

Before addressing the positives and negatives of equities, it's helpful to view the major factors that influence equity returns.

Factors Influencing Equity Returns

- Overall macroeconomic conditions
- Investment-specific characteristics, principally the present value of expected future cash flows
- Valuations, as measured by price to sales, price to earnings, price to free cash flow, and price to tangible book value
- Investors' behaviors, preferences, and risk tolerances
- Generic flow of funds

Knowing the factors that have an impact on equity returns, we can now turn our attention to the specific advantages and drawbacks of equities. They are outlined in the lists below.

Positives of Equities

- High total return potential
- Participation in share voting as a result of stock ownership
- Numerous asset classes to enhance a portfolio's risk and return profile

- Relatively liquid and efficient markets
- Ease of diversification

Negatives of Equities

- Potential for high volatility risk
- Difficulty in forecasting risk and return
- Fluctuating correlations
- Potential for high management fees
- Default or risk of bankruptcy

Volatility Risk and Correlations

There is little doubt that equity assets possess a high degree of risk. Moreover, some equity asset classes exhibit greater amounts of risk than other equity asset classes. For example, small-cap stocks possess more risk than large-cap stocks. However, additional risk means higher-return potential. The two go hand-in-hand. Small caps and micro caps have experienced substantial volatility risk from a historical perspective. Large caps and mid caps also exhibit volatility risk, but exhibit less volatility given they are more mature companies within more efficient markets. By allocating to investments with low correlations, investors can reduce portfolio volatility and smooth out large market-value swings.

Equity asset classes typically have high correlations with each other. Small-cap stocks had a correlation of close to 0.91 with large-cap stocks during the six-year period of 2004 to 2010. Accordingly, mid-cap stocks had a somewhat stronger correlation to large-cap stocks at 0.93 over the same time period. As for style, growth and value had a correlation of 0.92 during the aforementioned period of time. Regardless of the high correlations among equity asset classes, investors can gain asset allocation benefits since equity asset classes do not move in perfect lockstep with one another.

ETF Representation

Even though we have given relatively equal discussion to all size categories, there is no mistaking the substantially higher assets under management (AuM) with large-cap ETFs than with mid-cap and small-cap ETFs. As of the beginning of 2011, large-cap ETFs boasted nearly $247 billion in AuM. A number such as this illustrates clear domination of the respective market segment (i.e., asset class size). Mid-cap ETFs and small and micro caps had approximately $58 billion and $54 billion AuM, respectively. Furthermore, growth-focused ETFs held about $46 billion and value-focused ETFs about $40 billion in AuM, differences that are not especially important between each other.

Largest Broad-Based ETFs

Of the top five largest style and size ETFs, four of them are large-cap growth ETFs. These include the PowerShares QQQ, iShares Russell 1000 Growth, iShares Russell 1000 Value, iShares S&P 500 Growth, and the Vanguard Growth. Suffice to say that shareholders strongly prefer growth over value and large caps over mid and small caps. The first small-cap ETF to appear in the top 10 is the iShares Russell 2000 Value ETF, while the first mid-cap ETF is the similar iShares Russell Mid-Cap Value ETF. The very first mega-cap ETF does not enter the picture until number 21 on the top broad-based ETFs according to style and size. In aggregate, assets in large-cap ETFs are nearly 2½ times larger than mid caps and small caps combined. In summary, the top ETFs as measured by AuM are dominated by large-cap stocks with a bias toward growth over value.

PORTFOLIO ENHANCEMENT OPPORTUNITIES

Much research has been done in the area of what drives portfolio returns from both a macro and micro standpoint. Asset allocation has been clearly shown to be the primary determinant of portfolio performance over time. But what about the variables that also drive performance from a micro level? The following are three areas that have been shown to generate excess performance for investors. Each should be considered wisely and within the context of an investor's personal situation.

Volatility Premium

The greater the level of risk, the greater the potential for higher returns. This is the essence of investing. One method for evaluating volatility is beta, a financial measurement designed to illustrate the movement of a particular stock in relation to the overall market. Higher betas equate to greater price movements and therefore the potential for higher risk and higher returns. Research has concluded that nearly 70 percent of portfolio returns are driven by beta. As a result, allocating to high-beta investments in conjunction with a solid asset allocation and diversification plan will help to enhance risk-adjusted returns over time. The smaller the market cap, the higher the beta. If an investor can tolerate large price swings, overweighting small-cap stocks can prove financially rewarding. Beta is not the only measurement for volatility; thus you may find it more convenient to measure risk a different way, such as using standard deviation. Usually only small-cap and micro-cap stocks offer benefits according to market capitalization.

Style Premium

As previously mentioned, style refers to either a growth- or value-oriented stock. Each classification is defined by very specific factors, whereby each classification provides different portfolio benefits as a result. Many years ago, dividend yield and book value were the primary determinants for classifying stocks as growth or value. Over time, additional research was conducted, and now we have more sophisticated methods for classification. During the same time period, research was conducted into what type of stock, either growth or value, outperformed the other. Most research concludes that value stocks outpace growth stocks, but not to a significant degree. Moreover, these findings also show that volatility risk is lower for value stocks than for growth stocks. In consequence, value stocks provide a means to enhance portfolio returns while providing a means to reduce total portfolio risk—a very nice combination.

Although the correlations between growth and value stocks generally are quite high and thus unfavorable, there have been periods of time when the correlations have become very favorable.

For instance, during the late 1990s, correlations between value and growth stocks declined to near 0.5, which is still in the positive range but definitely offers better asset allocation benefits. As a result of these findings, investors should consider including value stocks in appropriate degrees in their portfolios.

Size Premium

The size of a stock is dictated by what is called market capitalization, which is measured by taking the outstanding stock of a particular company and multiplying it by the market price of the stock. The resulting market value allows for comparisons and classification into a definable group. Note that the new trend for calculating market capitalization is to replace total outstanding stock with what are called "free-float" shares outstanding. Free float refers to the total shares outstanding less what is held by private ownership, such as corporate insiders. This newer way to calculate market value will provide a better picture of a stock available to the investing public.

The three primary size categories are large caps, mid caps, and small caps—with micro caps a distant fourth. According to Morningstar, large caps represent the largest 70 percent of investable market cap, mid caps the next 20 percent, small caps the next 7 percent, and finally micro caps with the final 3 percent.

Research has demonstrated that small-cap stocks have out-performed large-cap stocks over time. More specifically, micro-cap stocks have outpaced large-cap stocks by a wide margin, even after adjusting for volatility. In summary, equity size does matter and can provide return-enhancement and risk-reduction benefits.

SELECT BROAD-BASED ETFS

Equity assets are the backbone of most well-diversified optimal port-folios. Equities provide the best way to safeguard against purchasing power risk, or the loss of asset value due to the corrosive impact of inflation. Figures 8-2 to 8-12 provide various ETF alternatives you may want to consider for your own portfolio. I strongly encourage you to evaluate them and determine for yourself if these ETF options make financial sense for your needs. Depending on your financial situation and goals, you may want to include a number of these in your portfolio or simply use one or two. Each of the equity segments in the figures is sorted by expense ratio and offers different market exposure and therefore distinct risk and reward opportunities.

FIGURE 8-2

List of Select Broad-Based ETFs: Large-Cap Blend

ETF	Symbol	Expense Ratio	Inception Date
LARGE-CAP BLEND			
Vanguard Total Stock Market	VTI	0.06%	5/24/01
Vanguard S&P 500	VOO	0.06%	9/7/10
Schwab U.S. Broad Market	SCHB	0.07%	11/3/09
Schwab U.S. Large-Cap	SCHX	0.08%	11/3/09
SPDR S&P 500	SPY	0.09%	1/22/93
iShares S&P 500 Index	IVV	0.09%	5/15/00
Wilshire 5000 Total Market	WFVK	0.12%	3/9/10
Vanguard Large Cap ETF	VV	0.12%	1/27/04
Vanguard Mega Cap 300 Index	MGC	0.13%	12/17/07
iShares Russell 1000 Index	IWB	0.15%	5/15/00
Vanguard Russell 1000 Index	VONE	0.15%	9/20/10
Vanguard Russell 3000 Index	VTHR	0.15%	9/20/10
iShares Russell Top 200 Index	IWL	0.15%	9/22/09
iShares MSCI USA Index	EUSA	0.15%	5/5/10
Vanguard Dividend Appreciation	VIG	0.18%	4/21/06
iShares Russell 3000 Index	IWV	0.20%	5/22/00
iShares S&P 100 Index	OEF	0.20%	10/23/00
iShares Dow Jones U.S. Index	IYY	0.20%	6/12/00
SPDR Dow Jones Large Cap	ELR	0.20%	11/8/05
Rydex Russell Top 50	XLG	0.20%	5/4/05
iShares S&P 1500 Index	ISI	0.20%	1/20/04
iShares Morningstar Large Core Index	JKD	0.20%	6/28/04
SPDR Dow Jones Total Market	TMW	0.20%	10/4/00
TXF Large Companies	TXF	0.20%	11/3/09
iShares NYSE Composite Index	NYC	0.25%	3/30/04

continued

FIGURE 8-2

List of Select Broad-Based ETFs: Large-Cap Blend (Cont.)

LARGE-CAP BLEND			
ETF	**Symbol**	**Expense Ratio**	**Inception Date**
WisdomTree Earnings 500	EPS	0.28%	2/23/07
WisdomTree Total Earnings	EXT	0.28%	2/23/07
ALPS Equal Sector Weight	EQL	0.34%	7/6/09
iPath Long Extended S&P 500 TR ETN	SFLA	0.35%	11/29/10
Rydex Russell 1000 Equal Weight	EWRI	0.40%	12/3/10
Rydex S&P Equal Weight	RSP	0.40%	4/24/03
iPath Long Extended Russell 1000 TR ETN	ROLA	0.50%	11/29/10
Pax MSCI North America ESG Index	NASI	0.50%	5/19/10
iShares MSCI USA ESG Select Index	KLD	0.50%	1/24/05
iShares KLD 400 Social Index	DSI	0.50%	11/14/06
PowerShares Dynamic Market	PWC	0.60%	5/1/03
PowerShares Dynamic Large Cap	PJF	0.65%	12/1/06
Guggenheim Ocean Tomo Patent	OTP	0.65%	12/15/06
PowerShares Buyback Achievers	PKW	0.70%	12/20/06
First Trust Large Cap Core AlphaDEX	FEX	0.70%	5/8/07
ELEMENTS Morningstar Wide Moat Focus ETN	WMW	0.75%	10/17/07
PowerShares Active Mega Cap	PMA	0.75%	4/11/08
ELEMENTS SPEC. Large Cap U.S. Sector ETN	EEH	0.75%	8/1/07
FaithShares Catholic Values	FCV	0.87%	12/8/09
FaithShares Christian Values	FOC	0.87%	12/8/09
FaithShares Methodist Values	FMV	0.87%	12/8/09
FaithShares Baptist Values	FZB	0.87%	12/14/09
FaithShares Lutheran Values	FKL	0.87%	12/14/09
RBS US Large Cap Trendpilot ETN	TRND	1.00%	12/6/10

FIGURE 8-3

List of Select Broad-Based ETFs: Large-Cap Growth

LARGE-CAP GROWTH			
ETF	**Symbol**	**Expense Ratio**	**Inception Date**
Vanguard Growth	VUG	0.12%	1/26/04
Vanguard Mega Cap 300 Growth Index	MGK	0.13%	12/17/07
Schwab U.S. Large-Cap Growth	SCHG	0.14%	12/11/09
Vanguard Russell 1000 Growth Index	VONG	0.15%	9/20/10
Vanguard S&P 500 Growth Index	VOOG	0.15%	9/7/10
iShares S&P 500 Growth Index	IVW	0.18%	5/22/00
iShares Russell Top 200 Growth Index	IWY	0.20%	9/22/09
PowerShares QQQ	QQQ	0.20%	3/10/99
SPDR S&P 500 Growth	SPYG	0.20%	9/25/00
iShares Russell 1000 Growth Index	IWF	0.20%	5/22/00
iShares Morningstar Large Growth Index	JKE	0.25%	6/28/04
iShares Russell 3000 Growth Index	IWZ	0.25%	7/24/00
Fidelity Nasdaq Composite Index Tracking	ONEQ	0.30%	9/25/03
Rydex S&P 500 Pure Growth	RPG	0.35%	3/1/06
WisdomTree Large Cap Growth	ROI	0.38%	12/4/08
First Trust Nasdaq-100 Equal Weight	QQEW	0.60%	4/19/06
First Trust Nasdaq-100 EX-Tech Sec	QQXT	0.60%	2/8/07
First Trust US IPO Index	FPX	0.60%	4/12/06
PowerShares Dynamic Large Cap Growth	PWB	0.61%	3/3/05
Guggenheim Ocean Tomo Growth Index	OTR	0.65%	4/2/07
Guggenheim Sector Rotation	XRO	0.65%	9/21/06
RP Focused Large Cap Growth	RWG	0.89%	10/2/09

FIGURE 8-4

List of Select Broad-Based ETFs: Large-Cap Value

LARGE-CAP VALUE			
ETF	Symbol	Expense Ratio	Inception Date
Vanguard Value	VTV	0.12%	1/26/04
Vanguard Mega Cap 300 Value Index	MGV	0.13%	12/17/07
Schwab U.S. Large-Cap Value	SCHV	0.14%	12/11/09
Vanguard S&P 500 Value Index	VOOV	0.15%	9/7/10
Vanguard Russell 1000 Value Index	VONV	0.15%	9/20/10
SPDR Dow Jones Industrial Average	DIA	0.18%	1/13/98
iShares S&P 500 Value Index	IVE	0.18%	5/22/00
Vanguard High-Dividend Yield	VYM	0.18%	11/10/06
iShares NYSE 100 Index	NY	0.20%	3/29/04
iShares Russell Top 200 Value Index	IWX	0.20%	9/22/09
SPDR S&P 500 Value	SPYV	0.20%	9/25/00
iShares Russell 1000 Value Index	IWD	0.20%	5/22/00
iShares Russell 3000 Value Index	IWW	0.25%	7/24/00
iShares Morningstar Large Value Index	JKF	0.25%	6/28/04
WisdomTree Large Cap Dividend	DLN	0.28%	6/16/06
WisdomTree Total Dividend	DTD	0.28%	6/16/06
SPDR S&P Dividend	SDY	0.35%	11/8/05
Rydex S&P 500 Pure Value	RPV	0.35%	3/1/06
WisdomTree Dividend EX-Financials	DTN	0.38%	6/16/06
WisdomTree Large Cap Value	EZY	0.38%	2/23/07
WisdomTree Equity Income	DHS	0.38%	6/16/06
PowerShares FTSE RAFI US 1000	PRF	0.39%	12/19/05
iShares Dow Jones Select Dividend Index	DVY	0.40%	11/3/03
First Trust Morningstar Dividend Leaders	FDL	0.45%	3/9/06
RevenueShares Large Cap	RWL	0.49%	2/22/08
PowerShares Dynamic Large Cap Value	PWV	0.60%	3/3/05
PowerShares Dividend Achievers	PFM	0.60%	9/15/05
Guggenheim Multi-Asset Income	CVY	0.65%	9/21/06
First Trust Strategic Value Index	FDV	0.65%	7/6/06
Guggenheim Defensive Equity	DEF	0.65%	12/15/06
First Trust Value Line Dividend Index	FVD	0.70%	8/19/03
ELEMENTS DJ High Yield Select 10 ETN	DOD	0.75%	11/7/07
ELEMENTS BG Large Cap ETN	BVL	0.75%	8/6/08
ELEMENTS BG Total Market ETN	BVT	0.75%	8/6/08
Grail American Beacon Large Value	GVT	0.79%	5/4/09

FIGURE 8-5

List of Select Broad-Based ETFs: Mid-Cap Blend

MID-CAP BLEND			
ETF	**Symbol**	**Expense Ratio**	**Inception Date**
Vanguard Mid-Cap	VO	0.12%	1/26/04
Vanguard Extended Market Index	VXF	0.12%	12/27/01
Vanguard S&P Mid-Cap 400 Index	IVOO	0.15%	9/7/10
Wilshire 4500 Completion	WXSP	0.18%	3/9/10
iShares Russell Midcap Index	IWR	0.20%	7/17/01
iShares S&P Mid Cap 400 Index	IJH	0.20%	5/22/00
iShares Morningstar Mid Core Index	JKG	0.25%	6/28/04
SPDR S&P Mid Cap 400	MDY	0.25%	5/4/95
SPDR Dow Jones Mid Cap	EMM	0.26%	11/8/05
WisdomTree Mid Cap Earnings	EZM	0.38%	2/23/07
Rydex Russell Mid Cap Equal Weight	EWRM	0.40%	12/3/10
JETS Contrarian Opportunities Index	JCO	0.58%	4/7/10
PowerShares Dynamic MagniQuant	PIQ	0.65%	10/12/06
PowerShares Dynamic Mid Cap	PJG	0.65%	12/1/06
Guggenheim Insider Sentiment	NFO	0.65%	9/21/06
First Trust Value Line Equity Allc Index	FVI	0.70%	12/5/06
First Trust Mid Cap Core AlphaDEX	FNX	0.70%	5/8/07
Guggenheim Raymond James SB-1 Equity	RYJ	0.72%	5/19/06
RBS US Mid Cap Trendpilot ETN	TRNM	1.00%	1/25/11

FIGURE 8-6

List of Select Broad-Based ETFs: Mid-Cap Growth

MID-CAP GROWTH			
ETF	**Symbol**	**Expense Ratio**	**Inception Date**
Vanguard Mid-Cap Growth	VOT	0.12%	8/17/06
Vanguard S&P Mid-Cap 400 Growth	IVOG	0.20%	9/7/10
iShares S&P Mid Cap 400 Growth Index	IJK	0.25%	7/24/00
iShares Russell Midcap Growth Index	IWP	0.25%	7/17/01
SPDR S&P 400 Mid Cap Growth	MDYG	0.26%	11/8/05
iShares Morningstar Mid Growth Index	JKH	0.30%	6/28/04
Rydex S&P Midcap 400 Pure Growth	RFG	0.35%	3/1/06
RevenueShares Navellier Overall A-100	RWV	0.60%	1/23/09
PowerShares Dynamic OTC	PWO	0.60%	5/1/03
PowerShares Dynamic Mid Cap Growth	PWJ	0.63%	3/3/05
Guggenheim Spin-Off	CSD	0.65%	12/15/06
PowerShares NXQ	PNXQ	0.70%	4/3/08
PowerShares DWA Technical Leaders	PDP	0.70%	3/1/07
PowerShares Morningstar Stock Investor	PYH	0.70%	12/1/06
First Trust Multi Cap Growth AlphaDEX	FAD	0.70%	5/8/07
PowerShares S&P 500 High Quality	PIV	0.70%	12/6/05
First Trust Value Line 100	FVL	0.70%	6/12/03

FIGURE 8-7

List of Select Broad-Based ETFs: Mid-Cap Value

MID-CAP VALUE			
ETF	**Symbol**	**Expense Ratio**	**Inception Date**
Vanguard Mid-Cap Value	VOE	0.12%	8/17/06
Vanguard S&P Mid-Cap 400 Value Index	IVOV	0.20%	9/7/10
iShares Russell Midcap Value Index	IWS	0.25%	7/17/01
iShares S&P Mid Cap 400 Value Index	IJJ	0.25%	7/24/00
SPDR S&P 400 Mid Cap Value	MDYV	0.26%	11/8/05
iShares Morningstar Mid Value Index	JKI	0.30%	6/28/04
Rydex S&P Midcap 400 Pure Value	RFV	0.35%	3/1/06
WisdomTree Mid Cap Dividend	DON	0.38%	6/16/06
RevenueShares Mid Cap	RWK	0.54%	2/22/08
PowerShares High-Yield Dividend Achievers	PEY	0.60%	12/9/04
PowerShares Dynamic Mid Cap Value	PWP	0.63%	3/3/05
Guggenheim Mid-Cap Core	CZA	0.65%	4/2/07
First Trust Multi Cap Value AlphaDEX	FAB	0.70%	5/8/07

FIGURE 8-8

List of Select Broad-Based ETFs: Small-Cap Blend

SMALL-CAP BLEND			
ETF	**Symbol**	**Expense Ratio**	**Inception Date**
Vanguard Small Cap	VB	0.12%	1/26/04
Schwab U.S. Small-Cap	SCHA	0.14%	11/3/09
Vanguard S&P Small-Cap 600 Index	VIOO	0.15%	9/7/10
Vanguard Russell 2000 Index	VTWO	0.15%	9/20/10
iShares S&P Small Cap 600 Index	IJR	0.20%	5/22/00
iShares Russell 2000 Index	IWM	0.20%	5/22/00
iShares Morningstar Small Core Index	JKJ	0.25%	6/28/04
			continued

FIGURE 8-8

List of Select Broad-Based ETFs: Small-Cap Blend (cont.)

SMALL-CAP BLEND			
ETF	**Symbol**	**Expense Ratio**	**Inception Date**
SPDR S&P 600 Small Cap	SLY	0.26%	11/8/05
WisdomTree Small Cap Earnings	EES	0.38%	2/23/07
Rydex Russell 2000 Equal Weight	EWRS	0.40%	12/3/10
iShares Russell Microcap Index	IWC	0.60%	8/12/05
First Trust Dow Jones Select Micro Cap	FDM	0.60%	9/27/05
PowerShares Dynamic Small Cap	PJM	0.65%	12/1/06
First Trust Small Cap Core AlphaDEX	FYX	0.70%	5/8/07

FIGURE 8-9

List of Select Broad-Based ETFs: Small-Cap Growth

SMALL-CAP GROWTH			
ETF	**Symbol**	**Expense Ratio**	**Inception Date**
Vanguard Small Cap Growth	VBK	0.12%	1/26/04
Vanguard Russell 2000 Growth Index	VTWG	0.20%	9/20/10
Vanguard S&P Small-Cap 600 Growth	VIOG	0.20%	9/7/10
iShares Russell 2000 Growth Index	IWO	0.25%	7/24/00
iShares S&P Small Cap 600 Growth	IJT	0.25%	7/24/00
SPDR S&P 600 Small Cap Growth	SLYG	0.25%	9/25/00
iShares Morningstar Small Growth Index	JKK	0.30%	6/28/04
Rydex S&P Small Cap 600 Pure Growth	RZG	0.35%	3/1/06
PowerShares Dynamic Small Cap Growth	PWT	0.63%	3/3/05
PowerShares FTSE Nasdaq Small Cap	PQSC	0.70%	4/3/08

FIGURE 8-10

List of Select Broad-Based ETFs: Small-Cap Value

SMALL-CAP VALUE			
ETF	Symbol	Expense Ratio	Inception Date
Vanguard Small Cap Value	VBR	0.12%	1/26/04
Vanguard Russell 2000 Value Index	VTWV	0.20%	9/20/10
Vanguard S&P Small-Cap 600 Value	VIOV	0.20%	9/7/10
iShares Russell 2000 Value Index	IWN	0.25%	7/24/00
iShares S&P Small Cap 600 Value Index	IJS	0.25%	7/24/00
SPDR S&P 600 Small Cap Value	SLYV	0.26%	9/25/00
iShares Morningstar Small Value Index	JKL	0.30%	6/28/04
Rydex S&P Small Cap 600 Pure Value	RZV	0.35%	3/1/06
WisdomTree Small Cap Dividend	DES	0.38%	6/16/06
PowerShares FTSE RAFI US 1500 Small-Mid	PRFZ	0.39%	9/20/06
RevenueShares Small Cap	RWJ	0.54%	2/22/08
PowerShares Dynamic Small Cap Value	PWY	0.63%	3/3/05
Wilshire Micro-Cap	WMCR	0.64%	9/21/06
PowerShares Zacks Micro Cap	PZI	0.70%	8/18/05
ELEMENTS BG Small Cap ETN	BSC	0.75%	8/6/08

FIGURE 8-11

List of Select Broad-Based ETFs: Asset Allocation

ASSET ALLOCATION			
ETF	Symbol	Expense Ratio	Inception Date
iShares S&P Aggressive Allocation	AOA	0.11%	11/4/08
iShares S&P Target Date Retirement	TGR	0.11%	11/4/08
iShares S&P Conservative Allocation	AOK	0.11%	11/4/08
iShares S&P Moderate Allocation	AOM	0.11%	11/4/08
PowerShares CEF Income Composite	PCEF	0.50%	2/19/10
TDX Independence In-Target	TDX	0.65%	10/1/07
Claymore CEF GS Connect ETN	GCE	0.95%	12/10/07

FIGURE 8-12

List of Select Broad-Based ETFs: Target Date

TARGET DATE			
ETF	Symbol	Expense Ratio	Inception Date
iShares S&P Target Date 2015	TZE	0.11%	11/4/08
iShares S&P Target Date 2020	TZG	0.11%	11/4/08
iShares S&P Target Date 2025	TZI	0.11%	11/4/08
iShares S&P Target Date 2030	TZL	0.11%	11/4/08
iShares S&P Target Date 2035	TZO	0.11%	11/4/08
iShares S&P Target Date 2040	TZV	0.11%	11/4/08
TDX Independence 2020	TDH	0.65%	10/1/07
TDX Independence 2030	TDN	0.65%	10/1/07
TDX Independence 2040	TDV	0.65%	10/1/07

## CHAPTER 9

Sector and Industry ETFs: From Basic Materials to Utilities

In addition to dividing equities into broad-based size and style categories, equities can also be divided into economic sectors and industry groups. The popularity of these more targeted groups has resulted in the strong growth of exchange-traded funds (ETFs) that track these equity segments. This is demonstrated by the fact that nearly 25 percent of all equity ETFs are sector and industry funds. Not only do sector and industry funds track U.S. markets; they also track international markets. In doing so, investors have solid investing alternatives to protect and grow their portfolios. As mentioned in Chapter 2, the first sector funds were introduced in 1998—called Select Sector SPDRs—by State Street Global Advisors based on 9 economic sectors (now technically 10 with the 2011 launch of the SPDR S&P Telecom ETF [symbol XTL]) of Standard & Poor's. Vanguard, PowerShares, WisdomTree, Rydex, and a host of others also offer sector and industry ETFs.

There are three primary reasons for investing in sector and industry ETFs. First, these funds provide investors with the means necessary to fill any gaps they might have in regard to their asset allocation.

Second, these funds give investors the opportunities to invest in more defined areas where they believe excess returns can be generated over and above the overall equity market. For example, if an investor believed basic materials stocks were close to breaking out from a technical standpoint, then that investor can overweight basic materials by purchasing the materials select sector SPDR (symbol XLB). Although the S&P 500 does provide exposure to basic materials, an investor may feel compelled to increase his or her exposure to fully take advantage of perceived underpriced segments in the equity market.

Third, sector and industry ETFs allow casual and institutional investors the means to hedge a portfolio, specifically a concentrated-stock portfolio. For example, a recently retired executive from a high-tech firm may hold a significant block of shares in his or her former employer. If the cost basis on that stock is low, then the executive may want to employ advanced strategies such as selling short a technology-sector ETF to hedge the downside risk of the concentrated position, given falling prices without selling the low-basis stock outright and incurring a significant capital gains tax liability.

Sector ETFs have two primary drawbacks. First, most sector ETFs have higher expense ratios than a broadly diversified ETF. The difference is typically small and still lower than comparable mutual funds, but differences do exist nonetheless. Second, the use of sector funds could motivate an investor to design a less than optimal portfolio and may even induce more frequent trading than under normal situations. Investing in sector or industry funds should be accomplished within the context of an optimally allocated, low-cost, and tax-efficient strategy.

SECTOR AND INDUSTRY CLASSIFICATION

There are thousands of stocks in the United States, and many more in the international marketplace. With so many stocks available, it makes sense to classify them into orderly and definable groups for ease of comparison and analysis. Dow Jones Indexes and Standard & Poor's are by far the two most important companies for their classification of stocks. Morningstar and a few other index sponsors provide their own proprietary methodologies as well.

Dow Jones Indexes

Dow Jones sector indexes include a diverse range of broad-market indexes available at the country, regional, and global levels. Each sector is defined by the Industry Classification Benchmark, a proprietary classification standard jointly maintained by Dow Jones Indexes and the FTSE Group. Under the Dow Jones methodology, a database of more than 60,000 global securities in 72 countries is classified according to one of four levels of specificity, including 10 broad industries, 19 supersectors, 41 sectors, and, at the most granular level, 114 subsectors. Each of the segments is designed to capture the risk and return characteristics of specific market segments by classifying and grouping together constituents that respond in relatively like-manner ways to economic, political, and environmental factors.

The 10 broad industries together with their constituent sectors are listed below. In addition, each current weighting within the Dow Jones U.S. Index, which represents approximately 95 percent of U.S. market capitalization, is given in parentheses.

1. **Basic Materials (3.86 Percent):** Chemicals, forest and paper, industrial metals and mining, and mining
2. **Consumer Goods (10.22 Percent):** Automobiles and parts, beverages, food producers, household goods and home construction, leisure goods, personal goods, and tobacco
3. **Consumer Services (11.85 Percent):** Food and drug retailers, general retailers, media, and travel and leisure
4. **Financials (16.52 Percent):** Banks, equity investment instruments, financial services, life insurance, nonequity investment instruments, nonlife insurance, real estate investment trusts, and real estate investment and services
5. **Health Care (10.52 Percent):** Health-care equipment and services and pharmaceuticals and biotechnology
6. **Industrials (12.99 Percent):** Aerospace and defense, construction and materials, electronic and electrical

equipment, general industrials, industrial engineering, industrial transportation, and support services
7. **Oil and Gas (11.18 Percent):** Alternative energy, oil and gas producers, and oil equipment and services
8. **Technology (16.35 Percent):** Software and computer services and technology hardware and equipment
9. **Telecommunications (2.97 Percent):** Fixed-line telecommunications and mobile telecommunications
10. **Utilities (3.53 Percent):** Electricity and gas, water, and multiutilities

Standard & Poor's

Introduced in cooperation with Morgan Stanley Capital International, the Global Industry Classification Standard (GICS) from S&P contains data on well over 30,000 global stocks. Under this system, GICS divides the S&P 1500 Index into 10 economic sectors, 23 industry groups, 59 industries, and 123 subindustries. The 10 economic sectors together with select constituent industries according to S&P include the following:

1. **Basic Materials:** Chemicals, metals and mining, and paper and forest products
2. **Consumer Discretionary:** Automobiles, apparel, leisure, and media
3. **Consumer Staples:** Food and drug retailing and household products
4. **Energy:** Energy equipment, oil and gas exploration, and refining
5. **Financials:** Banks, financial services, and all insurance
6. **Health Care:** Biotech, drugs, managed care, and medical products
7. **Industrials:** Aerospace, building, capital goods, defense, and transportation
8. **Information Technology:** Communication equipment, hardware, and software
9. **Telecommunication Services:** Telecommunication services and wireless
10. **Utilities:** Electric utilities and natural gas utilities

Morningstar

Taking a rather different approach, Morningstar classifies companies according to the industry in which the company's business activities generate the bulk of its revenue. Depending on the source of revenue, companies are classified under one of Morningstar's 129 industries, which themselves are classified into 1 of 12 sectors. Morningstar does not stop there, as it further classifies the 12 sectors in 1 of 3 supersectors—information economy (18.6 percent of total), service economy (48.4 percent of total), and manufacturing economy (33.1 percent of total). Individual ETFs exist to track the Morningstar supersector indexes.

According to Morningstar, the largest sector in the economy is financials, with a weighting of 21.4 percent of the total U.S. stock market capitalization. There is a tie for second place between health-care services and industrial materials at 12 percent each. Next in line are energy and consumer services, with weightings of 9.8 percent and 9 percent, respectively.

ETF Sector Assets Under Management

Given that both S&P and Dow Jones Indexes use similar methodologies for classifying stocks, we'll also proceed with 10 economic sectors for practicality purposes. Of the 10 economic sectors, energy is by far the leading sector as measured by assets under management (AuM) at $28.2 billion, as Figure 9-1 shows. Financials holds second place at $17.7 billion, while technology earns runner-up props. On the flip side of the coin, telecommunications earns the most irrelevant award with AuM of just $1.2 billion. Next closest in line is consumer staples with less than $5 billion in AuM.

Sector Volatility

If you are seeking a sector ETF with low volatility risk, then technology and financials are not for you. From a historical perspective, these two sectors—together with health care, consumer discretionary, and industrials—exhibit higher volatility risk than the average sector fund. As expected, consumer staples and utilities offer the lowest level of volatility risk as measured by standard

FIGURE 9-1

ETF AuM by Economic Sector

Economic Sector	Assets ($B)	% of Group
Basic Materials	7.6	7.3
Consumer Discretionary	4.6	4.4
Consumer Staples	6.4	6.2
Energy	28.2	27.2
Financials	17.7	17.1
Health Care	9.0	8.7
Industrials	6.4	6.2
Technology	16.0	15.4
Telecommunications	1.2	1.2
Utilities	6.7	6.5

Source: BlackRock, FactSet, and Bloomberg

deviation. Surprisingly, the energy sector is the third least volatile sector, or at least historically speaking.

Economic Cycles and Sector Rotation

Irrespective of the asset class, market segment, or economic sector, market leadership does not continue unabated over time. During certain periods of time, one economic sector will perform strongly, while during other periods of time, other economic sectors will perform strongly. Much of the reason why certain sectors do well or poorly is dependent on a country's place in the economic cycle. When the economy is doing well, then industrials-sector and energy-sector ETFs will perform accordingly. Conversely, when the economy is doing poorly, then utilities and consumer staples are in favor. Furthermore, when an economy is moving from contraction to expansion, technology and consumer discretionary ETFs will get extra attention from retail and institutional investors alike.

However, when an economy is transitioning from expansion to contraction, telecommunication and health-care ETFs will typically outperform. Figure 9-2 illustrates this market dynamic.

FIGURE 9-2

Economic Cycles and Sector Rotation

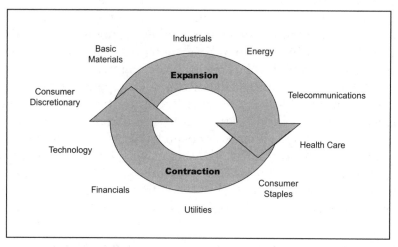

Source: Frush Financial Group

Largest Sector ETFs

The sector ETFs with the most AuMs just happen to be the oldest sector ETFs as well. By far, the largest sector ETF is the SPDR Energy ETF, followed by the SPDR Financial ETF and SPDR Technology ETF. Thereafter the assets fall off precipitously, with the next two largest sector ETFs being the SPDR Industrial ETF and SPDR Utilities ETF. Consumer staples, health care, basic materials, and finally consumer discretionary SPDRs round out the bottom of the SPDR lineup as measured by AuM. Only the Oil Service HOLDRs and JPMorgan Alerian MLP ETN break up the rankings of SPDRs. Nonetheless, it is quite obvious that the State Street SPDR lineup is dominating the sector ETF lineup.

Sector Risk and Return Profiles

As of early 2011, out of all the sectors, the consumer discretionary sector exhibited the best three-year risk-to-reward trade-off. Although the consumer staple sector had a modestly higher return, 4.5 percent as compared with 3.2 percent, over the same three-year period, the sector also exhibited higher volatility risk, as measured by standard deviation (the best measure of investment risk). The only two other economic sectors to experience positive performance over the last three years were the technology sector and the basic materials sector. However, no other economic sector exhibited higher volatility risk than basic materials. The financial sector had nearly the same level of risk as basic materials, but also experienced the worst annualized returns (–13.2 percent) by a very wide margin of all sectors. High risk and terrible returns defined financials over the period 2008 to 2010. Industrials and the energy sector also had higher than composite levels of risk together with negative annualized returns. The sector with the lowest degree of volatility risk was utilities, but still this sector had a negative return. The data illustrate that it was difficult to generate positive annualized returns over the past three-year period.

SELECT SECTOR AND INDUSTRY ETFs

Figures 9-3 to 9-12 provide some ETF alternatives you may want to consider for your own portfolio. I strongly encourage you to evaluate the list and determine for yourself if these investment options make sense for your needs. The figures focus on the 10 economic sectors, with each sector offering different portfolio risk and return enhancement opportunities. Each segment in the figures is sorted by expense ratio.

FIGURE 9-3

List of Select Sector and Industry ETFs: Basic Materials

BASIC MATERIALS			
ETF	Symbol	Expense Ratio	Inception Date
Materials Select Sector SPDR	XLB	0.20%	12/16/98
Vanguard Materials	VAW	0.24%	1/26/04
PowerShares S&P Small Cap Materials	PSCM	0.29%	4/7/10
SPDR S&P Metals & Mining	XME	0.35%	6/19/06
SPDR S&P Global Natural Resources	GNR	0.40%	9/13/10
iShares Dow Jones US Basic Materials	IYM	0.47%	6/12/00
iShares S&P North American Natural Resources	IGE	0.48%	10/22/01
iShares S&P Global Materials	MXI	0.48%	9/12/06
iShares MSCI ACWI EX US Materials Index	AXMT	0.48%	7/13/10
iShares S&P Global Timber & Forestry	WOOD	0.48%	6/24/08
Rydex S&P Equal Weight Materials	RTM	0.50%	11/1/06
SPDR S&P International Materials Sector	IRV	0.52%	7/16/08
WisdomTree International Basic Materials	DBN	0.58%	10/13/06
Market Vectors RVE Hard Assets Producers	HAP	0.63%	8/29/08
PowerShares Dynamic Basic Materials	PYZ	0.65%	10/12/06
iShares MSCI Emerging Markets Materials	EMMT	0.69%	1/20/10
First Trust Materials Alpha DEX	FXZ	0.70%	5/8/07
PowerShares Global Water	PIO	0.75%	6/13/07
IQ Global Resources	GRES	0.79%	10/27/09
EGShares Emerging Markets Metals/Mining	EMT	0.85%	5/21/09

FIGURE 9-4

List of Select Sector and Industry ETFs: Consumer
Discretionary

CONSUMER DISCRETIONARY			
ETF	**Symbol**	**Expense Ratio**	**Inception Date**
Consumer Discretionary Select Sector SPDR	XLY	0.20%	12/16/98
Vanguard Consumer Discretionary	VCR	0.24%	1/26/04
PowerShares S&P SmallCap Consumer Discretionary	PSCD	0.29%	4/7/10
SPDR S&P Retail	XRT	0.35%	6/19/06
SPDR S&P Homebuilders	XHB	0.35%	1/31/06
iShares Dow Jones US Home Construction	ITB	0.47%	5/1/06
iShares MSCI ACWI EX US Consumer Discretionary	AXDI	0.48%	7/13/10
iShares Dow Jones US Consumer Services	IYC	0.48%	6/12/00
iShares S&P Global Consumer Discretionary	RXI	0.48%	9/12/06
Rydex S&P Equal Weight Consumer Discretionary	RCD	0.50%	11/1/06
SPDR S&P International Consumer Discretionary Sector	IPD	0.51%	7/16/08
PowerShares Dynamic Leisure & Entertainment	PEJ	0.63%	6/23/05
PowerShares Dynamic Retail	PMR	0.63%	10/26/05
PowerShares Dynamic Consumer Discretionary	PEZ	0.65%	10/12/06
First Trust Consumer Discretionary AlphaDEX	FXD	0.70%	5/8/07

FIGURE 9-5

List of Select Sector and Industry ETFs: Consumer Staples

CONSUMER STAPLES			
ETF	**Symbol**	**Expense Ratio**	**Inception Date**
Consumer Staples Select Sector SPDR	XLP	0.20%	12/16/98
Vanguard Consumer Staples	VDC	0.24%	1/26/04
PowerShares S&P Small Cap Consumer Staples	PSCC	0.29%	4/7/10
iShares MSCI ACWI EX US Consumer Staples	AXSL	0.48%	7/13/10
iShares S&P Global Consumer Staples	KXI	0.48%	9/12/06
iShares Dow Jones US Consumer Goods	IYK	0.48%	6/12/00
Rydex S&P Equal Weight Consumer Staples	RHS	0.50%	11/1/06
SPDR S&P International Consumer Staples Sector	IPS	0.51%	7/16/08
PowerShares Dynamic Food & Beverage	PBJ	0.63%	6/23/05
PowerShares Dynamic Consumer Staples	PSL	0.65%	10/12/06
First Trust Consumer Staples AlphaDEX	FXG	0.70%	5/8/07
EGShares Emerging Markets Consumer	ECON	0.85%	9/14/10

FIGURE 9-6

List of Select Sector and Industry ETFs: Energy

ENERGY			
ETF	Symbol	Expense Ratio	Inception Date
Energy Select Sector SPDR	XLE	0.20%	12/16/98
Vanguard Energy	VDE	0.24%	9/23/04
PowerShares S&P Small Cap Energy	PSCE	0.29%	4/7/10
SPDR S&P Oil & Gas Equipment & Services	XES	0.35%	6/19/06
SPDR S&P Oil & Gas Exploration & Production	XOP	0.35%	6/19/06
iShares Dow Jones US Oil Equipment Index	IEZ	0.47%	5/1/06
iShares MSCI ACWI EX US Energy Index	AXEN	0.48%	7/13/10
iShares S&P Global Clean Energy Index	ICLN	0.48%	6/24/08
iShares Dow Jones US Oil & Gas Exploration Index	IEO	0.48%	5/1/06
iShares S&P Global Nuclear Energy Index	NUCL	0.48%	6/24/08
iShares S&P Global Energy	IXC	0.48%	11/12/01
iShares Dow Jones US Energy	IYE	0.48%	6/12/00
Rydex S&P Equal Weight Energy	RYE	0.50%	11/1/06
SPDR S&P International Energy Sector	IPW	0.51%	7/16/08
Market Vectors Uranium + Nuclear Energy	NLR	0.57%	8/13/07
Market Vectors Coal	KOL	0.58%	1/10/08
WisdomTree International Energy	DKA	0.58%	10/13/06
First Trust Global Wind Energy	FAN	0.60%	6/16/08
First Trust ISE-Revere Natural Gas	FCG	0.60%	5/8/07
First Trust Nasdaq Cln Edg Green Energy	QCLN	0.60%	2/8/07
PowerShares Dynamic Oil & Gas Services	PXJ	0.63%	10/26/05
PowerShares Dynamic Energy Exploration & Production	PXE	0.63%	10/26/05
Market Vectors Solar Energy	KWT	0.65%	4/21/08
Jefferies TR/J CRB Wildcatters Exploration & Production Eq	WCAT	0.65%	1/20/10

ENERGY			
ETF	Symbol	Expense Ratio	Inception Date
PowerShares Dynamic Energy	PXI	0.65%	10/12/06
PowerShares Cleantech	PZD	0.67%	10/24/06
PowerShares WilderHill Progressive Energy	PUW	0.70%	10/24/06
PowerShares WilderHill Clean Energy	PBW	0.70%	3/3/05
Guggenheim Canadian Energy Income	ENY	0.70%	7/3/07
First Trust Energy AlphaDEX	FXN	0.70%	5/8/07
PowerShares Global Nuclear Energy	PKN	0.75%	4/3/08
PowerShares Global Coal	PKOL	0.75%	9/18/08
PowerShares Global Wind Energy	PWND	0.75%	7/1/08
PowerShares Global Clean Energy	PBD	0.75%	6/13/07
JPMorgan Alerian MLP Index ETN	AMJ	0.85%	4/2/09
ALPS Alerian MLP	AMLP	0.85%	8/25/10
UBS E-TRACS MLP Wells Fargo ETN	MLPW	0.85%	10/29/10
UBS E-TRACS Alerian MLP Infrastructure ETN	MLPI	0.85%	4/1/10
Credit Suisse Cushing 30 MLP Index ETN	MLPN	0.85%	4/13/10
UBS E-TRACS Alerian Nat Gas MLP ETN	MLPG	0.85%	7/13/10

FIGURE 9-7

List of Select Sector and Industry ETFs: Financials

FINANCIALS			
ETF	Symbol	Expense Ratio	Inception Date
Financial Select Sector SPDR	XLF	0.20%	12/16/98
Vanguard Financials	VFH	0.24%	1/26/04
PowerShares S&P Small Cap Financials	PSCF	0.29%	4/7/10
SPDR KBW Mortgage Finance	KME	0.35%	4/29/09
SPDR KBW Capital Markets	KCE	0.35%	11/8/05
SPDR KBW Regional Banking	KRE	0.35%	6/19/06
			continued

FIGURE 9-7

List of Select Sector and Industry ETFs: Financials (cont.)

FINANCIALS			
ETF	**Symbol**	**Expense Ratio**	**Inception Date**
SPDR KBW Insurance	KIE	0.35%	11/8/05
SPDR KBW Bank	KBE	0.35%	11/8/05
PowerShares KBW International Financial	KBWX	0.40%	12/1/10
iShares Dow Jones US Insurance	IAK	0.47%	5/1/06
iShares MSCI Europe Financials Index	EUFN	0.48%	1/20/10
iShares Dow Jones US Financial Sector	IYF	0.48%	5/22/00
iShares S&P Global Financials	IXG	0.48%	11/12/01
iShares Dow Jones US Financial Services	IYG	0.48%	6/12/00
iShares MSCI ACWI EX US Financials Index	AXFN	0.48%	1/20/10
iShares MSCI Far East Financials Index	FEFN	0.48%	1/20/10
iShares Dow Jones US Broker-Dealers	IAI	0.48%	5/1/06
iShares Dow Jones US Regional Banks	IAT	0.48%	5/1/06
RevenueShares Financials Sector	RWW	0.49%	11/10/08
Rydex S&P Equal Weight Financials	RYF	0.50%	11/1/06
SPDR S&P International Financial Sector	IPF	0.51%	7/16/08
First Trust Nasdaq ABA Community Bank	QABA	0.60%	6/29/09
PowerShares Dynamic Insurance	PIC	0.63%	10/26/05
PowerShares Dynamic Banking	PJB	0.65%	10/12/06
PowerShares Dynamic Financials	PFI	0.65%	10/12/06
iShares MSCI Emerg Markets Financials	EMFN	0.69%	1/20/10
First Trust Financials AlphaDEX	FXO	0.70%	5/8/07
PowerShares Listed Private Equity	PSP	0.70%	10/24/06
EGShares Emerging Markets Financials	EFN	0.85%	9/16/09
PowerShares KBW Hi Dividend Yield Financial	KBWD	0.93%	12/1/10

FIGURE 9-8

List of Select Sector and Industry ETFs: Health Care

HEALTH CARE			
ETF	Symbol	Expense Ratio	Inception Date
Health Care Select Sector SPDR	XLV	0.20%	12/16/98
Vanguard Health Care	VHT	0.24%	1/26/04
PowerShares S&P Small Cap Health Care	PSCH	0.29%	4/7/10
SPDR S&P Biotech	XBI	0.35%	1/31/06
SPDR S&P Health Care Equipment	XHE	0.35%	1/26/11
SPDR S&P Pharmaceuticals	XPH	0.36%	6/19/06
iShares Dow Jones US Medical Devices	IHI	0.47%	5/1/06
iShares Dow Jones US Healthcare Provider	IHF	0.47%	5/1/06
iShares Dow Jones US Pharmaceuticals	IHE	0.47%	5/1/06
iShares MSCI ACWI EX US Health Care	AXHE	0.48%	7/13/10
iShares Dow Jones US Healthcare	IYH	0.48%	6/12/00
iShares S&P Global Healthcare	IXJ	0.48%	11/13/01
iShares Nasdaq Biotechnology	IBB	0.48%	2/5/01
Rydex S&P Equal Weight HealthCare	RYH	0.50%	11/1/06
SPDR S&P International HealthCare Sector	IRY	0.51%	7/16/08
First Trust NYSE Arca Biotech Index	FBT	0.60%	6/19/06
PowerShares Dynamic Biotech & Genome	PBE	0.61%	6/23/05
PowerShares Dynamic Pharmaceuticals	PJP	0.63%	6/23/05
PowerShares Dynamic Healthcare	PTH	0.65%	10/12/06
First Trust Health Care AlphaDEX	FXH	0.70%	5/8/07
PowerShares Global Biotech	PBTQ	0.75%	9/18/08

FIGURE 9-9

List of Select Sector and Industry ETFs: Industrials

INDUSTRIALS			
ETF	Symbol	Expense Ratio	Inception Date
Industrial Select Sector SPDR	XLI	0.20%	12/16/98
Vanguard Industrials	VIS	0.24%	9/23/04
PowerShares S&P Small Cap Industrials	PSCI	0.29%	4/7/10
SPDR S&P Transportation	XTN	0.35%	1/26/11
iShares DJ US Aerospace & Defense	ITA	0.47%	5/1/06
iShares S&P Global Infrastructure Index	IGF	0.48%	12/10/07
iShares S&P Global Industrials	EXI	0.48%	9/12/06
Rydex S&P Equal Weight Industrials	RGI	0.50%	11/1/06
Market Vectors Environmental Services	EVX	0.55%	10/10/06
PowerShares Dynamic Building & Const	PKB	0.63%	10/26/05
PowerShares Water Resources	PHO	0.64%	12/6/05
PowerShares Dynamic Industrials	PRN	0.65%	10/12/06
Guggenheim Shipping	SEA	0.65%	6/11/10
PowerShares Aerospace & Defense	PPA	0.66%	10/26/05
Guggenheim Airline	FAA	0.75%	1/26/09

FIGURE 9-10

List of Select Sector and Industry ETFs: Technology

TECHNOLOGY			
ETF	Symbol	Expense Ratio	Inception Date
Technology Select Sector SPDR	XLK	0.20%	12/16/98
Vanguard Information Technology	VGT	0.24%	1/26/04
PowerShares S&P Small Cap Information Technology	PSCT	0.29%	4/7/10
SPDR S&P Semiconductor	XSD	0.35%	1/31/06
iShares Dow Jones US Technology	IYW	0.47%	5/15/00
iShares MSCI ACWI EX US Information Technology Index	AXIT	0.48%	7/13/10

TECHNOLOGY			
ETF	**Symbol**	**Expense Ratio**	**Inception Date**
iShares S&P Global Technology	IXN	0.48%	11/12/01
iShares S&P NA Technology-Software	IGV	0.48%	7/10/01
iShares S&P NA Technology	IGM	0.48%	3/13/01
iShares S&P NA Technology-Multimedia Network	IGN	0.48%	7/10/01
iShares PHLX SOX Semiconductor Sector	SOXX	0.48%	7/10/01
SPDR Morgan Stanley Technology	MTK	0.50%	9/25/00
Rydex S&P Equal Weight Technology	RYT	0.50%	11/1/06
SPDR S&P International Technology Sector	IPK	0.52%	7/16/08
First Trust Dow Jones Internet Index	FDN	0.60%	6/19/06
First Trust Nasdaq-100-Technology Index	QTEC	0.60%	4/19/06
PowerShares Nasdaq Internet	PNQI	0.60%	6/12/08
PowerShares Dynamic Software	PSJ	0.63%	6/23/05
PowerShares Dynamic Semiconductors	PSI	0.63%	6/23/05
PowerShares Dynamic Networking	PXQ	0.63%	6/23/05
PowerShares Dynamic Technology	PTF	0.65%	10/12/06
PowerShares Lux Nanotech	PXN	0.70%	10/26/05
First Trust Technology AlphaDEX	FXL	0.70%	5/8/07

FIGURE 9-11

List of Select Sector and Industry ETFs: Telecommunications

TELECOMMUNICATIONS			
ETF	**Symbol**	**Expense Ratio**	**Inception Date**
Vanguard Telecom Services	VOX	0.24%	9/23/04
iShares MSCI ACWI EX US Telecom	AXTE	0.48%	7/13/10
iShares Dow Jones US Telecom	IYZ	0.48%	5/22/00
iShares S&P Global Telecom	IXP	0.48%	11/12/01
SPDR S&P Telecom	XTL	0.50%	1/26/11
SPDR S&P International Telecom Sector	IST	0.52%	7/16/08
PowerShares Dynamic Media	PBS	0.63%	6/23/05
First Trust Nasdaq CEA Smartphone	FONE	0.70%	2/17/11

FIGURE 9-12

List of Select Sector and Industry ETFs: Utilities

UTILITIES			
ETF	Symbol	Expense Ratio	Inception Date
Utilities Select Sector SPDR	XLU	0.20%	12/16/98
Vanguard Utilities	VPU	0.24%	1/26/04
PowerShares S&P Small Cap Utilities	PSCU	0.29%	4/7/10
iShares MSCI ACWI EX US Utilities Index	AXUT	0.48%	7/13/10
iShares Dow Jones US Utilities	IDU	0.48%	6/12/00
iShares S&P Global Utilities	JXI	0.48%	9/12/06
Rydex S&P Equal Weight Utilities	RYU	0.50%	11/1/06
SPDR S&P International Utilities Sector	IPU	0.52%	7/16/08
WisdomTree International Utilities	DBU	0.58%	10/13/06
First Trust ISE Water	FIW	0.60%	5/8/07
PowerShares Dynamic Utilities	PUI	0.63%	10/26/05
First Trust Utilities AlphaDEX	FXU	0.70%	5/8/07

## CHAPTER 10

Fixed-Income ETFs: Bonding With Corporates, Municipals, Treasuries, and More

Quick, which market is larger—the equities market or the fixed-income market? The answer is the fixed-income market, hands down (see Figure 10-1 for some advantages and disadvantages). Given the breadth and depth of the expansive fixed-income market, investors have significant alternatives from which to choose—regardless if the investors are seeking current income or if they are attempting to enhance a portfolio from a risk and return trade-off perspective. There are multiple segments within the fixed-income market, from mortgage-backed bonds to corporate bonds and from government bonds to foreign bonds. Each one of these segments exhibits different risk and return potential, a favorable situation for investors.

A bond represents a loan to a corporation or government entity in order to raise capital to finance many different kinds of expenditures. In most cases, assets of the issuer back each fixed-income security, thus providing the purchaser with some level of protection in the case of default. These assets, or debt instruments, hold the issuer to a contractual obligation to make periodic interest payments to the purchaser on predetermined dates in predetermined amounts until the security reaches maturity or is called by the issuer. Furthermore, the issuer is obligated to repay principal at maturity.

FIGURE 10 - 1

Positives and Negatives of Fixed-Income Investing

Positives	Negatives
▶ Current and Predictable Income	▶ Lower Return Potential
▶ Low Correlations to Other Assets	▶ Default and Credit Risk
▶ Safety of Principal	▶ Interest Rate Risk
▶ Treasuries Default Free	▶ Higher Transaction Costs
▶ Priority of Claims on Assets	▶ Liquidity Risk
▶ Typically Low Volatility	▶ Greater Price Inefficiencies
▶ Tax Advantages	▶ Prepayment Risk
▶ Quick Access to Funds	▶ Purchasing Power Risk
▶ Possible Conversion to Stock	▶ Reinvestment Risk

Source: Frush Financial Group

The first fixed-income exchange-traded funds (ETFs) that were brought to market were based on U.S Treasuries. Today, the dominant fixed-income ETFs are either actively traded investment-grade bonds or based on broad bond market indexes with significant emphasis on the largest and most creditworthy issuers. Unlike equity ETFs, some fixed-income ETFs do not employ in-kind creation and redemption. This occurrence is a direct result of bonds and other fixed-income securities being much less liquid and thus not appropriate for buying and selling by an authorized participant. Furthermore, market prices are much less reliable with fixed-income securities than with equity securities.

Using fixed-income ETFs in your portfolio will provide you with immediate exposure to targeted fixed-income segments with a highly diversified and low-expense investment. Investing in an ETF instead of direct purchases is ideal when the fixed-income segment is more complex, such as high-yield corporate bonds. Spreading the risk from one particular bond across a pool of bonds will ensure that you do not experience excessive losses tied to singular issues.

Fixed-Income Risk and Return

There is a strong and positive correlation between length of maturity and risk, as Figure 10-2 illustrates. The longer you hold an investment, the longer you are exposed to risk. The longer you are exposed to risk, the greater the probability you can experience partial or total losses. Greater compensation in the form of higher returns is then in order. For those with lower-risk profiles—due to either low tolerance, low capacity, or low need—investing in shorter-term fixed-income investments is therefore prudent. Unfortunately, lower-risk potential is synonymous with lower-return potential.

Yield is the annual rate of return for a fixed-income investment derived from dividing the annual interest payments by the purchase price or market value (depending on when and how

FIGURE 10-2

Bond Risk and Yields

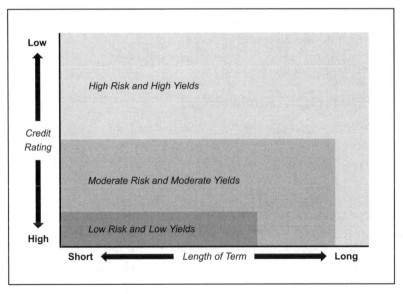

Source: Frush Financial Group

you are evaluating the security). Typically, the longer the time to maturity for a fixed-income security, the higher its yield. Thus, short-term securities tend to have lower yields than do long-term securities. This is not always the case, but tends to hold true for the vast majority of time. Why do securities with longer maturities have higher yields? The principal and most accepted theory—since there are other theories—says that investors demand higher rates of return for each progressively longer period of time they must forgo current consumption and place their invested capital at risk for extended periods of time. As such, bond issuers know they need to increase the interest rate on longer-term investments to entice investors.

To illustrate how investors demand higher rates of return for securities with longer maturities, the concept of the yield curve was created. A yield curve is the graphical representation of the relationship between fixed-income yields and their time to maturity. Under normal economic conditions, yield curves are upward sloping; thus the yields increase as the time to maturity increases. This is known as a "normal" yield curve. When the yields for both short-term and long-term bonds are the same, the yield curve is said to be "flat." However, when the yields on long-term bonds are lower than the yields on short-term bonds, the yield curve is said to be "inverted."

FIXED-INCOME MARKET

Fixed-income investments are available in a wide variety of segments. Each segment is different from the next, which is ideal since your goal is to invest in assets that are fundamentally different from one another. Three of the primary factors impacting most investors' decisions when evaluating fixed-income investments are tax considerations, length of maturity consideration, and credit risk or default risk consideration, which is the uncertainty that an issuer will not be able to make scheduled interest payments or repayments of principal at maturity.

Although bonds are typically issued with a variety of maturities, they can be categorized into one of three segments.

These segments include short-term bonds, intermediate-term bonds, and long-term bonds. Short-term bonds have maturities of 1 to 3 years, intermediate-term bonds have maturities anywhere between 4 and 10 years, and long-term bonds have maturities greater than 10 years. Accordingly, long-term bonds tend to have higher yields than intermediate-term bonds, which tend to have higher yields than short-term bonds. (See Figure 10-3 for leading characteristics of bonds).

Although considered a separate asset class from fixed income, cash and equivalents define a very broad category of assets that are highly liquid, are very safe, and can be converted easily into cash, such as money market funds—or that are already in that form, such as coins and bills. In practice, cash and equivalents have a maturity date within one year. The returns of this asset class generally correlate to the rate of inflation. Thus, as inflation rates fall, so too do the rates on money market funds and certificates of deposit. Cash and equivalents are differentiated by their issuer, maturity date, interest rate (referred to as coupon rate), credit quality, and tax status (taxable or nontaxable).

Although market values for fixed-income securities are more stable than those for equities and other investments, they do change over time. The primary factors impacting market values include the degree and direction of changing interest rates, fiscal and monetary policies, the macroeconomic health of the national and local economies, the generic flow of funds into or out of fixed income, and the supply-and-demand balance for specific fixed-income issues.

Some common fixed-income segments include the following:

- Treasury bills, notes, and bonds
- Municipal bonds
- Agency bonds
- Corporate bonds
- Mortgage-backed securities
- Asset-backed securities
- Money markets
- Certificates of deposit

FIGURE 10-3

Leading Characteristics of Bonds

Municipal	**Corporate**
▶ Federal tax exempt	▶ Fully taxable
▶ State and city tax exempt if buying home state and city	▶ Pay the highest yields
▶ Less risk than corporate, but more risk than Treasuries	▶ Greater risk than other bonds
▶ Two types—revenue and general obligation	▶ Three types--asset-backed, debenture, and convertible
Treasuries	**Agency**
▶ Subject to federal taxes, but state and local tax exempt	▶ Can be taxable on the federal, state, and local levels
▶ Lowest yields of all bonds	▶ Modestly higher yields than Treasuries
▶ Lowest risk of all bonds	▶ Modestly higher risk than Treasuries
▶ Three types—bills (<1 year), notes (2–10 years), and bonds (10+ years)	▶ Issued by federal, state, and local agencies

Source: Frush Financial Group

FIXED-INCOME VOLATILITY

Given their greater inherent risk, long-term bonds yield returns that are more volatile than those of both intermediate-term and short-term bonds. Not only are the returns of long-term bonds more volatile, but also are the market values. Fortunately, holding higher-risk, more volatile long-term bonds typically compensates an investor with higher returns over the maturity holding period. The same can be said for intermediate-term bonds versus short-term bonds. This is an outstanding example of the golden rule of investing—risk and return are inescapably linked.

FIXED-INCOME CORRELATIONS

One of the leading benefits of fixed income is the low and thus favorable correlations with equities. By combining fixed income and equities in the same portfolio, an investor will enhance his or her portfolio's risk-adjusted return. Short-term bonds have the lowest correlations to equities, while long-term bonds have higher correlations to equities. As the length of maturity increases, the correlation to equities also increases—however, the increase is only marginal.

Historically, short-term bonds have a correlation to equities of slightly less than zero. Intermediate-term bonds have a correlation of close to 0.1, and long-term bonds have a correlation of about 0.2 to equities. Correlations in the range of –0.3 to +0.3 are considered noncorrelated and thus have no pattern of moving together. Accordingly, correlations to other fixed-income securities depend on the maturity. Short-term bonds have moderate to high correlations to intermediate-term bonds, which in turn have strong correlations to long-term bonds. The greatest differential is between short-term bonds and long-term bonds.

These findings support the inclusion of fixed-income investments in a portfolio in which an investor wants to enhance overall diversification and improve the risk-adjusted return. The greatest benefit is provided when short-term bonds are added to an otherwise diversified multiasset-class portfolio where equities are the backbone of the portfolio.

PORTFOLIO ENHANCEMENT OPPORTUNITIES

We now turn our attention to four opportunities within the fixed-income market where excess return premiums are available, taking into consideration each opportunity's unique risk and reward profile. These four opportunities include credit premiums, tax-status premiums, maturity premiums, and high-yield premiums. Given each investor's unique financial situation, exercising care when pursuing any of these opportunities is most appropriate. Also, always remember that although an asset class may exhibit high risk, it is the synergistic benefits that truly matter. The total portfolio—including aggregate return and risk—is more important than the sum of its constituent parts. We will begin with credit premiums and the incremental returns investors can receive for assuming higher risk.

Credit Premiums

Credit risk refers to the uncertainty that a particular issuer will not make required annual interest payments or return principal at maturity. Companies with greater financial troubles are considered to have greater credit risk than companies with a more favorable financial picture. As an investor, you should be compensated for taking on this extra risk.

But how do you measure the credit risk of any particular company? Fortunately you don't have to do this, as this work is handled by three recognizable and relatively competent credit rating agencies—Standard & Poor's, Moody's, and Fitch. Each agency delves into the financials of many publicly traded companies (and their issued securities) and governments across the globe to issue a relevant credit rating. All three credit rating agencies have similar ratings levels, but dissimilarities do exist (see Figure 10-4). Ratings of BBB or better are considered investment grade at both Standard & Poor's and Fitch, whereas a rating of Baa or higher at Moody's is considered investment grade. These differences are more cosmetic than substantive.

FIGURE 10-4

Bond Credit Ratings

Credit Risk	Moody's	Standard & Poor's	Fitch
Investment Grade		**Rating**	
Highest Quality	Aaa	AAA	AAA
High Quality	Aa	AA	AA
Upper-Medium Grade	A	A	A
Medium Grade	Baa	BBB	BBB
Noninvestment Grade		**Rating**	
Somewhat Speculative	Ba	BB	BB
Speculative	B	B	B
Highly Speculative	Caa	CCC	CCC
Most Speculative	Ca	CC	CC
Imminent Default	C	C	C
Default	C	D	D

Source: Frush Financial Group

U.S. Treasuries and federal agency bonds have the least amount of credit risk and therefore receive the highest ratings. They typically yield the lowest as a consequence, however. Municipalities and many corporations tend to receive the next highest ratings, followed by questionable companies and even some municipalities. Bonds from questionable or distressed issuers are considered high-yield, or "junk," bonds. These types of investments offer a unique premium and are discussed in more detail later in this section.

The difference in bond ratings has a corresponding impact on the yield of bonds. Higher-rated bonds have lower yields, and lower-rated bonds have higher yields. The variation in yields provides us with credit spreads. These spreads widen during periods of economic weakness and narrow during periods of economic strength. Research has shown that the average correlation between credit risk premiums and equity risk premiums is only about 25 percent. As a result, investing in bonds will enhance the risk and return trade-off profile of a portfolio. Bonds exhibiting greater credit risk provide excess return potential, but also with a slight increase in risk.

Opportunities With Tax-Exempt Securities

For taxable investors, taxes on capital gains and ordinary income are the performance penalty variables that generally have the most impact on the bottom-line return. As a result, minimizing the impact of taxes should be of utmost priority. For some investors, investing in tax-exempt securities (e.g., municipal bonds) may be a smart and beneficial move. Investors in the highest income tax bracket will benefit the most from tax-exempt securities. Likewise, investors in lower income tax brackets are typically better served by investing in taxable securities since the after-tax return is typically higher than the rate of return on a comparable, but tax-exempt and lower-yielding, municipal bond.

In addition to your tax bracket, the type of account you have also plays a role in determining whether or not taxable or tax-exempt investments make good financial sense. For example, if you hold a tax-exempt account, then investing in tax-exempt securities is generally a waste. Since you do not have to pay taxes on interest received from tax-exempt securities, they make far more sense in taxable accounts. The same holds true for taxable securities. Their impact is greater in tax-exempt accounts since taxes are not levied on the income received.

So how do you compare the yields on tax-exempt bonds with those on fully taxable bonds? The best way is to compute what is called the tax-equivalent yield. Doing so allows you to make apples-to-apples comparisons. To compute a tax-equivalent yield, simply divide the yield on a tax-exempt bond by 1 minus your tax rate, as follows:

$$\textit{Tax-equivalent yield} = \frac{\textit{tax-exempt municipal bond yield}}{1 - \textit{tax rate}}$$

For instance, if you were considering a municipal bond yielding 4 percent and your tax rate is 30 percent, then your tax-equivalent yield is 5.71 percent [4 percent/(1 − 0.3)]. Thus, for you to consider a fully taxable corporate bond instead of the tax-exempt municipal bond, you will require at least a yield of 5.71 percent, all else being equal.

Income from municipal bonds is exempt from all federal, state, and local income taxes for an investor residing in the state of issuance. Investors can purchase municipal bonds issued by other states, but doing so results in the loss of the state tax exemption. Home states would prefer that you not invest in bonds issued in one of the other 49 states. Irrespective of this drawback, many investors purchase non–home state municipal bonds to diversify credit risk. Furthermore, investing in municipal bonds is really about the federal tax exemption, not the state tax exemption, since the federal tax rate is much higher than state income tax rates, which is nil in some states.

Maturity Premium Opportunities

Under normal economic conditions, bonds with longer maturities pay higher interest rates than bonds with shorter maturities. This premium is the result of the additional risk that investors must assume, as the principal is repaid at a much later date. In addition to credit risk, longer maturities also exhibit greater interest rate risk, or risk that rising market interest rates will create less demand for a lower interest rate bond. Less demand will cause the price of a bond to fall in response. The longer the time to maturity, the greater the premium for holding a particular bond.

Duration is a mathematical concept used in the investment field to measure the price sensitivity of a bond to changing market interest rates. Bonds with higher durations are more susceptible to changing interest rates—and therefore experience greater changes in market value when market interest rates do change—than bonds with lower durations. The length of maturity outstanding and coupon interest rate for a particular fixed-income security are the primary determinants of duration. Both longer times to maturity and lower interest rates equate to higher duration—and thus greater market-value sensitivity to interest rate changes—while the opposite is true for shorter times to maturity and higher interest rates.

Fixed-income spreads refer to differences in yields between shorter-term bonds and longer-term bonds. These spreads are constantly changing and can approach 1 percent—sometimes even higher. During strong economic periods, yield spreads will narrow as investors have greater confidence in the stability of higher-risk companies and their ability to pay interest and principal payments. In contrast, yield spreads typically widen during periods of economic weakness as investors become skeptical over the prospects of riskier companies and therefore favor more secure companies, which issue corresponding lower-yielding bonds, however. This situation is illustrated in Figure 10-5.

FIGURE 10-5

Relationship Between Bond Yields and Economic Health

Bond Quality	Good Economy	Weak Economy
High-Quality Bonds	Sell = yields ▲	Buy = yields ▼
Low-Quality Bonds	Buy = yields ▼	Sell = yields ▲

From a pure return standpoint, longer-term bonds may provide more benefit as they typically have higher yields. However, from a risk-adjusted standpoint, shorter-term bonds may be more ideal given their lower correlation to equity investments. The benefit of shorter-term bonds increases when portfolios have greater allocations to equities.

High-Yield Opportunities

Although frequently referred to as junk bonds, high-yield bonds play an important role in a properly allocated portfolio. High-yield bonds are speculative in nature, but when invested in a well-diversified portfolio, risk is controlled. Research has shown that although some issuers will default on their bonds, this impact is not great enough to offset the excess return you can capture by investing in a pool of high-yield bonds. High-yield bonds receive their name and status when one of the aforementioned three credit rating agencies assigns a non-investment-grade rating.

Research has demonstrated that the factors influencing equity and high-yield bond returns have little in common. Ironically, though, default risk for high-yield bonds and equity securities is typically highly correlated, thus diminishing the asset allocation benefits. However, the correlations frequently do fluctuate and even have become negative at times, which is an ideal situation for investors. The best method for investing in high-yield bonds is through a pooled investment—namely, ETFs and even some mutual funds—given the higher than normal risk that is inherent in each of the high-yield bonds.

SELECT FIXED-INCOME ETFs

An optimal portfolio emphasizes multiasset classes with allocations to equities, fixed income, and real assets. Creating this kind of portfolio will provide significant risk and return trade-off benefits, specifically the enhancement of total returns with only a moderate and manageable increase in portfolio risk.

Figures 10-6 to 10-19 provide ETF investment options you may want to consider for your own portfolio. I strongly encourage you to evaluate the options and determine for yourself if these ETFs make financial and suitability sense for your needs. Depending on your financial situation and goals, you may want to incorporate multiple fixed-income ETFs or concentrate on just a couple of the broader segment ETFs. The market is divided into 14 diverse segments, each offering different market exposure and therefore distinct risk and reward opportunities. Note that each segment in the figures is sorted by expense ratio.

FIGURE 10-6

List of Select Fixed-Income ETFs: Short-Term Government

SHORT-TERM GOVERNMENT			
ETF	Symbol	Expense Ratio	Inception Date
PIMCO 1-3 Year US Treasury Index	TUZ	0.09%	6/1/09
Schwab Short-Term U.S. Treasury	SCHO	0.12%	8/5/10
iShares Barclays 1-3 Year Treasury Bond	SHY	0.15%	7/22/02
iShares Barclays Short Treasury Bond	SHV	0.15%	1/5/07
Vanguard Short-Term Government Bond	VGSH	0.15%	11/19/09
PowerShares Active Low Duration	PLK	0.29%	4/11/08

FIGURE 10-7

List of Select Fixed-Income ETFs: Short Term

SHORT TERM			
ETF	**Symbol**	**Expense Ratio**	**Inception Date**
Vanguard Short-Term Bond	BSV	0.11%	4/3/07
SPDR Barclays Capital Short Term Corporate Bond	SCPB	0.13%	12/16/09
SPDR Barclays Capital 1-3 Month T-Bill	BIL	0.14%	5/25/07
Vanguard Short-Term Corporate Bond	VCSH	0.15%	11/19/09
iShares Barclays 1-3 Year Credit Bond	CSJ	0.20%	1/5/07
SPDR Barclays Capital Mortgage Backed Bond	MBG	0.21%	1/15/09
Guggenheim BulletShares 2012 Corporate Bond	BSCC	0.24%	6/7/10
Guggenheim BulletShares 2013 Corporate Bond	BSCD	0.24%	6/7/10
Claymore U.S. Capital Markets Micro-Term	ULQ	0.32%	2/12/08
PIMCO Enhanced Short Maturity Strategy	MINT	0.35%	11/16/09

FIGURE 10-8

List of Select Fixed-Income ETFs: Intermediate-Term Government

INTERMEDIATE-TERM GOVERNMENT			
ETF	**Symbol**	**Expense Ratio**	**Inception Date**
Schwab Interm-Tm U.S. Treasury	SCHR	0.12%	8/5/10
SPDR Barclays Capital Interm-Tm Treasury	ITE	0.14%	5/23/07
PIMCO 3-7 Year U.S. Treasury Index	FIVZ	0.15%	10/30/09
Vanguard Interm-Tm Government Bond	VGIT	0.15%	11/19/09
iShares Barclays 3-7 Year Treasury Bond	IEI	0.15%	1/5/07
iShares Barclays Agency Bond	AGZ	0.20%	11/5/08

FIGURE 10-9

List of Select Fixed-Income ETFs: Intermediate Term

INTERMEDIATE-TERM			
ETF	**Symbol**	**Expense Ratio**	**Inception Date**
Vanguard Total Bond Market	BND	0.11%	4/3/07
Vanguard Intermediate-Term Bond	BIV	0.11%	4/3/07
SPDR Barclays Capital Aggregate Bond	LAG	0.13%	5/23/07
Vanguard Mortgage-Backed Securities	VMBS	0.15%	11/19/09
Vanguard Intermediate-Term Corporate Bond	VCIT	0.15%	11/19/09
SPDR Barclays Cap Intermediate Term Corporate Bond	ITR	0.15%	2/10/09
iShares Barclays Intermediate Credit Bond	CIU	0.20%	1/5/07
iShares Barclays Credit Bond	CFT	0.20%	1/5/07
PIMCO Invest Grade Corporate Bond	CORP	0.20%	9/20/10
iShares Barclays Aggregate Bond	AGG	0.20%	9/22/03
Guggenheim BulletShares 2014 Corporate Bond	BSCE	0.24%	6/7/10
Guggenheim BulletShares 2015 Corporate Bond	BSCF	0.24%	6/7/10
Guggenheim BulletShares 2016 Corporate Bond	BSCG	0.24%	6/7/10
Guggenheim BulletShares 2017 Corporate Bond	BSCH	0.24%	6/7/10
iShares Barclays MBS Bond	MBB	0.25%	3/13/07
Claymore U.S. Capital Markets Bond	UBD	0.32%	2/12/08

FIGURE 10-10

List of Select Fixed-Income ETFs: Long-Term Government

LONG-TERM GOVERNMENT			
ETF	**Symbol**	**Expense Ratio**	**Inception Date**
Vanguard Extended Duration Bond	EDV	0.13%	12/6/07
SPDR Barclays Capital Long Term Treasury	TLO	0.14%	5/23/07
PIMCO Broad U.S. Treasury Index	TRSY	0.15%	10/29/10
PIMCO 7-15 Year U.S. Treasury Index	TENZ	0.15%	9/10/09
iShares Barclays 20+ Year Treasury Bond	TLT	0.15%	7/22/02
Vanguard Long-Term Government Bond	VGLT	0.15%	11/19/09
PIMCO 25+ Yr Zero Cpn U.S. Treasury	ZROZ	0.15%	10/30/09
iShares Barclays 10-20 Year Treasury Bond	TLH	0.15%	1/5/07
PowerShares 1-30 Laddered Treasury	PLW	0.25%	10/11/07

FIGURE 10-11

List of Select Fixed-Income ETFs: Long Term

LONG TERM			
ETF	**Symbol**	**Expense Ratio**	**Inception Date**
Vanguard Long-Term Bond Index	BLV	0.11%	4/3/07
Vanguard Long-Term Corp Bond	VCLT	0.15%	11/19/09
SPDR Barclays Capital Long Corporate Term Bond	LWC	0.15%	3/10/09
iShares iBoxx $ Invest Grade Corporate Bond	LQD	0.15%	7/22/02
iShares 10+ Year Credit Bond	CLY	0.20%	12/8/09
PowerShares Build America Bond	BAB	0.28%	11/17/09
SPDR Nuveen Barclays Capital Build American Bond	BABS	0.36%	5/12/10
PIMCO Build America Bond Strategy	BABZ	0.45%	9/20/10

FIGURE 10-12

List of Select Fixed-Income ETFs: Municipal

MUNICIPAL			
ETF	Symbol	Expense Ratio	Inception Date
Market Vectors Short Municipal Index	SMB	0.19%	2/22/08
SPDR Nuveen Barclays Capital CA Municipal Bond	CXA	0.20%	10/10/07
SPDR Nuveen Barclays Capital Municipal Bond	TFI	0.20%	9/11/07
SPDR Nuveen Barclays Capital NY Municipal Bond	INY	0.20%	10/11/07
SPDR Nuveen Barclays Capital S/T Municipal Bond	SHM	0.20%	10/10/07
SPDR Nuveen S&P VRDO Municipal Bond	VRD	0.21%	9/23/09
Market Vectors Intermediate Municipal	ITM	0.23%	12/4/07
Market Vectors Pre-Refunded Municipal	PRB	0.24%	2/2/09
Market Vectors Long Municipal Index	MLN	0.24%	1/2/08
iShares S&P CA AMT-Free Municipal Bond	CMF	0.25%	10/4/07
iShares S&P National AMT-Free Municipal Bond	MUB	0.25%	9/7/07
iShares S&P NY AMT-Free Municipal Bond	NYF	0.25%	10/4/07
PowerShares VRDO Tax-Free Weekly	PVI	0.25%	11/15/07
iShares S&P S/T National AMT-Free Municipal Bond	SUB	0.25%	11/5/08
PowerShares Insured California Municipal Bond	PWZ	0.28%	10/11/07
PowerShares Insured National Municipal Bond	PZA	0.28%	10/11/07
PowerShares Insured New York Municipal Bond	PZT	0.28%	10/11/07
iShares 2012 S&P AMT-Free Municipal Series	MUAA	0.30%	1/7/10
iShares 2013 S&P AMT-Free Municipal Series	MUAB	0.30%	1/7/10
iShares 2014 S&P AMT-Free Municipal Series	MUAC	0.30%	1/7/10

continued

FIGURE 10-12

List of Select Fixed-Income ETFs: Municipal (Cont.)

MUNICIPAL			
ETF	**Symbol**	**Expense Ratio**	**Inception Date**
iShares 2015 S&P AMT-Free Municipal Series	MUAD	0.30%	1/7/10
iShares 2016 S&P AMT-Free Municipal Series	MUAE	0.30%	1/7/10
iShares 2017 S&P AMT-Free Municipal Series	MUAF	0.30%	1/7/10
Grail McDonnell Intermediate Municipal Bond	GMMB	0.35%	1/29/10
PIMCO Intermediate Municipal Bond Strategy	MUNI	0.35%	11/30/09
Market Vectors High-Yield Municipal	HYD	0.35%	2/4/09
PIMCO Short Term Municipal Bond Strategy	SMMU	0.35%	2/1/10

FIGURE 10-13

List of Select Fixed-Income ETFs: High Yield

HIGH YIELD			
ETF	**Symbol**	**Expense Ratio**	**Inception Date**
SPDR Barclays Capital High Yield Bond	JNK	0.40%	11/28/07
iShares iBoxx $ High Yield Corporate Bond	HYG	0.50%	4/4/07
PowerShares Fundamental High Yield Corporate Bond	PHB	0.50%	11/15/07
Peritus High Yield	HYLD	1.37%	11/30/10

FIGURE 10-14

List of Select Fixed-Income ETFs: Inflation Protected

INFLATION PROTECTED			
ETF	**Symbol**	**Expense Ratio**	**Inception Date**
Schwab U.S. TIPS	SCHP	0.14%	8/5/10
SPDR Barclays Capital TIPS	IPE	0.19%	5/25/07
iShares Barclays 0-5 Year TIPS Bond	STIP	0.20%	12/1/10
PIMCO Broad U.S. TIPS Index	TIPZ	0.20%	9/3/09
PIMCO 15+ Year U.S. TIPS Index	LTPZ	0.20%	9/3/09
iShares Barclays TIPS Bond	TIP	0.20%	12/4/03
PIMCO 1-5 Year U.S. TIPS Index	STPZ	0.20%	8/20/09

FIGURE 10-15

List of Select Fixed-Income ETFs: Preferred Stock

PREFERRED STOCK			
ETF	**Symbol**	**Expense Ratio**	**Inception Date**
SPDR Wells Fargo Preferred Stock	PSK	0.45%	9/16/09
iShares S&P U.S. Preferred Stock Index	PFF	0.48%	3/26/07
PowerShares Preferred	PGX	0.50%	1/31/08
PowerShares Financial Preferred	PGF	0.65%	12/1/06

FIGURE 10-16

List of Select Fixed-Income ETFs: Convertibles

CONVERTIBLES			
ETF	**Symbol**	**Expense Ratio**	**Inception Date**
SPDR Barclays Capital Convertible Securities	CWB	0.40%	4/14/09

FIGURE 10-17

List of Select Fixed-Income ETFs: World

WORLD			
ETF	Symbol	Expense Ratio	Inception Date
iShares S&P/Citi International Treasury Bond	IGOV	0.35%	1/21/09
SPDR Barclays Cap S/T International Treasury Bond	BWZ	0.35%	1/15/09
iShares S&P/Citi 1-3 Yr International Treasury Bond	ISHG	0.35%	1/21/09
PowerShares International Corporate Bond	PICB	0.50%	6/3/10
SPDR Barclays Capital International Treasury Bond	BWX	0.50%	10/2/07
SPDR DB International Government Inflation-Protected Bond	WIP	0.50%	3/13/08
SPDR Barclays Capital International Corporate Bond	IBND	0.55%	5/19/10

FIGURE 10-18

List of Select Fixed-Income ETFs: Emerging Markets

EMERGING MARKETS			
ETF	Symbol	Expense Ratio	Inception Date
SPDR Barclays Capital Emerging Markets Local Bond	EBND	0.50%	2/23/11
PowerShares Emerging Markets Sovereign Debt	PCY	0.50%	10/11/07
WisdomTree Emerging Markets Local Debt	ELD	0.55%	8/9/10
WisdomTree Asia Local Debt	ALD	0.55%	3/16/11
iShares JPMorgan USD Emerging Markets Bond	EMB	0.60%	12/17/07
Market Vectors Emerging Markets Local Curr Bond	EMLC	0.60%	7/22/10

FIGURE 10-19

List of Select Fixed-Income ETFs: Multisector

MULTISECTOR			
ETF	**Symbol**	**Expense Ratio**	**Inception Date**
iShares Barclays Intermediate Government/Credit Bond	GVI	0.20%	1/5/07
iShares 10+ Year Government/ Credit Bond	GLJ	0.20%	12/8/09
iShares Barclays Government/ Credit Bond	GBF	0.20%	1/5/07
Grail McDonnell Core Taxable Bond	GMTB	0.35%	1/29/10

CHAPTER 11

Global ETFs: Country, Region, Style, and Broad-Market Opportunities

Global financial markets have experienced dynamic changes over the last couple of decades. U.S. equities now account for less than half of the total global equity market capitalization. This figure is down from more than two-thirds just a couple of decades ago. As a result, investors who incorporate international assets into their portfolios will find greater opportunities to protect and grow their investments. More specifically, they will improve the risk and return trade-off profile inherent in their portfolio by adding international assets to their asset mix. Consider, for example, two football teams—one with 30 players and one with 100 players. Since only 11 players per team are on the field at any one time, the team with 100 players has a higher chance of finding better players than the team with 30 players, all else being equal. Of course, this is not the case in all situations, but it is for the vast majority of instances. It is simply the law of numbers. By the way, the numbers 30 and 100 were not selected at random. The number 30 represents the approximate percentage of the total global equity market the U.S. market represents, while the number 100 simply represents the entire global equity market.

Historically, most individual investors did not pay attention to investing globally for three principal reasons:

1. Investors did not realize the benefits.
2. Transaction costs were substantial.
3. Information for making investment decisions was unreliable or, worse yet, absent.

Over the years, both transaction costs and availability of information have become more favorable, and many investors have realized the benefits of adding international investments to their portfolios. Adding international assets to an investment portfolio does not come without risk, however. There are new and different risks confronting the global investor. In addition, some risks that a U.S. investor faces are significantly magnified in foreign markets. For example, market liquidity is not as robust in most foreign countries as it is in the United States. Even with that being said, adding international assets to an investment portfolio still has greater potential rewards than potential risks.

BENEFITS OF GLOBAL ASSET ALLOCATION

The ability of investors to reduce portfolio risk is limited in portfolios comprising purely U.S. assets. Investors are able to reduce total risk by minimizing investment-specific risk with U.S.-only assets, but investors cannot reduce systematic risk, or risk attributed to the market and other uncontrollable external factors. When investors add international assets to their portfolios, the market portfolio changes to encompass both the U.S. market and the international market. Thus, reducing market risk is at the heart of global asset allocation.

The reduction of total risk from global asset allocation is driven by the less than perfect correlations between U.S. assets and international assets. Asset classes that are not perfectly positively correlated with each other will provide return-enhancing and risk-reducing benefits.

Global correlations are different from country to country, some highly correlated to U.S. assets and some not. More developed countries tend to have higher correlations with U.S. investments and those of other developed countries due in large part to the significant degree of economic integration. The more interaction among countries, the more influence each country has on the economic conditions of the other. Conversely, the less interaction countries have with each other, the more insulated they are from one another's economic influences—both positive and negative.

The greatest benefits from adding international assets to a portfolio come from those countries that have the lowest correlations to assets in the United States. However, the governments of many less-developed countries often place harsh regulations and severe restrictions on the investment and repatriation of capital from their countries. Higher potential returns come with higher potential risks.

GLOBAL ASSET ALLOCATION RISKS

In aggregate, international investments generally offer higher return potential than U.S. investments, but also come with higher risk. Irrespective of the higher risk, international investments are still advantageous since they are not perfectly positively correlated with U.S. investments and thus provide return-enhancing and risk-reducing benefits to your portfolio.(See Figure 11-1 for a list of the 10 largest international ETFs.)

International investments tend to be more risky than U.S. investments for the following major reasons.

Currency Fluctuation Risk

Exchange rates between the U.S. dollar and foreign currencies are constantly in flux due to supply and demand for each currency. As a result, currency exchange rates can substantially increase or decrease the net return (expressed in U.S. dollars) of your investment made abroad even if the market value of your investment in foreign terms did not change during the holding period.

For example, suppose that a U.S. real estate investment group purchases a commercial property in Canada for 5 million Canadian dollars. If one year later the value of the property remains at 5 million Canadian dollars and the Canadian dollar has declined in value against the U.S. dollar, then the U.S. real estate investment group will experience a negative holding period return. Why? If the U.S. real estate investment group were to sell the property, it would require more Canadian dollars to buy U.S. dollars to repatriate the capital.

FIGURE 11-1

Largest International Category ETFs

ETF	Symbol	Assets ($B)
Vanguard MSCI Emerging Markets	VWO	49.4
iShares MSCI Emerging Markets	EEM	41.6
iShares MSCI EAFE Index	EFA	40.6
iShares MSCI Brazil Index	EWZ	13.2
iShares FTSE China 25 Index Fund	FXI	8.4
Vanguard FTSE All-World EX-US	VEU	7.9
iShares MSCI Japan Index	EWJ	7.3
Vanguard MSCI EAFE	VEA	6.9
iShares MSCI Canada Index	EWC	6.5
iShares MSCI South Korea Index	EWY	5.4

Source: Morningstar, April 2011

Political Risk

Political risk refers to the uncertainty that political decisions, policies, events, and conditions in a foreign country will adversely impact the market values of investments made in that particular country. Political risk takes many forms such as confiscation of property, economic instability, repatriation of profits, war, revolution, kidnapping and ransom, extortion, and lack of or unreliability of financial information.

Lack-of-Liquidity Risk

You may find it challenging to trade securities in less-developed countries due to their smaller market size and resulting lower inherent supply and demand. In fact, at times there may be little to no demand for an investment that you need to sell. As a result, you may be forced to liquidate your investment at a much lower price than expected, thus impacting your return.

Merging-of-Asset-Correlations Risk

Today, nearly 50 percent of the global market capitalization and 40 percent of global sales are attributed to multinational corporations. Over time, as global economies and multinational companies become progressively more integrated, correlations become stronger thus diminishing the benefit of investing globally. This trend will only become more pronounced as international corporations increase their global operations either through organic growth or through the acquisition of foreign companies. As long as correlations are not perfectly correlated, then there is opportunity to enhance returns while reducing risk.

Foreign Tax Risk

When an international company pays a dividend to stockholders, the country where the company is domiciled will assess a withholding tax, generally around 15 percent. For taxable investors, any foreign taxes paid can be deducted and written off against U.S. taxes as long as the foreign country and the United States have signed a tax treaty. However, U.S-based tax-exempt investors are not subject to tax on ordinary interest and dividend income. Accordingly, when tax-exempt investors pay taxes on foreign income, then they cannot write off the taxes paid against U.S. taxes since they will not have paid taxes anyway. Thus, international investing may not hold the same benefits for all types of investors.

GLOBAL MARKET STRUCTURE AND ETFs

The entire investing marketplace begins with the global market portfolio, which comprises all investable opportunities and securities across the world. The global market portfolio can be divided and further subdivided into smaller and smaller markets (see Figure 11-2). For example, the global market portfolio can be divided into developed markets and emerging markets, both of which can be subdivided into various geographic regions. Finally, geographic regions can be subdivided into single-basket countries, each of which constitutes the underlying foundation of the global market structure. Index sponsors, such as Morgan Stanley Capital International (MSCI), create indexes based on individual countries, regions, styles, and the broad market. Rights are then sold to exchange-traded fund (ETF) providers, who have launched numerous ETFs based on many of the indexes. As a result, investors have excellent ways to gain international investment exposure to geographic areas and markets of their desire.

Country Indexes

As previously mentioned, countries make up the core of the global market portfolio. The most widely recognized indexes tracking individual countries are the MSCI indexes. These indexes capture at least 85 percent of the market capitalization of each country they track. Specifically, MSCI categorizes publicly traded securities into industry groups and then selects stocks from each group to create the country market index. Thus, industry replication is the most important factor in MSCI's methodology. These indexes and other global ETFs are provided in Figures 11-4 to 11-17.

Simplified Global Market Structure

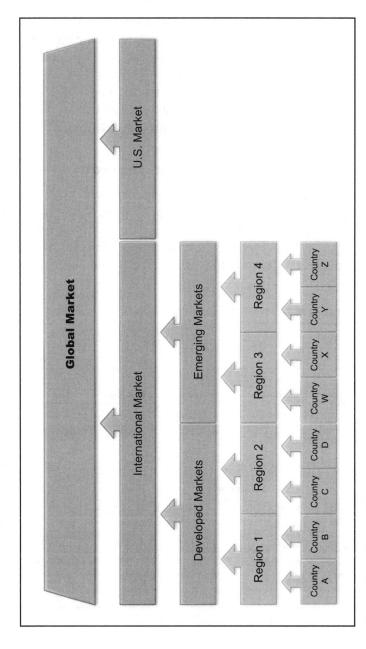

Source: Frush Financial Group

Regional Indexes

Although there are a number of regional indexes, the two most popular track Europe and Asia Pacific, given their economic might. As such, the MSCI Europe and MSCI Pacific are two of the most widely used indexes by ETF providers. Other regions with investable indexes include the Middle East and Africa and Latin America. Many of the new regional indexes are divided into developed and emerging markets, such as the emerging Eastern Europe market.

Developed Markets

Developed markets comprise those countries that have stable governments, large economies, robust banking systems, effective legal systems, and, most important, strong and liquid investment markets. Countries that meet these provisions typically have a minimum of $20,000 per capita annual GDP (see Figure 11-3).

FIGURE 11-3

Countries With GDP Greater Than $20,000 per Capita

Rank	Country	Amount	Rank	Country	Amount
1	Luxembourg	$108,832	11	Canada	$46,215
2	Norway	$84,444	12	Ireland	$45,689
3	Qatar	$76,168	13	Austria	$44,987
4	Switzerland	$67,246	14	Finland	$44,489
5	United Arab Emirates	$59,717	15	Singapore	$43,117
6	Denmark	$56,147	16	Japan	$42,820
7	Australia	$55,590	17	Belgium	$42,630
8	Sweden	$48,875	18	France	$41,019
9	United States	$47,284	19	Germany	$40,631
10	Netherlands	$47,172	20	Iceland	$39,026

Source: International Monetary Fund, 2010

Combining the aforementioned MSCI Europe and MSCI Pacific sums to the MSCI EAFE Index, which is the most recognizable index of developed markets. EAFE stands for Europe, Australasia, and the Far East and is composed of approximately 1,000 large-company stocks (slightly over half attributed to Europe) from more than 20 developed markets around the globe.

Emerging Markets

Emerging markets are countries where business activity is rapidly expanding. Although there are more than 150 countries meeting some classification standard of emerging market status—with over 100 having some resemblance of a stock market—there are only about 40 officially recognized emerging markets in the world, with China and India the largest such markets. MSCI recognizes 21 countries, Standard & Poor's recognizes 19 countries, and Dow Jones recognizes the most, at 35 countries.

International Market

The leading index for tracking the international market is the FTSE All-World ex-U.S. Index. This index—appropriately named— tracks all developed and emerging markets around the world with the exception of the United States. Other popular international market indexes include the Citigroup Primary Market Index and the Citigroup Broad Market Index.

Global Market

The global market is simply a combination of the international market plus the United States market. Dividing the global market portfolio into the two markets provides investors with ways to make targeted investments without overlap. The S&P Global 1200 and S&P Global 100 are two excellent indexes for tracking the global market portfolio. The FTSE All-World Index Series provides solid coverage of the global market as measured by market capitalization.

YOUR ALLOCATION TO GLOBAL ASSETS

There is a significant debate about how much you should allocate to international assets. The best answer is to base the allocation on your risk profile. For those investors who aspire for a higher return and are willing and able to assume a higher risk, they can allocate a substantial portion of their portfolio to international assets, perhaps as high as 50 percent. Conversely, for those investors who have lower risk profiles and lower return aspirations, they can allocate a much smaller portion, if any, of their portfolio to international assets—perhaps anywhere from 5 to 15 percent.

Given the risks of investing globally, adding international assets to an investment portfolio requires greater analysis and evaluation. Seeking professional advice on such matters is typically a good decision.

SELECT GLOBAL ETFs

Figures 11-4 to 11-17 provide some ETF options you may want to consider for your own portfolio. I strongly encourage you to evaluate the ETFs listed here and determine for yourself if these investment options make sense for your needs. Depending on your financial situation and goals, you may want to incorporate a number of these or simply use one or two to track the broad markets, such as the developing markets and the emerging markets. The international market is divided into 14 diverse segments, each offering different market exposure and therefore distinct risk and reward opportunities. Note that each segment in the figures is sorted by expense ratio.

FIGURE 11-4

List of Select Global ETFs: China

CHINA			
ETF	**Symbol**	**Expense Ratio**	**Inception Date**
iShares MSCI Hong Kong Index	EWH	0.53%	3/12/96
SPDR S&P China	GXC	0.61%	3/19/07
Global X China Industrials	CHII	0.65%	12/1/09
Global X China Financials	CHIX	0.65%	12/11/09
Global X China Materials	CHIM	0.65%	1/14/10
Global X China Technology	CHIB	0.65%	12/9/09
iShares MSCI China Small Cap Index	ECNS	0.65%	9/28/10
Global X China Consumer	CHIQ	0.65%	12/1/09
Global X China Energy	CHIE	0.65%	12/16/09
Guggenheim China All-Cap	YAO	0.70%	10/19/09
Guggenheim China Technology	CQQQ	0.70%	12/8/09
Guggenheim China Real Estate	TAO	0.70%	12/18/07
PowerShares Golden Dragon Halter USX China	PGJ	0.70%	12/9/04
iShares FTSE China 25 Index Fund	FXI	0.72%	10/5/04
iShares FTSE China (HK Listed) Index	FCHI	0.72%	6/24/08
Market Vectors China	PEK	0.72%	10/13/10
Guggenheim China Small Cap	HAO	0.75%	1/30/08
EGShares China Infrastructure	CHXX	0.85%	2/17/10

FIGURE 11-5

List of Select Global ETFs: Diversified Emerging Markets

DIVERSIFIED EMERGING MARKETS			
ETF	**Symbol**	**Expense Ratio**	**Inception Date**
Vanguard MSCI Emerging Markets	VWO	0.22%	3/4/05
BLDRS Emerging Markets 50 ADR Index	ADRE	0.30%	11/13/02
Schwab Emerging Markets Equity	SCHE	0.30%	1/14/10
			continued

FIGURE 11-5

List of Select Global ETFs: Diversified Emerging Markets (Cont.)

DIVERSIFIED EMERGING MARKETS			
ETF	Symbol	Expense Ratio	Inception Date
SPDR S&P BRIC 40	BIK	0.52%	6/19/07
SPDR S&P Emerging Markets Dividend	EDIV	0.59%	2/23/11
Market Vectors Indonesia Index	IDX	0.60%	1/15/09
SPDR S&P Emerging Markets	GMM	0.60%	3/19/07
SPDR S&P Emerging Middle East & Africa	GAF	0.60%	3/19/07
iShares MSCI South Africa Index	EZA	0.61%	2/3/03
iShares MSCI Turkey Invest Market	TUR	0.61%	3/26/08
SPDR S&P Emerging Europe	GUR	0.61%	3/19/07
iShares MSCI Indonesia Invstble Market	EIDO	0.61%	5/5/10
iShares MSCI Israel Cap Invstble Market	EIS	0.61%	3/26/08
iShares MSCI Thailand Invstble Market	THD	0.62%	3/26/08
WisdomTree Emerging Markets SmallCap Diversified	DGS	0.63%	10/30/07
Guggenheim BRIC	EEB	0.63%	9/21/06
WisdomTree Emerging Markets Equity Inc	DEM	0.63%	7/13/07
First Trust BICK Index	BICK	0.64%	4/12/10
SPDR S&P Emerging Markets Small Cap	EWX	0.66%	5/12/08
iShares MSCI Emerging Markets Index	EEM	0.68%	4/7/03
iShares MSCI Emerging Markets Eastern Europe	ESR	0.69%	9/30/09
iShares MSCI BRIC Index	BKF	0.69%	11/12/07
PowerShares MENA Frontier Countries	PMNA	0.70%	7/9/08
Guggenheim Frontier Markets	FRN	0.70%	6/12/08
Rydex MSCI Emerging Markets Equity Weight	EWEM	0.70%	12/3/10
EGShares Emerging Markets Large Cap	EEG	0.75%	7/22/09
Market Vectors Africa Index	AFK	0.83%	7/10/08
Market Vectors Vietnam	VNM	0.84%	8/11/09
PowerShares FTSE RAFI Emerging Markets	PXH	0.85%	9/27/07
WisdomTree Middle East Dividend	GULF	0.88%	7/16/08
PowerShares DWA Emerging Markets Technical Leaders	PIE	0.90%	12/28/07
Market Vectors Egypt Index	EGPT	0.94%	2/16/10
Market Vectors Gulf States Index	MES	0.98%	7/22/08

FIGURE 11-6

List of Select Global ETFs: Diversified Pacific/Asia

DIVERSIFIED PACIFIC/ASIA			
ETF	Symbol	Expense Ratio	Inception Date
Vanguard MSCI Pacific	VPL	0.14%	3/4/05
BLDRS Asia 50 ADR Index	ADRA	0.30%	11/13/02
iShares S&P Asia 50 Index	AIA	0.52%	11/13/07

FIGURE 11-7

List of Select Global ETFs: Europe

EUROPE			
ETF	Symbol	Expense Ratio	Inception Date
Vanguard MSCI European	VGK	0.14%	3/4/05
BLDRS Europe 100 ADR Index	ADRU	0.30%	11/13/02
SPDR STOXX Europe 50	FEU	0.31%	10/15/02
SPDR EURO STOXX 50	FEZ	0.31%	10/15/02
Global X FTSE Norway 30	NORW	0.50%	11/9/10
Global X FTSE Nordic Region	GXF	0.50%	8/17/09
iShares MSCI Ireland Capped Investable Market	EIRL	0.53%	5/5/10
iShares MSCI Germany Index	EWG	0.53%	3/12/96
iShares MSCI Sweden Index	EWD	0.53%	3/12/96
iShares MSCI Switzerland Index	EWL	0.53%	3/12/96
iShares MSCI Netherlands Investable Market	EWN	0.53%	3/12/96
iShares MSCI United Kingdom Index	EWU	0.53%	3/12/96
iShares MSCI EMU Index	EZU	0.54%	7/25/00
iShares MSCI Belgium Investable Market	EWK	0.54%	3/12/96
iShares MSCI France Index	EWQ	0.54%	3/12/96
iShares MSCI Spain Index	EWP	0.54%	3/12/96
			continued

FIGURE 11-7

List of Select Global ETFs: Europe (Cont.)

EUROPE			
ETF	Symbol	Expense Ratio	Inception Date
iShares MSCI Austria Investable Market	EWO	0.54%	3/12/96
iShares MSCI Italy Index	EWI	0.54%	3/12/96
WisdomTree Europe Small Cap Dividend	DFE	0.58%	6/16/06
SPDR S&P Russia	RBL	0.59%	3/10/10
First Trust STOXX Euro Select Dividend	FDD	0.60%	8/27/07
iShares S&P Europe 350 Index	IEV	0.60%	7/25/00
iShares MSCI Poland Investable Market	EPOL	0.61%	5/25/10
Market Vectors Russia	RSX	0.65%	4/24/07
iShares MSCI Russia Capped Index	ERUS	0.65%	11/9/10
Market Vectors Poland	PLND	0.67%	11/24/09

FIGURE 11-8

List of Select Global ETFs: Foreign Large Blend

FOREIGN LARGE BLEND			
ETF	Symbol	Expense Ratio	Inception Date
Vanguard MSCI EAFE	VEA	0.12%	7/20/07
Schwab International Equity	SCHF	0.14%	11/3/09
Vanguard Total International Stock	VXUS	0.20%	1/26/11
Vanguard FTSE All-World EX-US	VEU	0.22%	3/2/07
BLDRS Developed Markets 100 ADR Index	ADRD	0.30%	11/13/02
Guggenheim EW Euro-Pacific LDRs	EEN	0.35%	3/1/07
iShares MSCI ACWI EX US Index	ACWX	0.35%	3/26/08
SPDR MSCI ACWI (EX-US)	CWI	0.35%	1/10/07
iShares MSCI EAFE Index	EFA	0.35%	8/14/01
SPDR S&P World EX-US	GWL	0.35%	4/20/07
Pax MSCI EAFE ESG Index	EAPS	0.55%	1/28/11
Rydex MSCI EAFE Equal Weight	EWEF	0.55%	12/3/10

ETF	Symbol	Expense Ratio	Inception Date
WisdomTree World EX-US Growth	DNL	0.58%	6/16/06
Guggenheim International Multi-Asset Inc	HGI	0.70%	7/11/07
PowerShares Dynamic Developed International Opportunities	PFA	0.75%	6/13/07
PowerShares DWA Developed Markets Technical Leaders	PIZ	0.80%	12/28/07
JETS DJ Islamic Market International Index	JVS	0.92%	7/1/09

FIGURE 11-9

List of Select Global ETFs: Foreign Large Growth

FOREIGN LARGE GROWTH			
ETF	Symbol	Expense Ratio	Inception Date
iShares MSCI EAFE Growth Index	EFG	0.40%	8/1/05
WCM/BNY Mellon Focused Growth ADR	AADR	1.27%	7/20/10

FIGURE 11-10

List of Select Global ETFs: Foreign Large Value

FOREIGN LARGE VALUE			
ETF	Symbol	Expense Ratio	Inception Date
WisdomTree DEFA	DWM	0.19%	6/16/06
iShares MSCI EAFE Value Index	EFV	0.40%	8/1/05
SPDR S&P Intl Dividend	DWX	0.46%	2/12/08
WisdomTree Intl Hedged Equity	HEDJ	0.47%	12/31/09
WisdomTree Intl Large Cap Dividend	DOL	0.48%	6/16/06
RevenueShares ADR	RTR	0.49%	11/20/08
iShares Dow Jones Intl Select Dividend	IDV	0.50%	6/11/07
iShares MSCI Canada Index	EWC	0.53%	3/12/96
PowerShares Intl Dividend Achievers	PID	0.57%	9/15/05
WisdomTree Intl Dividend EX-Financials	DOO	0.58%	6/16/06
WisdomTree DEFA Equity Income	DTH	0.58%	6/16/06
PowerShares FTSE RAFI Dev Mkts EX-US	PXF	0.75%	6/25/07

FIGURE 11-11

List of Select Global ETFs: Foreign Small/Mid Growth

FOREIGN SMALL/MID GROWTH			
ETF	Symbol	Expense Ratio	Inception Date
Vanguard FTSE All-World EX-US Small Cap	VSS	0.33%	4/2/09
Schwab International Small-Cap Equity	SCHC	0.35%	1/14/10
Guggenheim International Small Cap LDRs	XGC	0.45%	4/2/07
iShares FTSE Developed Small Cap EX-North America	IFSM	0.50%	11/12/07
SPDR S&P International Small Cap	GWX	0.60%	4/20/07
IQ Canada Small Cap	CNDA	0.71%	3/23/10
Global X S&P/TSX Venture 30 Canada	TSXV	0.75%	3/16/11

FIGURE 11-12

List of Select Global ETFs: Foreign Small/Mid Value

FOREIGN SMALL/MID VALUE			
ETF	Symbol	Expense Ratio	Inception Date
iShares MSCI EAFE Small Cap Index	SCZ	0.40%	12/10/07
SPDR S&P International Mid Cap	MDD	0.46%	5/7/08
WisdomTree International SmallCap Dividend	DLS	0.58%	6/16/06
WisdomTree International MidCap Dividend	DIM	0.58%	6/16/06
PowerShares FTSE RAFI Developed Markets EX-US S/M	PDN	0.75%	9/27/07

FIGURE 11-13

List of Select Global ETFs: Japan

JAPAN			
ETF	**Symbol**	**Expense Ratio**	**Inception Date**
WisdomTree Japan Hedged Equity	DXJ	0.48%	6/16/06
iShares S&P/TOPIX 150 Index	ITF	0.50%	10/23/01
SPDR Russell/Nomura PRIME Japan	JPP	0.51%	11/9/06
iShares MSCI Japan Small Cap Index	SCJ	0.53%	12/20/07
iShares MSCI Japan Index	EWJ	0.54%	3/12/96
SPDR Russell/Nomura Small Cap Japan	JSC	0.56%	11/9/06
WisdomTree Japan SmallCap Dividend	DFJ	0.58%	6/16/06

FIGURE 11-14

List of Select Global ETFs: Latin America

LATIN AMERICA			
ETF	**Symbol**	**Expense Ratio**	**Inception Date**
iShares S&P Latin America 40 Index	ILF	0.50%	10/25/01
iShares MSCI All Peru Capped Index	EPU	0.51%	6/19/09
iShares MSCI Mexico Investable Market	EWW	0.53%	3/12/96
iShares MSCI Chile Investable Market	ECH	0.61%	11/12/07
SPDR S&P Emerging Latin America	GML	0.61%	3/19/07
iShares MSCI Brazil Index	EWZ	0.61%	7/10/00
Market Vectors Latin America Small-Cap Index	LATM	0.63%	4/6/10
Market Vectors Brazil Small-Cap	BRF	0.64%	5/12/09
iShares MSCI Brazil Small Cap Index	EWZS	0.65%	9/28/10
Global X Brazil Mid Cap	BRAZ	0.69%	6/22/10
Global X FTSE Argentina 20	ARGT	0.75%	3/3/11
Global X Brazil Financials	BRAF	0.77%	7/29/10
Global X Brazil Consumer	BRAQ	0.77%	7/8/10
EGShares Brazil Infrastructure	BRXX	0.85%	2/24/10
Global X FTSE Colombia 20	GXG	0.86%	2/5/09

FIGURE 11-15

List of Select Global ETFs: Pacific/Asia, Excluding Japan

PACIFIC/ASIA, EX. JAPAN			
ETF	**Symbol**	**Expense Ratio**	**Inception Date**
WisdomTree Pacific EX-Japan Total Div	DND	0.48%	6/16/06
iShares MSCI Pacific EX-Japan	EPP	0.50%	10/25/01
iShares MSCI Australia Index	EWA	0.53%	3/12/96
iShares MSCI Singapore Index	EWS	0.53%	3/12/96
iShares MSCI Malaysia Index	EWM	0.53%	3/12/96
iShares MSCI New Zealand Investable Market	ENZL	0.55%	9/1/10
WisdomTree Pacific EX-Japan Equity Inc	DNH	0.58%	6/16/06
SPDR S&P Emerging Asia Pacific	GMF	0.60%	3/19/07
First Trust ISE Chindia	FNI	0.60%	5/8/07
iShares MSCI South Korea Index	EWY	0.61%	5/9/00
Global X FTSE ASEAN 40	ASEA	0.65%	2/17/11
iShares MSCI Philippines Investable Market	EPHE	0.65%	9/28/10
iShares MSCI All Country Asia EX-Japan	AAXJ	0.68%	8/13/08
IQ Australia Small Cap	KROO	0.71%	3/23/10
PowerShares India	PIN	0.78%	3/5/08
IQ South Korea Small Cap	SKOR	0.79%	4/14/10
PowerShares FTSE RAFI Asia Pacific EX-Japan	PAF	0.80%	6/25/07
EGShares India Infrastructure	INXX	0.85%	8/11/10
Market Vectors India Small-Cap	SCIF	0.85%	8/24/10
EGShares India Small Cap	SCIN	0.85%	7/7/10
WisdomTree India Earnings	EPI	0.88%	2/22/08
iPath MSCI India Index ETN	INP	0.89%	12/19/06
iShares S&P India Nifty 50 Index	INDY	0.89%	11/18/09

FIGURE 11-16

List of Select Global ETFs: World Allocation

WORLD ALLOCATION			
ETF	Symbol	Expense Ratio	Inception Date
iShares S&P Growth Allocation	AOR	0.11%	11/4/08
PowerShares Ibbotson Alternative Completion	PTO	0.25%	5/20/08
PowerShares RiverFront Tactical Growth & Income	PCA	0.25%	5/20/08
One Fund	ONEF	0.53%	5/11/10
Cambria Global Tactical	GTAA	1.32%	10/25/10
Dent Tactical	DENT	1.50%	9/15/09

FIGURE 11-17

List of Select Global ETFs: World

WORLD			
ETF	Symbol	Expense Ratio	Inception Date
iShares MSCI Kokusai Index	TOK	0.25%	12/10/07
Vanguard Total World Stock Index	VT	0.25%	6/24/08
WisdomTree Global Equity Income	DEW	0.26%	6/16/06
iShares MSCI ACWI Index	ACWI	0.35%	3/26/08
iShares S&P Global 100 Index	IOO	0.40%	12/5/00
SPDR DJ Global Titans	DGT	0.50%	9/25/00
Market Vectors Rare Earth/Str Metals	REMX	0.57%	10/27/10
First Trust DJ Global Select Dividend	FGD	0.60%	11/21/07
Guggenheim S&P Global Dividend Opps	LVL	0.65%	6/25/07
Market Vectors Gaming	BJK	0.65%	1/22/08
Guggenheim Solar	TAN	0.66%	4/15/08
Guggenheim S&P Global Water Index	CGW	0.70%	5/14/07
Guggenheim Timber	CUT	0.70%	11/9/07
PowerShares Global Progressive Transport	PTRP	0.75%	9/18/08

## CHAPTER 12

Real Asset ETFs: The REIT Moves With Commodities and Currencies

Real assets, or what are sometimes referred to as alternative investments or hard assets, provide additional ways for you to maximize your portfolio's risk-adjusted return. This asset class goes beyond traditional equities and fixed-income investments that many investors overlook. Your investing does not need to be limited to just traditional stocks and bonds. This asset class has been gaining in popularity over the recent few years primarily because exchange-traded funds (ETFs) have made real asset investing quicker and easier. More and more investors have been allocating a portion of their portfolios to real assets, namely, real estate and especially commodities, given their unique benefits.

In contrast to the other primary asset classes, real assets are more dissimilar in their inherent characteristics than they are similar. Furthermore, real assets are tangible, unlike the intangible assets in the other primary asset classes. Real assets typically do well in times of high inflation, often capturing more investment inflows during periods of overall market weakness.

One of the primary reasons underlying the purchase of real assets is to protect your purchasing power—thus a hedge against inflation. Another strong reason investors should consider real assets is because they tend to have very low, and sometimes negative, correlations with equities and bonds. It is for these reasons that including real assets in your portfolio has the potential to enhance returns and reduce investment risk over time.

Although there are clear benefits to investing in real assets, there are also a number of drawbacks and challenges to overcome. By far, the most significant is higher total cost. Real asset ETFs typically have higher than normal expenses, such as trading commissions, bid-ask spreads, management fees, and asset-specific expenses (e.g., contango with commodity futures). As a result, you need to fully investigate the potential benefits and evaluate them against the potential costs. It is possible to run into situations where the total cost outweighs the potential benefits.

MARKETPLACE FRAMEWORK

The primary categories encompassed in this asset class include real estate, commodities, private equity, foreign currencies, and collectibles such as artwork, rare stamps, classic cars, vintage wines, and military antiques and collectibles. From a practicality standpoint, we will only focus on the primary categories. Although hedge fund investments themselves do not constitute a true asset class, a brief discussion is provided since they do offer noncorrelated benefits similar to the benefits of real assets.

Common Real Asset and Related Types

- Real estate
- Commodities
- Private equity
- Foreign currencies
- Collectibles
- Hedge funds

FACTORS INFLUENCING RETURNS

Several factors influence the total returns of real assets. By far, the largest factor is simple macro supply and demand. Supply is dictated by pure availability of a certain asset, while demand is driven by perceived value. For this reason, many of the real asset classes are valued according to subjective value unique to individual investors. Collectibles are a prime example of this. One investor may place a significant value on a collectible asset, while another investor may not. A list of the primary factors influencing returns for real assets includes the following. Note that one factor may influence returns for one asset, but not necessarily for another.

- Supply and production obstacles
- Demand and quantity demanded
- Rate of inflation or deflation
- Regulatory oversight
- Geopolitical issues

- Currency exchange rates
- Transaction costs
- Management fees and expenses
- Shipping and holding costs
- Generic inflow and outflow of capital

DIFFERENT TYPES OF REAL ASSETS

Given the vast dissimilarities among the various assets that are categorized as real assets, a breakout of each primary asset is necessary. Each asset does not have the same return potential or level of risk. Furthermore, the drawbacks and costs of investing in each are also very different. These are important characteristics to keep in mind when evaluating each investment potential.

Real Estate

Real estate is land, including the air above and the ground below, the permanent buildings or structures attached, and all the natural resources contained within the domain. Real estate is enticing, as it offers low correlations to both equities and fixed income. A properly allocated portfolio should include real estate investments in addition to stocks, bonds, and other investments. This combination of assets has proved to be one of the most effective ways of building a successful portfolio over time. These returns—together with low correlations—are sufficient evidence for building a multiasset-class portfolio that holds real estate.

Investors have two avenues for investing in real estate. First, an investor can buy real estate directly, using capital from his or her investment portfolio, or an investor can invest in real estate investment trusts (REITs). REITs are highly liquid, convenient, well diversified, and they offer an ideal way to gain immediate exposure to real estate opportunities. REITs are either privately held or traded on U.S. stock exchanges like common stocks and ETFs. Many REITs hold office buildings, apartments, shopping malls, business centers, industrial buildings, and hotels. The total holdings in REITs still only account for less than 2 percent of the total stock market capitalization.

Directly investing in real estate offers you total control over your investment. Decisions on what leasing terms to use, how much to charge for leases and rents, what discretionary expenses to incur, and when and how to liquidate are squarely at your discretion. However, directly owning real estate is not for everyone. It requires a significant time commitment and unique market knowledge, for starters.

For the vast majority of investors, passively investing in real estate is the preferred and best option—enter REITs. The popularity of REITs has exploded over the last couple of decades due to tax law changes enacted in the early 1990s. According to NAREIT (National Association of Real Estate Investment Trusts), assets in REITs rose from $7.7 billion in 1985 to over $375 billion only 25 years later in 2010 (see Figure 12-1). At the same time, the number of REITs increased from 82 to 153. Furthermore, the total value of all REITs accounts for less than 10 percent of the total investable U.S. real estate.

Under U.S. tax provisions, REITs must distribute at least 90 percent of their earnings to shareholders in the form of dividends or else be subject to corporate taxes on the REIT level. It is for this reason that REITs typically pay strong dividends, a benefit that drives their demand with investors. The market price of REITs typically rises with increases in the inflation rate since REIT income is principally derived from leases and rents, which are indexed to the inflation rate. In addition, rising inflation can cause stock prices to fall; thus the simple flow of funds out of stocks and into REITs may push up market prices even more.

From a performance standpoint, there have been periods where REITs have outperformed stocks and periods where stocks

FIGURE 12-1

Snapshot of the REIT Industry

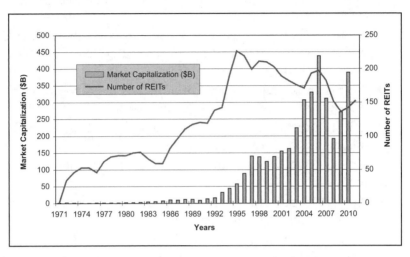

Source: National Association of Real Estate Investment Trusts

have outperformed REITs. Since the tax law changes affecting REITs in the early 1990s, the correlation between stocks and REITs has declined in contrast to historical correlations. Today, the correlation between the two is about 0.4 with a short-term ceiling of 0.5—this equates to risk and return-enhancement potential. Several low-cost REIT ETFs are available for your choosing. A list of available ETFs is provided in Figures 12-5 to 12-10. I highly suggest you consider one of them for your real estate exposure.

Qualifications, Advantages, and Disadvantages
REITs must satisfy the following requirements in order to qualify for the advantage of being a pass-through entity for U.S. corporate income tax purposes:

- A REIT must be structured as a corporation, trust, or association. Otherwise it will be taxable as a domestic corporation.
- A REIT cannot be a financial institution or an insurance company.

- REITs must be jointly owned by 100 persons or more.
- They must be managed by a board of directors or trustees.
- They must have transferable shares or transferable certificates of interest.
- No more than 50 percent of the shares can be held by five or fewer individuals during the last half of each taxable year (5/50 rule).
- A REIT must have 95 percent of its income derived from dividends, interest, and property income.
- A REIT must distribute at least 90 percent of its taxable income in the form of dividends.
- At least 75 percent of total investment assets must be in real estate.
- At least 75 percent of a REIT's gross income must be derived from rents or mortgage interest.
- No more than 20 percent of a REIT's assets may consist of stocks in taxable REIT subsidiaries.

The advantages and disadvantages of REITs are summarized in the lists below:

Positives of REITs

- Low correlations to other asset classes
- High current income potential
- Solid price appreciation potential

Negatives of REITs

- Higher transaction costs
- Greater market inefficiencies
- Liquidity concerns

Commodities

Commodities are the raw materials, hard assets, and tangible products that underscore our civilization in nearly every way possible. Commodities are the building blocks for virtually everything we eat, everything we use for energy, everything we use in construction, and many of the things we use on a daily basis. Commodities are what gave civilization life from the very beginning with the cultivation of wheat and barley. Moreover, commodities were instrumental in the development of civilization, and we recognize this importance by naming these early periods for them—copper age, bronze age, and steel age.

As a general rule, all commodities are defined by three characteristics—the first being standardization. This means that you can take one unit of a particular commodity and replace it with another unit of the same commodity without issue. Thus, commodities are said to be interchangeable. The second characteristic is tradability, which refers to two distinct features: (1) the existence of a robust marketplace consisting of many buyers and sellers and (2) the unique futures market, a trading structure not found in traditional investments. The final characteristic is deliverability, which refers to the actual physical exchange of the commodity from the seller to the buyer.

The commodity class called financials is the only exception to the rules that commodities must be raw materials and must provide deliverability. For the most part, financials are considered commodities and include indexes, rates, and emissions allowance credits.

Commodity Classes

The global marketplace is vast, with many different commodities. Commodities are classified in one of six major sectors—metals, energy fuels, livestock, agricultural, exotics, and (as noted earlier) financials. Within certain sectors, commodities are further divided into classes such as precious metals and industrial metals (see Figure 12-2).

Characteristics, Advantages, and Disadvantages

Commodities are characterized in the following ways:

- Commodities are *standardized* by commodity class.
- Commodities are recognized for their unique *tradability.*
- Commodities offer *deliverability* as a settlement option.

- Commodities exhibit a high level of *inelastic demand.*
- Commodities are *finite and limited.*
- Commodities encompass a highly *global marketplace.*
- Commodities require *long production lead times.*
- Commodities offer investors an *investing safe haven* during uncertain times.
- Commodities provide a *hedge against inflation.*
- Commodities exhibit *favorable correlations* to other asset classes.

The advantages and disadvantages of commodities are summarized in the two lists that follow:

Positives of Commodities

- Enhanced portfolio optimization
- Inflation protection
- Potential for aggressive returns
- Zero risk of product obsolescence
- Minimal company management issues

FIGURE 12-2

List of Individual Commodities by Class

Commodity Class	Individual Commodity
Precious Metals	Gold, silver, platinum
Industrial (or Base) Metals	Aluminum, copper, lead, nickel, palladium, tin, zinc
Energies (or Energy Fuels)	Coal, crude oil, electric power, heating oil, natural gas, unleaded gasoline, uranium ore
Agriculture: Grains and Oil Seeds	Corn, soybeans, soybean oil, soybean meal, wheat
Agriculture: Softs	Cocoa, coffee, cotton, orange juice, sugar
Livestock	Feeder cattle, lean hogs, live cattle, pork bellies
Exotics	Ethanol, lumber, rubber, wool
Financials	Emissions allowance credits, indexes, rates

Negatives of Commodities

- Market risk
- Volatility risk
- Geopolitical risk
- Environmental risk
- Regulatory risk
- Weather and force majeure risk
- Terrorism risk
- Liquidity risk
- Overexposure risk
- Knowledge and expertise risk

Figure 12-3 outlines basic supply and demand fundamentals for commodities.

FIGURE   1 2 - 3

Commodity Supply-and-Demand Fundamentals

Bullish Demand Fundamentals	Bullish Supply Fundamentals
► Increasing Global Population	► Limited Quantity of Raw Materials
► Development of Global Economies	► Finite Amount of Agricultural Acreage
► Standard of Living Advances	► Increasing Production Difficulties

Source: Frush Financial Group

Currencies

The foreign exchange market, or forex for short, is a global, worldwide, decentralized, over-the-counter market to facilitate the trading of currencies. Crisscrossing the globe, financial centers serve as anchors of trading among a wide range of different types of buyers and sellers. Transactions are executed around the clock, with the exception of the weekends.

The first currency ETF—introduced in the United States as a grantor trust based on euro deposits—was launched in late 2005 and instantly gave casual investors a quick and easy way to speculate in the currency market. Currency ETFs have gained in popularity for many reasons, most notably to gain or hedge against the fall of the U.S. dollar relative to foreign currencies. Currency ETFs also provide attractive dividends since the ETF provider takes the assets invested in an ETF and deposits the money denominated in foreign currency with banks to gain interest. Investing in currencies can be a hedge against rising inflation and the subsequent devaluation of the U.S. dollar (or other home country currency for that matter) against countries with lower rates of inflation. However, currencies can also be used as speculative bets, given fast-moving international turmoil. The U.S. dollar is by far the most actively traded global currency, followed by the euro and then the Japanese yen (see Figure 12-4).

Private Equity

Sometimes referred to as private investments, private equity is a very broad term that actually describes any form of equity investment in companies that are not freely traded, nor listed on stock exchanges. Some of the primary types of private equity include venture capital (VC), mezzanine capital, leveraged buyouts (LBOs), managed buyouts (MBOs), fund of funds, growth capital, and angel investing. These types of private equity are generally illiquid and therefore considered long-term investments. Many private equity funds seek investments in startup companies that offer high return (and high risk) potential. Taking these companies public through an initial public offering is the overall goal. At the same time, some private equity funds hunt for distressed publicly traded companies, with the aim of taking them private and sometime thereafter returning them to publicly traded status and making a hefty profit in the process.

FIGURE 12-4

Most-Traded Currencies

Rank	Currency	%
1	United States Dollar	84.9%
2	Euro	39.1%
3	Japanese Yen	19.0%
4	British Pound Sterling	12.9%
5	Australian Dollar	7.6%
6	Swiss Franc	6.4%
7	Canadian Dollar	5.3%
8	Hong Kong Dollar	2.4%
9	Swedish Krona	2.2%
10	New Zealand Dollar	1.6%
	Other Currencies	*18.6%*

The total sum is 200% due to trading currency pairs.

Source: 2010 Triennial Central Bank Survey

There are typically a number of restrictions on the transfer of ownership, but private equity investments are not subject to the same high-level government scrutiny that publicly traded companies are accustomed to.

Private equities are generally organized as partnerships where there are one or more general partners and numerous limited partners. Once a particular partnership has reached its target size, the partnership is closed to new investors, including new capital from existing investors. Since the early 1990s, private equities have experienced strong growth, with solid year-over-year rising capital growth rates. Although the allure of private equities is high, keep in mind the high risk and the high investment hurdles and barriers to liquidation. This alternative asset is not for everyone, but some investors may find it quite lucrative.

Hedge Funds

As mentioned previously, a hedge fund is not a true asset class. Rather, it's a shell account much like a mutual fund or ETF. However, since hedge funds are an alternative investment to equities and fixed income, a quick discussion is appropriate. Hedge funds are pooled investment vehicles that are managed by professional money managers. Thus, the concept of hedge funds is quite similar to that of mutual funds. The difference for practical investment purposes is how they invest and what they invest in.

Hedge funds are private funds in which investments are made typically using aggressive or nontraditional strategies. Such strategies include selling short, using significant leverage, employing computer program trading, and incorporating derivatives such as options, swaps, and futures. Other differences include management disclosures, fees, and government restrictions on the number of investment participants. By law, hedge funds are restricted to a limited number of investors, and as a result, the vast majority of hedge funds target institutions and wealthy individuals to fill the open slots.

The lack of regulatory oversight provides hedge fund managers with significant flexibility with investment holdings and investment strategies. Although debated, the number of hedge funds in existence today is around 7,000, with over $2 trillion of assets under management.

Many styles of hedge funds have low correlations to both equities and fixed income, thus making them attractive options for enhancing portfolios. Unfortunately, many hedge funds have excessive annual management fees (comparable to an expense ratio) from 1 to 2 percent and a 20 percent take of any gains they generate for their investors above certain hurdles. Performance incentive fees are both good and bad. Good because they give hedge fund managers an extra incentive to deliver strong performance, but bad since not only can the fees be a significant cost to investors, but also because the fees financially motivate hedge fund managers to take higher risk than perhaps they would under normal situations in the hope of capturing higher returns.

Advantages and Disadvantages of Hedge Funds
The positives and negatives of hedge funds are outlined here:

Positives of Hedge Funds

- Strong return potential
- Low correlations to other asset classes
- Multiple styles and strategies for different investors

Negatives of Hedge Funds

- High management and incentive fees
- Significant financial qualification requirements
- High risk compared with that of other investments

PORTFOLIO ALLOCATION CONSIDERATIONS

Given the different opportunities with real assets, investors can customize their portfolios in a way most suitable for achieving their objectives. Utilizing multiple asset classes is central to enhancing portfolio returns while reducing portfolio risk. Some real assets offer excellent ways to amplify a portfolio, such as real estate, while others only offer limited returns with disproportionately higher risk. Some real assets are altogether not needed, as their costs are simply too high to justify. Excessive costs have the potential of outweighing the benefits you can earn. Care, skill, and patience are thus needed to evaluate each asset class and determine how it will enhance your overall portfolio.

SELECT REAL ASSET ETFs

Figures 12-5 to 12-10 provide some investment options you may want to consider for your own portfolio. I strongly encourage you to evaluate the following ETFs and depending on your financial situation and goals, you may want to incorporate a number of these or simply use one or two. Each of the following segments offers different market exposure and therefore distinct risk and reward opportunities. Note that each segment in the figures is sorted by expense ratio.

FIGURE 12-5

List of Select Real Asset ETFs: Broad-Basket Commodities

BROAD-BASKET COMMODITIES

ETF	Symbol	Expense Ratio	Inception Date
UBS E-TRACS DJ-UBS Commodity ETN	DJCI	0.50%	10/29/09
UBS E-TRACS CMCI TR ETN	UCI	0.65%	4/1/08
Jefferies TR/J CRB Global Commodity	CRBQ	0.65%	9/21/09
iPath DJ-UBS Commodity Index TR ETN	DJP	0.75%	6/6/06
iShares S&P GSCI Commodity-Indexed Trust	GSG	0.75%	7/10/06
ELEMENTS Rogers Intl Commodity ETN	RJI	0.75%	10/17/07
PowerShares DB Commodity Long ETN	DPU	0.75%	4/28/08
iPath S&P GSCI Total Return Index ETN	GSP	0.75%	6/6/06
PowerShares DB Commodity Index Tracking	DBC	0.81%	2/3/06
United States Commodity Index	USCI	0.95%	8/10/10
GreenHaven Continuous Commodity Index	GCC	1.08%	1/24/08
GS Connect S&P GSCI Commodity ETN	GSC	1.25%	7/31/07

FIGURE 12-6

List of Select Real Asset ETFs: Agriculture and Livestock

AGRICULTURE AND LIVESTOCK

ETF	Symbol	Expense Ratio	Inception Date
Market Vectors Agribusiness ETF	MOO	0.55%	8/31/07
UBS E-TRACS CMCI Livestock TR ETN	UBC	0.65%	4/1/08
UBS E-TRACS CMCI Food TR ETN	FUD	0.65%	4/1/08
Jefferies TR/J CRB Global Agriculture	CRBA	0.65%	10/27/09
UBS E-TRACS CMCI Agriculture TR ETN	UAG	0.65%	4/1/08
PowerShares Global Agriculture	PAGG	0.75%	9/18/08
iPath DJ-UBS Sugar TR Sub-Idx ETN	SGG	0.75%	6/24/08

ETF	Symbol	Expense Ratio	Inception Date
ELEMENTS Rogers International Commodity Agriculture ETN	RJA	0.75%	10/17/07
iPath DJ-UBS Coffee TR Sub-Idx ETN	JO	0.75%	6/24/08
PowerShares DB Agriculture Long ETN	AGF	0.75%	4/14/08
iPath DJ-UBS Grains TR Sub-Idx ETN	JJG	0.75%	10/23/07
iPath DJ-UBS Agriculture TR Sub-Idx ETN	JJA	0.75%	10/23/07
iPath DJ-UBS Cocoa TR Sub-Idx ETN	NIB	0.75%	6/24/08
ELEMENTS MLCX Grains Idx TR ETN	GRU	0.75%	2/5/08
ELEMENTS MLCX Biofuels Idx TR ETN	FUE	0.75%	2/5/08
iPath DJ-UBS Livestock TR Sub-Idx ETN	COW	0.75%	10/23/07
iPath DJ-UBS Cotton TR Sub-Idx ETN	BAL	0.75%	6/24/08
iPath DJ-UBS Softs TR Sub-Idx ETN	JJS	0.75%	6/24/08
PowerShares DB Agriculture	DBA	0.85%	1/5/07
Teucrium Corn	CORN	1.00%	6/9/10

FIGURE 12-7

List of Select Real Asset ETFs: Energy

ENERGY			
ETF	Symbol	Expense Ratio	Inception Date
PowerShares DB Oil	DBO	0.54%	1/5/07
Market Vectors Global Alternatve Energy ETF	GEX	0.60%	5/3/07
UBS E-TRACS CMCI Energy TR ETN	UBN	0.65%	4/1/08
Global X Uranium	URA	0.69%	11/4/10
iPath S&P GSCI Crude Oil TR Idx ETN	OIL	0.75%	8/15/06
ELEMENTS Rogers International Commodity Energy ETN	RJN	0.75%	10/17/07
United States Brent Oil	BNO	0.75%	6/2/10
iPath DJ-UBS Energy TR Sub-Idx ETN	JJE	0.75%	10/23/07
			continued

FIGURE 12-7

List of Select Real Asset ETFs: Energy (Cont.)

ENERGY			
ETF	**Symbol**	**Expense Ratio**	**Inception Date**
PowerShares DB Crude Oil Long ETN	OLO	0.75%	6/16/08
iPath DJ-UBS Natural Gas TR Sub-Idx ETN	GAZ	0.75%	10/23/07
United States Oil	USO	0.78%	4/10/06
PowerShares DB Energy	DBE	0.80%	1/5/07
EGShares Emerging Markets Energy	EEO	0.85%	5/21/09
United States Gasoline	UGA	0.90%	2/26/08
United States Heating Oil	UHN	0.90%	4/9/08
United States 12 Month Oil	USL	1.10%	12/6/07
United States 12 Month Natural Gas	UNL	1.12%	11/18/09
United States Natural Gas	UNG	1.18%	4/18/07

FIGURE 12-8

List of Select Real Asset ETFs: Metals

METALS			
ETF	**Symbol**	**Expense Ratio**	**Inception Date**
iShares Gold Trust	IAU	0.25%	1/21/05
ETFS Physical Silver Shares	SIVR	0.30%	7/24/09
UBS E-TRACS CMCI Gold TR ETN	UBG	0.30%	4/1/08
ETFS Physical Swiss Gold Shares	SGOL	0.39%	9/9/09
SPDR Gold Shares	GLD	0.40%	11/18/04
UBS E-TRACS CMCI Silver TR ETN	USV	0.40%	4/1/08
iShares Silver Trust	SLV	0.50%	4/21/06
PowerShares DB Gold	DGL	0.52%	1/5/07
Market Vectors Gold Miners	GDX	0.53%	5/16/06
PowerShares DB Silver	DBS	0.54%	1/5/07
Market Vectors Junior Gold Miners	GDXJ	0.54%	11/10/09

ETF	Symbol	Expense Ratio	Inception Date
Market Vectors Steel	SLX	0.55%	10/10/06
ETFS Physical Precious Metals Basket Shares	GLTR	0.60%	10/22/10
ETFS Physical Palladium Shares	PALL	0.60%	1/8/10
ETFS Physical Platinum Shares	PPLT	0.60%	1/8/10
ETFS Physical White Metals Basket Shares	WITE	0.60%	12/1/10
Jefferies TR/J CRB Global Industrial Metals	CRBI	0.65%	10/27/09
Global X Copper Miners	COPX	0.65%	4/20/10
Global X Gold Explorers	GLDX	0.65%	11/3/10
UBS E-TRACS Long Platinum TR ETN	PTM	0.65%	5/8/08
UBS E-TRACS CMCI Industrial Metals ETN	UBM	0.65%	4/1/08
Global X Aluminum	ALUM	0.69%	1/4/11
First Trust ISE Global Copper Index	CU	0.70%	3/11/10
First Trust ISE Global Platinum Index	PLTM	0.70%	3/11/10
PowerShares Global Steel	PSTL	0.75%	9/18/08
Global X Lithium	LIT	0.75%	7/23/10
PowerShares DB Base Metals Long ETN	BDG	0.75%	6/16/08
iPath Global Carbon ETN	GRN	0.75%	6/24/08
iPath DJ-UBS Copper TR Sub-Idx ETN	JJC	0.75%	10/23/07
iPath DJ-UBS Industrial Metals TR Sub-Idx ETN	JJM	0.75%	10/23/07
iPath DJ-UBS Nickel TR Sub-Idx ETN	JJN	0.75%	10/23/07
iPath DJ-UBS Precious Metals TR Sub-Idx ETN	JJP	0.75%	6/24/08
iPath DJ-UBS Tin TR Sub-Idx ETN	JJT	0.75%	6/24/08
iPath DJ-UBS Aluminum TR Sub-Idx ETN	JJU	0.75%	6/24/08
iPath DJ-UBS Lead TR Sub-Idx ETN	LD	0.75%	6/24/08
iPath DJ-UBS Platinum TR Sub-Idx ETN	PGM	0.75%	6/24/08
PowerShares Global Gold & Precious Metals	PSAU	0.75%	9/18/08
ELEMENTS Rogers International Commodity Metal ETN	RJZ	0.75%	10/17/07
PowerShares DB Base Metals	DBB	0.76%	1/5/07
PowerShares DB Precious Metals	DBP	0.77%	1/5/07
RBS Gold Trendpilot ETN	TBAR	1.00%	2/17/11

FIGURE 12-9

List of Select Real Asset ETFs: Currencies

CURRENCIES			
ETF	**Symbol**	**Expense Ratio**	**Inception Date**
WisdomTree Dreyfus Euro	EU	0.35%	5/14/08
WisdomTree Dreyfus Japanese Yen	JYF	0.35%	5/21/08
iPath EUR/USD Exchange Rate ETN	ERO	0.40%	5/8/07
iPath GBP/USD Exchange Rate ETN	GBB	0.40%	5/8/07
CurrencyShares Australian Dollar Trust	FXA	0.40%	6/21/06
CurrencyShares Canadian Dollar Trust	FXC	0.40%	6/21/06
CurrencyShares Russian Ruble Trust	XRU	0.40%	11/10/08
CurrencyShares Swedish Krona Trust	FXS	0.40%	6/21/06
CurrencyShares Swiss Franc Trust	FXF	0.40%	6/21/06
CurrencyShares Euro Trust	FXE	0.40%	12/9/05
CurrencyShares Mexican Peso Trust	FXM	0.40%	6/21/06
CurrencyShares Japanese Yen Trust	FXY	0.40%	2/12/07
iPath JPY/USD Exchange Rate ETN	JYN	0.40%	5/8/07
CurrencyShares British Pound Sterling Trust	FXB	0.40%	6/21/06
WisdomTree Dreyfus Chinese Yuan	CYB	0.45%	5/14/08
WisdomTree Dreyfus New Zealand Dollar	BNZ	0.45%	6/25/08
WisdomTree Dreyfus Indian Rupee	ICN	0.45%	5/14/08
WisdomTree Dreyfus Brazilian Real	BZF	0.45%	5/14/08
WisdomTree Dreyfus South African Rand	SZR	0.45%	6/25/08
Market Vectors Indian Rupee/USD ETN	INR	0.55%	3/14/08
WisdomTree Dreyfus Emerging Currency	CEW	0.55%	5/6/09
WisdomTree Dreyfus Commodity Currency	CCX	0.55%	9/24/10
Market Vectors Chinese Renminbi/ USD ETN	CNY	0.55%	3/14/08
iPath Optimized Currency Carry ETN	ICI	0.65%	1/31/08
PowerShares DB US Dollar Index Bullish	UUP	0.81%	2/20/07
PowerShares DB G10 Currency Harvest	DBV	0.81%	9/18/06
Barclays GEMS Asia-8 ETN	AYT	0.89%	4/2/08
Barclays GEMS Index ETN	JEM	0.89%	2/1/08
Barclays Asian & Gulf Currency Reval ETN	PGD	0.89%	2/5/08

FIGURE 12-10

List of Select Real Asset ETFs: Real Estate

REAL ESTATE			
ETF	Symbol	Expense Ratio	Inception Date
Vanguard REIT Index	VNQ	0.12%	9/23/04
SPDR DJ Wilshire REIT	RWR	0.25%	4/23/01
Wilshire US REIT	WREI	0.32%	3/9/10
iShares Cohen & Steers Realty Majors	ICF	0.35%	1/29/01
PowerShares KBW Premium Yield Equity REIT	KBWY	0.35%	12/1/10
Vanguard Global EX-US Real Estate	VNQI	0.35%	11/1/10
iShares Dow Jones US Real Estate	IYR	0.47%	6/12/00
iShares FTSE EPRA/NAREIT Dev Asia	IFAS	0.48%	11/12/07
iShares FTSE EPRA/NAREIT Dev EU	IFEU	0.48%	11/12/07
iShares FTSE EPRA/NAREIT Dev Real Estate EX-US	IFGL	0.48%	11/12/07
iShares FTSE EPRA/NAREIT North America	IFNA	0.48%	11/12/07
iShares FTSE NAREIT Industrial Office Capped	FNIO	0.48%	5/1/07
iShares FTSE NAREIT Mortgage Plus Capped Index	REM	0.48%	5/1/07
iShares FTSE NAREIT Real Estate 50	FTY	0.48%	5/1/07
iShares FTSE NAREIT Residential Plus Capped Index	REZ	0.48%	5/1/07
iShares FTSE NAREIT Retail Capped Index RTL	0.48%	5/1/07	
iShares S&P Developed EX-US Property Index	WPS	0.48%	7/30/07
First Trust S&P REIT Index	FRI	0.50%	5/8/07
SPDR Dow Jones Global Real Estate	RWO	0.51%	5/7/08
Cohen & Steers Global Realty Majors	GRI	0.55%	5/7/08
WisdomTree International Real Estate	DRW	0.58%	6/5/07
First Trust FTSE EN Developed Markets Real Estate	FFR	0.60%	8/27/07
SPDR Dow Jones International Real Estate	RWX	0.60%	12/15/06
PowerShares Active U.S. Real Estate	PSR	0.80%	11/20/08

CHAPTER 13

Specialty ETFs: Leveraged, Inverse, and Long-Short Funds

Some of the newest innovations sweeping the exchange-traded fund (ETF) marketplace are leveraged, inverse, and long-short ETFs. The explosion of these types of ETFs is comparable to how traditional ETFs themselves were launched and quickly began to dominate the general investing landscape. Unfortunately, there is much confusion and bad press over these types of ETFs.

Leveraged ETFs have much in common with traditional ETFs, but with one major difference—the underlying leverage an ETF provider uses to magnify the performance of the tracking index. Leveraged long, inverse, and long-short ETFs incorporate stocks and bonds just like traditional ETFs. Upward of 85 to 90 percent of their holdings are in stocks we are familiar with. The remaining assets are made up of either derivatives or stocks used as collateral for purposes of generating the desired leverage or inverse capabilities.

Leveraged inverse, fixed-income, and commodity funds are less representative of their tracking index, however. Furthermore, these specialty ETFs track everyday indexes that we all know and follow. Nonetheless, the mere presence of leverage and inverse capabilities makes these specialty ETFs higher risk and thus not suitable for many investors. So consider the full risk of these ETFs before adding them to your portfolio.

LEVERAGED AND INVERSE ETFs

Leveraged long and inverse ETFs are available on the most well-known market indexes, including the S&P 500, the Nasdaq-100, and the Dow Jones Industrial Average. Furthermore, nearly all the economic sectors, such as basic materials and financials, and broad-based style and size market indexes are also tracked by leveraged and inverse ETFs. Most of the current leveraged and inverse ETFs in the marketplace today only track market indexes—with little consideration given to proprietary custom indexes.

Leveraged long ETFs seek daily investment results, before fees and expenses, that correspond to 2× to 3× the daily performance of the underlying tracking index. The two most prominent ETF providers of leveraged and inverse funds are ProFunds (ProShares) and Direxion. By scanning the select specialty ETFs presented in Figures 13-1 to 13-3, you will quickly see how the two dominate this ETF category. Due to intense Security and Exchange Commission (SEC) scrutiny of leveraged and inverse ETFs, ProFunds and Direxion place a significant emphasis on reinforcing the "daily" performance claim. From time to time, a leveraged or inverse ETF will not properly track its underlying index. There can be significant deviations over the long term, but the returns from day to day are typically much more aligned with the underlying index.

The singular reason for purchasing a leveraged ETF is for the higher performance potential over the underlying tracking index. If an investor were to own a leveraged technology ETF and technology stocks were to rise by 1 percent, then the ETF should return 2 percent, given a 2× leverage. However, the leverage also works against the same investor if the market or, more specifically, technology stocks were to fall. A 5 percent decline over one month, for instance, would equate to a 10 percent decline for the leveraged long ETF. Investors need a tough stomach to take the high inherent volatility and therefore higher risk.

For investors that really want to dial up the level of risk, investing in a triple-leveraged ETF that tracks a traditionally volatile asset class (without leverage) can really churn your stomach. For example, small-cap stocks have historically been more volatile than the overall equity market, with a beta near 1.25. Tack on not double leverage, but triple leverage, to small caps, and you have a high-risk and high-reward potential ETF. This investment is obviously not for the majority of people—especially novice investors—but may be suitable in small amounts for an experienced investor with a high-risk profile.

While leveraged ETFs magnify the performance of the underlying tracking index—thus providing long equity exposure—inverse ETFs, for all practical purposes, sell short their underlying tracking index—thus providing short equity exposure. Moreover, inverse ETFs can aim for a 1-for-1 inverse price movement, or they can employ leverage like the long ETFs and produce 2-for-1 (2×) or 3-for-1 (3×) inverse price movement of the underlying index. For example, investors have the choice of investing in the ProShares Short S&P 500 (symbol SH), which aims to generate a 1-for-1 inverse return of the S&P 500, or the ProShares Ultra Short S&P 500 (symbol SDS), which aims to generate a 2-for-1, or 2×, inverse return of the S&P 500. In doing so, inverse ETFs take even leveraged ETFs to a higher level. Leveraged ETFs and, more important, inverse leveraged ETFs are highly volatile and thus are considered two of the most risky types of ETFs in the marketplace.

From two perspectives, inverse ETFs get a bad rap from some investors and the SEC. First, inverse ETFs do not have unlimited risk—in contrast to selling short. When you sell short, the stock you sold short can rise in value exponentially over time, generating incremental losses. However, the downside risk for an inverse ETF is limited to the invested capital. That's a material difference between the two bearish strategies.

Second, inverse ETFs afford investors—retail and institution alike—the opportunity to hedge their long portfolio holdings. Theoretically speaking, adding a short position—whether by using an inverse ETF or selling short a security—will proportionately decrease the volatility risk inherent in a portfolio. The greater the weighting given to the inverse ETF, the larger the reduction in total portfolio risk. Of course, this example is assuming a reasonable exposure to an inverse ETF and not more than 50 percent of the total portfolio assets. Even a small allocation to an inverse ETF can materially decrease volatility risk. You would be surprised at how blind the regulators seem to be to this benefit.

In addition to the aforementioned specific ETFs in the marketplace, other categories of leveraged and inverse ETFs include the following:

- Sizes (large, mid, small caps)
- Styles (growth, value, blend)
- Sectors and industries
- International markets
- Fixed-income segments
- Commodity classes
- Currencies
- Absolute return strategies
- Volatility measures

Leveraged and inverse ETFs track indexes from a number of index sponsors, including the following most frequently tracked:

- Barclays Capital
- Credit Suisse
- Dow Jones
- FTSE
- MSCI
- Russell Investments
- Standard & Poor's

How They Gain Their Leverage

Leveraged long and inverse ETFs track well-known market indexes. However, in addition to the holdings of the index, these ETFs employ derivatives such as futures contracts and index swaps to generate the leverage or inverse capabilities they desire. Investing in these types of derivatives requires very little cash deposited, and the cash that is used is typically either from dividends and interest income received from the underlying securities or from borrowed cash using the securities in the ETF as loans. The result is a little to no cost increase in the market exposure to the underlying securities the ETF is attempting to track. Without the use of derivatives, leverage and inverse capabilities could not exist.

Drawbacks and Disadvantages

Some investors and regulatory agencies do not especially like leveraged long and inverse ETFs. However, these types of ETFs do exactly what the ETF provider says they are going to do. This may be at odds with what an investor may have hoped for, given misconceptions before investing. Notwithstanding the debate over the suitability of these specialty funds, there are four drawbacks and disadvantages that investors need to be aware of.

First and foremost, leveraged long and inverse ETFs move upward to three times faster than the pace of market movement. Of course, this is disclosed to investors before investment, but the degree of price change still surprises investors. High volatility is high risk, and so investors need to be prepared for the incredible percentage swings these funds may exhibit in any one or more trading sessions.

Second, leveraged long and inverse ETFs have higher expenses than comparable nonleveraged ETFs. Most of these ETFs charge near 1 percent expense ratios, which is approaching active-management mutual fund territory.

Third, these specialty ETFs may not do exactly what an investor originally planned. The aim of these ETFs is to generate a return that is two or three times the daily return of the tracking index. The ETF providers make no claims to long-term returns.

Finally, leveraged long and inverse ETFs typically do not offer dividends like those that comparable nonleveraged ETFs might offer. Although the underlying securities pay dividends, the cash is used to finance the purchase of derivatives to generate the desired leverage or inverse capabilities. Nonetheless, most investors do not invest in these types of ETFs for ordinary dividend payments, and so it should not be a significant issue.

Largest Leveraged and Inverse ETFs

As of early 2011, there is one specialty ETF that is far and away the largest in the group. This leading ETF is nearly three times larger than the second-place specialty ETF. Care to take a guess at what it might be? Considering the economic and political environment of the early 2010s, it's no surprise that the ETF with the most assets under management is the ProShares UltraShort 20+ U.S. Treasury ETF. Not only is this an inverse play on the perceived opportunity in the direction of market interest rates, but also it's a bet that is essentially backed up with leverage. The word *ultra* in the name implies the use of leverage on top of the inverse capabilities. This all means that investors in aggregate have strong convictions on the direction of interest rates—up.

The number two specialty ETF is the ProShares UltraShort S&P 500 ETF. Again, investors are demonstrating their combined disbelief in the direction of macroeconomics. At number three is the Direxion Financial Bull ETF with approximately $19 billion under management. Ironically, the ProShares Ultra S&P 500 sits at number four. This promarket fund is in contrast to the antimarket ETF we saw at number two. Finally, rounding out the top five is the ProShares Short S&P 500 ETF. This ETF is similar to the aforementioned ETF with leverage eliminated. Perhaps the market is more fragmented than one might think.

LONG-SHORT ETFs

Although we will not get into the specific details of long-short funds, these specialty ETFs take simultaneous long and short positions in their underlying holdings with the objective of reducing correlation to the equity market and smoothing out returns during market swings. This type of ETF can be considered a combination of long ETF and inverse ETF in one—without the leverage, however.

The long-short strategy is widely popular with hedge funds as they seek to deliver absolute returns. Mutual funds have also embraced this type of fund, but the costs of these ETFs are higher and they are less tax efficient than comparable ETFs. On balance, long-short ETFs have higher expense ratios compared with those of both leveraged long and inverse ETFs. This type of specialty ETF is a nice option for investors who take a hands-off approach to investing. For more self-directed investors, employing separate long and short (inverse) ETFs is ideal, as it affords hands-on management. There is nothing particularly wrong with long-short ETFs; they are simply more appropriate for a distinct set of investors who desire specialized management. A list of available long-short ETFs is provided in Figure 13-3.

SELECT SPECIALTY ETFs

Figures 13-1 to 13-3 provide bullish, bearish, and long-short ETF alternatives you may want to consider for your own portfolio. As mentioned previously, these types of ETFs are considered higher risk and are not suitable for many investors. Carefully consider whether or not your portfolio really needs leverage or inverse exposure to satisfy the performance you desire. Investing is not about knocking the cover off the baseball on each at-bat. Rather, it's about striving for consistent base hits and a subsequently higher batting average. Nonetheless, Figures 13-1 to 13-3 provide a list of leveraged long, inverse, and long-short ETFs. Note that each segment in the figures is sorted by expense ratio.

FIGURE 13-1

List of Select Specialty ETFs: Bullish

BULLISH			
ETF	**Symbol**	**Expense Ratio**	**Inception Date**
Market Vectors Double Long Euro ETN	URR	0.65%	5/6/08
Rydex 2x S&P 500	RSU	0.71%	11/5/07
PowerShares DB Commodity Double Long ETN	DYY	0.75%	4/28/08
PowerShares DB Gold Double Long ETN	DGP	0.75%	2/27/08
UBS E-TRACS 2x Long Alerian MLP Infrastructure/ETN	MLPL	0.85%	7/6/10
ProShares Ultra S&P500	SSO	0.92%	6/19/06
ProShares Ultra DJ-UBS Commodity	UCD	0.95%	11/24/08
ProShares Ultra DJ-UBS Crude Oil	UCO	0.95%	11/24/08
ProShares Ultra Gold	UGL	0.95%	12/1/08
ProShares Ultra Silver	AGQ	0.95%	12/1/08
ProShares Ultra Telecommunications	LTL	0.95%	3/25/08
Direxion Daily Retail Bull 2X Shares	RETL	0.95%	7/14/10
ProShares Ultra Consumer Services	UCC	0.95%	1/30/07
ProShares Ultra Consumer Goods	UGE	0.95%	1/30/07
ProShares Ultra Euro	ULE	0.95%	11/24/08
ProShares Ultra Yen	YCL	0.95%	11/24/08
Direxion Daily BRIC Bull 2X Shares	BRIL	0.95%	3/11/10
Direxion Daily Emerging Markets Bull 3X Shares	EDC	0.95%	12/17/08
			continued

FIGURE 13-1

List of Select Specialty ETFs: Bullish (Cont.)

BULLISH			
ETF	Symbol	Expense Ratio	Inception Date
ProShares Ultra MSCI Emerging Markets	EET	0.95%	6/2/09
Direxion Daily Energy Bull 3X Shares	ERX	0.95%	11/6/08
Direxion Daily Natural Gas Related Bull 2X Shares	FCGL	0.95%	7/14/10
ProShares Ultra Oil & Gas	DIG	0.95%	1/30/07
ProShares Ultra MSCI Europe	UPV	0.95%	4/27/10
Direxion Daily Financial Bull 3X Shares	FAS	0.95%	11/6/08
ProShares Ultra Financials	UYG	0.95%	1/30/07
ProShares Ultra KBW Regional Banking	KRU	0.95%	4/20/10
Direxion Daily Dev Market Bull 3X Shares	DZK	0.95%	12/17/08
ProShares Ultra MSCI EAFE	EFO	0.95%	6/4/09
ProShares Ultra Health Care	RXL	0.95%	1/30/07
ProShares Ultra Nasdaq Biotechnology	BIB	0.95%	4/6/10
ProShares Ultra Industrials	UXI	0.95%	1/30/07
Direxion Daily 7-10 Year Treasury Bull 3X Shares	TYD	0.95%	4/16/09
ProShares Ultra MSCI Japan	EZJ	0.95%	6/2/09
Direxion Daily Large Cap Bull 3X Shares	BGU	0.95%	11/5/08
ProShares Ultra Dow30	DDM	0.95%	6/19/06
ProShares Ultra Russell3000	UWC	0.95%	6/30/09
ProShares UltraPro Dow30	UDOW	0.95%	2/9/10
ProShares UltraPro S&P500	UPRO	0.95%	6/23/09
ProShares Ultra QQQ	QLD	0.95%	6/19/06
ProShares Ultra Russell1000 Growth	UKF	0.95%	2/20/07
ProShares UltraPro QQQ	TQQQ	0.95%	2/9/10
ProShares Ultra Russell1000 Value	UVG	0.95%	2/20/07
Direxion Daily Latin America Bull 3X Shares	LBJ	0.95%	12/3/09
ProShares Ultra MSCI Brazil	UBR	0.95%	4/27/10
ProShares Ultra MSCI Mexico	UMX	0.95%	4/27/10
Direxion Daily 20+ Year Treasury Bull 3X Shares	TMF	0.95%	4/16/09
ProShares Ultra 20+ Year Treasury	UBT	0.95%	1/19/10
ProShares Ultra 7-10 Year Treasury	UST	0.95%	1/19/10

ETF	Symbol	Expense Ratio	Inception Date
Direxion Daily Mid Cap Bull 3X Shares	MWJ	0.95%	1/8/09
ProShares UltraPro MidCap400	UMDD	0.95%	2/9/10
ProShares Ultra Russell MidCap Growth	UKW	0.95%	2/20/07
ProShares Ultra Russell MidCap Value	UVU	0.95%	2/20/07
ProShares Ultra Basic Materials	UYM	0.95%	1/30/07
Direxion Daily India Bull 2X Shares	INDL	0.95%	3/11/10
ProShares Ultra MSCI Pacific EX-Japan	UXJ	0.95%	4/27/10
Direxion Daily Gold Miners Bull 2X Shares	NUGT	0.95%	12/8/10
Direxion Daily Real Estate Bull 3X Shares	DRN	0.95%	7/16/09
ProShares Ultra Real Estate	URE	0.95%	1/30/07
Direxion Daily Small Cap Bull 3X Shares	TNA	0.95%	11/5/08
ProShares Ultra Russell2000	UWM	0.95%	1/23/07
ProShares Ultra SmallCap600	SAA	0.95%	1/23/07
ProShares UltraPro Russell2000	URTY	0.95%	2/9/10
ProShares Ultra Russell2000 Growth	UKK	0.95%	2/20/07
ProShares Ultra Russell2000 Value	UVT	0.95%	2/20/07
Direxion Daily Semicondct Bull 3X Shares	SOXL	0.95%	3/11/10
Direxion Daily Technology Bull 3X Shares	TYH	0.95%	12/17/08
ProShares Ultra Semiconductors	USD	0.95%	1/30/07
ProShares Ultra Technology	ROM	0.95%	1/30/07
ProShares Ultra Utilities	UPW	0.95%	1/30/07

FIGURE 13-2

List of Select Specialty ETFs: Bearish

BEARISH			
ETF	Symbol	Expense Ratio	Inception Date
iPath Short Extended S&P 500 TR ETN	SFSA	0.35%	11/29/10
Barclays Short B Leveraged Inverse S&P 500 TR ETN	BXDB	0.40%	11/17/09
Barclays Short C Leveraged Inverse S&P 500 TR ETN	BXDC	0.40%	11/17/09

continued

FIGURE 13-2

List of Select Specialty ETFs: Bearish (Cont.)

BEARISH			
ETF	**Symbol**	**Expense Ratio**	**Inception Date**
Barclays Short D Leveraged Inverse S&P 500 TR ETN	BXDD	0.40%	11/17/09
iPath Short Extended Russell 1000 TR ETN	ROSA	0.50%	11/29/10
iPath Short Extended Russell 2000 TR ETN	RTSA	0.50%	11/29/10
Market Vectors Double Short Euro ETN	DRR	0.65%	5/6/08
UBS E-TRACS Short Platinum ER ETN	PTD	0.65%	5/8/08
Rydex Inverse 2x S&P 500	RSW	0.71%	11/5/07
iPath US Treasury 10-Year Bear ETN	DTYS	0.75%	8/9/10
iPath US Treasury 2-Year Bear ETN	DTUS	0.75%	8/9/10
iPath US Treasury Flattener ETN	FLAT	0.75%	8/9/10
iPath US Treasury Long Bond Bear ETN	DLBS	0.75%	8/9/10
JPMorgan 2X Short US 10 Year Treasury Futures ETN	DSXJ	0.75%	10/1/10
PowerShares DB Agriculture Double Short ETN	AGA	0.75%	4/14/08
PowerShares DB Agriculture Short ETN	ADZ	0.75%	4/14/08
PowerShares DB Base Metals Double Short ETN	BOM	0.75%	6/16/08
PowerShares DB Base Metals Short ETN	BOS	0.75%	6/16/08
PowerShares DB Commodity Double Short ETN	DEE	0.75%	4/28/08
PowerShares DB Commodity Short ETN	DDP	0.75%	4/28/08
PowerShares DB Crude Oil Double Short ETN	DTO	0.75%	6/16/08
PowerShares DB Crude Oil Short ETN	SZO	0.75%	6/16/08
PowerShares DB Gold Double Short ETN	DZZ	0.75%	2/27/08
PowerShares DB Gold Short ETN	DGZ	0.75%	2/27/08
iPath Short Enhanced MSCI EAFE ETN	MFSA	0.80%	11/29/10
iPath Short Enhanced MSCI Emrg Mkts ETN	EMSA	0.80%	11/29/10
PowerShares DB US Dollar Index Bearish	UDN	0.80%	2/20/07

ETF	Symbol	Expense Ratio	Inception Date
JPMorgan 2X Short US Long Treasury Futures ETN	DSTJ	0.85%	10/1/10
UBS E-TRACS 1x Short Alerian MLP Infrastructure ETN	MLPS	0.85%	9/28/10
ProShares UltraShort S&P500	SDS	0.90%	7/11/06
ProShares Short S&P500	SH	0.92%	6/19/06
United States Short Oil	DNO	0.92%	9/24/09
Direxion Daily 20+ Year Treasury Bear 3X Shares	TMV	0.95%	4/16/09
Direxion Daily 7-10 Year Treasury Bear 3X Shares	TYO	0.95%	4/16/09
Direxion Daily BRIC Bear 2X Shares	BRIS	0.95%	3/11/10
Direxion Daily China Bear 3X Shares	CZI	0.95%	12/3/09
Direxion Daily Dev Mkts Bear 3X Shares	DPK	0.95%	12/17/08
Direxion Daily Emrg Mkts Bear 3X Shares	EDZ	0.95%	12/17/08
Direxion Daily Energy Bear 3X Shares	ERY	0.95%	11/6/08
Direxion Daily Financial Bear 3X Shares	FAZ	0.95%	11/6/08
Direxion Daily India Bear 2X Shares	INDZ	0.95%	3/11/10
Direxion Daily Large Cap Bear 3X Shares	BGZ	0.95%	11/5/08
Direxion Daily Latin America Bear 3X Shares	LHB	0.95%	12/3/09
Direxion Daily Mid Cap Bear 3X Shares	MWN	0.95%	1/8/09
Direxion Daily Real Estate Bear 3X Shares	DRV	0.95%	7/16/09
Direxion Daily Semiconductor Bear 3X Shares	SOXS	0.95%	3/11/10
Direxion Daily Small Cap Bear 3X Shares	TZA	0.95%	11/5/08
Direxion Daily Technology Bear 3X Shares	TYP	0.95%	12/17/08
PowerShares DB 3x Short 25+ Year Treasury Bond ETN	SBND	0.95%	6/28/10
ProShares Short 20+ Year Treasury	TBF	0.95%	8/18/09
ProShares Short Basic Materials	SBM	0.95%	3/16/10
ProShares Short Dow30	DOG	0.95%	6/19/06
ProShares Short Financials	SEF	0.95%	6/10/08
ProShares Short FTSE China 25	YXI	0.95%	3/16/10
ProShares Short KBW Regional Banking	KRS	0.95%	4/20/10

continued

FIGURE 13-2

List of Select Specialty ETFs: Bearish (Cont.)

BEARISH			
ETF	Symbol	Expense Ratio	Inception Date
ProShares Short MidCap400	MYY	0.95%	6/19/06
ProShares Short MSCI EAFE	EFZ	0.95%	10/23/07
ProShares Short MSCI Emrg Mkts	EUM	0.95%	10/30/07
ProShares Short Oil & Gas	DDG	0.95%	6/10/08
ProShares Short QQQ	PSQ	0.95%	6/19/06
ProShares Short Real Estate	REK	0.95%	3/16/10
ProShares Short Russell2000	RWM	0.95%	1/23/07
ProShares Short SmallCap600	SBB	0.95%	1/23/07
ProShares UltraPro Short Dow30	SDOW	0.95%	2/9/10
ProShares UltraPro Short MidCap400	SMDD	0.95%	2/9/10
ProShares UltraPro Short QQQ	SQQQ	0.95%	2/9/10
ProShares UltraPro Short Russell2000	SRTY	0.95%	2/9/10
ProShares UltraPro Short S&P500	SPXU	0.95%	6/23/09
ProShares UltraShort 20+ Year Treasury	TBT	0.95%	4/29/08
ProShares UltraShort 7-10 Year Treasury	PST	0.95%	4/29/08
ProShares UltraShort Basic Materials	SMN	0.95%	1/30/07
ProShares UltraShort Consumer Goods	SZK	0.95%	1/30/07
ProShares UltraShort Consumer Services	SCC	0.95%	1/30/07
ProShares UltraShort DJ-UBS Commodity	CMD	0.95%	11/24/08
ProShares UltraShort DJ-UBS Crude Oil	SCO	0.95%	11/24/08
ProShares UltraShort Dow30	DXD	0.95%	7/11/06
ProShares UltraShort Euro	EUO	0.95%	11/24/08
ProShares UltraShort Financials	SKF	0.95%	1/30/07
ProShares UltraShort FTSE China 25	FXP	0.95%	11/6/07
ProShares UltraShort Gold	GLL	0.95%	12/1/08
ProShares UltraShort Health Care	RXD	0.95%	1/30/07
ProShares UltraShort Industrials	SIJ	0.95%	1/30/07
ProShares UltraShort MidCap400	MZZ	0.95%	7/11/06
ProShares UltraShort MSCI Brazil	BZQ	0.95%	6/16/09

BEARISH			
ETF	**Symbol**	**Expense Ratio**	**Inception Date**
ProShares UltraShort MSCI EAFE	EFU	0.95%	10/23/07
ProShares UltraShort MSCI Emrg Mkts	EEV	0.95%	10/30/07
ProShares UltraShort MSCI Europe	EPV	0.95%	6/16/09
ProShares UltraShort MSCI Japan	EWV	0.95%	11/6/07
ProShares UltraShort MSCI Mexico	SMK	0.95%	6/16/09
ProShares UltraShort MSCI Pacific EX-Japan	JPX	0.95%	6/16/09
ProShares UltraShort Nasdaq Biotech	BIS	0.95%	4/6/10
ProShares UltraShort Oil & Gas	DUG	0.95%	1/30/07
ProShares UltraShort QQQ	QID	0.95%	7/11/06
ProShares UltraShort Real Estate	SRS	0.95%	1/30/07
ProShares UltraShort Russell Mid Cap Growth	SDK	0.95%	2/20/07
ProShares UltraShort Russell Mid Cap Value	SJL	0.95%	2/20/07
ProShares UltraShort Russell1000 Growth	SFK	0.95%	2/20/07
ProShares UltraShort Russell1000 Value	SJF	0.95%	2/20/07
ProShares UltraShort Russell2000	TWM	0.95%	1/23/07
ProShares UltraShort Russell2000 Growth	SKK	0.95%	2/20/07
ProShares UltraShort Russell2000 Value	SJH	0.95%	2/20/07
ProShares UltraShort Russell3000	TWQ	0.95%	6/30/09
ProShares UltraShort Semiconductors	SSG	0.95%	1/30/07
ProShares UltraShort Silver	ZSL	0.95%	12/1/08
ProShares UltraShort SmallCap600	SDD	0.95%	1/23/07
ProShares UltraShort Technology	REW	0.95%	1/30/07
ProShares UltraShort Telecommunications	TLL	0.95%	3/25/08
ProShares UltraShort Utilities	SDP	0.95%	1/30/07
ProShares UltraShort Yen	YCS	0.95%	11/24/08
Direxion Daily Natural Gas Related Bear 2X Shares	FCGS	1.01%	7/14/10
Direxion Daily Retail Bear 2X Shares	RETS	1.01%	7/14/10
Active Bear	HDGE	1.85%	1/26/11

FIGURE 13-3

List of Specialty ETFs: Long-Short

LONG-SHORT			
ETF	Symbol	Expense Ratio	Inception Date
Credit Suisse Long/Short Liquid Index ETN	CSLS	0.45%	2/22/10
Credit Suisse 2X Merger Arbitage Liquid Index ETN	CSMB	0.55%	3/7/11
Credit Suisse Merger Arbitage Liquid Index ETN	CSMA	0.55%	10/1/10
ELEMENTS S&P CTI ETN	LSC	0.75%	6/10/08
FactorShares 2X: Gold Bull/S&P500 Bear	FSG	0.75%	2/24/11
FactorShares 2X: Oil Bull/S&P500 Bear	FOL	0.75%	2/24/11
FactorShares 2X: S&P500 Bull/ Treasury Bond Bear	FSE	0.75%	2/24/11
FactorShares 2X: S&P500 Bull/USD Bear	FSU	0.75%	2/24/11
FactorShares 2X: Treasury Bond Bull/ S&P500 Bear	FSA	0.75%	2/24/11
iPath CBOE S&P 500 BuyWrite Index ETN	BWV	0.75%	5/22/07
PowerShares Nasdaq-100 BuyWrite	PQBW	0.75%	6/12/08
PowerShares S&P 500 BuyWrite	PBP	0.75%	12/20/07
ProShares VIX Mid-Term Futures	VIXM	0.85%	1/3/11
ProShares VIX Short-Term Futures	VIXY	0.85%	1/3/11
UBS E-TRACS Daily Long-Short VIX ETN	XVIX	0.85%	11/30/10
iPath Inverse S&P 500 VIX S/T Fut ETN	XXV	0.89%	7/16/10
iPath Long Enhanced S&P 500 VIX MT Futures ETN	VZZ	0.89%	11/29/10
iPath S&P 500 VIX Mid-Term Futures ETN	VXZ	0.89%	1/29/09
iPath S&P 500 VIX Short-Term Futures ETN	VXX	0.89%	1/29/09
VelocityShares Long VIX Medium Term ETN	VIIZ	0.89%	11/29/10
VelocityShares Long VIX Short Term ETN	VIIX	0.89%	11/29/10

ETF	Symbol	Expense Ratio	Inception Date
iShares Diversified Alternatives Trust	ALT	0.95%	10/6/09
ProShares Credit Suisse 130/30	CSM	0.95%	7/13/09
WisdomTree Managed Futures	WDTI	0.95%	1/5/11
ProShares RAFI Long/Short	RALS	0.95%	12/9/10
VelocityShares Daily Inverse VIX MT ETN	ZIV	1.35%	11/29/10
VelocityShares Daily Inverse VIX ST ETN	XIV	1.35%	11/29/10
Mars Hill Global Relative Value	GRV	1.49%	7/8/10
VelocityShares Daily 2x VIX Med Term ETN	TVIZ	1.65%	11/29/10
VelocityShares Daily 2x VIX ST ETN	TVIX	1.65%	11/29/10

PART 3

Use of Exchange-Traded Funds

## CHAPTER 14

Risk and Return: Fundamentals of Investing 101

No one particularly likes risk, especially when risk translates into portfolio losses like the ones so many of us experienced in 2008. Avoiding or minimizing risk wherever and whenever possible is therefore a top priority. However, doing so is not entirely feasible in the world of investing since there is a clear and profound relationship between risk and return. Risk is an inherent part of any investment undertaking, making it critical to understand and manage this inescapable trade-off between risk and return.

Unfortunately, we hear the very opposite practically every day. We have all seen those crazy infomercials (if you want to call them by that name) that claim reward can be earned with little to no risk. Reward without risk is not possible—if it were, then we would all be millionaires with multiple homes and multiple cars, if that's your thing. Abnormally high returns are not uncommon; however, they are not predictable nor consistent over time. Consequently, if you desire a return that outpaces both inflation and taxes, then you must be prepared to assume some level of risk in your portfolio. You get what you pay for and reap what you sow. Figure 14-1 illustrates the relationship in basic terms between risk and return and the application to portfolio construction.

Investment return and investment risk and the way they work together are the foundations of asset allocation and its application

FIGURE 14-1

Relationship Between Risk and Return

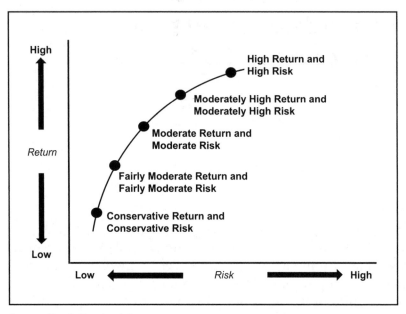

Source: Frush Financial Group

to building an optimal portfolio. Depending on your objectives and constraints, you may invest in assets that exhibit low risk and therefore the potential for low, but stable, returns; or you may invest in assets that exhibit high risk and therefore the potential for high, but oftentimes, volatile returns. In basic asset allocation theory, the higher the potential risk you take, the higher the potential return you should expect to generate over time. Rational investors will not assume a higher level of risk in the hopes of earning a return that a less risky investment will generate.

The trade-off between risk and return is not defined in black-and-white terms. There are multiple shades of gray. As a result, the golden question is how to enhance your returns while minimizing risk. Although risk cannot be entirely eliminated from a portfolio, it can be controlled and managed with a proper asset allocation and diversification policy. Portfolios that are optimally designed, built, and managed will exhibit a higher risk-adjusted return than portfolios that do not subscribe to proper asset allocation policy, regardless of having high-potential-return investments in that portfolio. This is exemplified by modern portfolio theory, which suggests that investors should not evaluate each investment on a stand-alone basis and instead focus on the ability of each investment to enhance the overall risk and return profile of a portfolio. After learning the risk and reward profiles of each asset class, you will then be able to build your own portfolio with an acceptable level of risk and expected return.

The next section of this chapter will discuss investment return, followed by an in-depth discussion of investment risk.

INVESTMENT RETURN

Generating investment return is of primary concern to investors. Why would you invest otherwise? Without appropriate compensation in the form of gains and income, people would not invest their hard-earned money and forgo immediate consumption. Earning the highest return for the least amount of risk assumed is at the core of asset allocation. Investment return can come in many different ways, and it means different things to different people. Although we will be discussing quantitative measures of return, do not forget that return can also be expressed in qualitative terms as well—such as emotional comfort, security, and a feeling of independence and control.

It is vitally important that you consider the potential level of return you wish to generate and the level of risk you need to assume in order to obtain that return. Additionally, investing more money in a higher-potential-return investment or asset class does not necessarily mean your return will be any higher than that of someone who invested in a somewhat lower-potential-return asset class. The reason is because it is not the individual investments in your portfolio that are key; rather it is how the component investments work together to form a complete portfolio. For this reason, it is wise to build a portfolio made up of multiple asset classes rather than allocating to only the current high-return-potential asset class or classes. Generally speaking, a higher probability of return also means a higher probability of losing some or all of an investment. Some people are willing to assume that risk, while others are not. This is what makes investing and portfolio construction unique from person to person.

The profit or loss from an investment is composed of both appreciation—or depreciation—in market value over a specific holding period and income (dividends and interest) received during the same time period. Summing the two profit or loss components and dividing by the market value of the investment at the beginning of the period equals total return. This measure takes into account both the change in price of the security and any cash flow received during the holding period. It is commonplace in the investment field to measure return using the total return calculation. An example of calculating total return is as follows.

Suppose you purchase 1,000 shares of JPMorgan Chase common stock at $40 a share. One year later you sell your 1,000 shares at $44 per share. In addition, during your 1-year holding period, JPMorgan Chase paid you a $1 per share dividend. Therefore, the total return of your investment, excluding transaction costs and taxes, is 12.5 percent ($4 appreciation plus $1 dividend divided by $40 cost basis).

The concept of investment return can be divided into two distinctions: actual return and expected return. Actual return is the return you have generated, whether realized or unrealized, in a past holding period. Expected return is an estimate of what you should generate, both appreciation and income, in a future holding period. Both actual and expected returns are commonly expressed in annualized percentages. Determining actual return is important, since doing so gives you a handle on how well—or poorly—your investments had fared and how best to move forward with any changes, such as rebalancing. Similarly, determining expected return is important, as it enables you to fully analyze the profit potential for the level of risk you might take.

The process of forecasting expected returns is a difficult task and typically performed only by very sophisticated and institutional investors. The following are the basic steps for identifying expected return:

1. Forecast all possible material outcomes and scenarios that may occur.
2. Assign probabilities of occurrence to each material outcome.
3. Forecast a return for each specific material outcome.
4. Multiply the probabilities with their related forecasted return.
5. Sum the results (equals the expected return).

Take the following scenario: Say an analyst estimates that Ford Motor Company has a 25 percent probability of returning 15 percent, a 50 percent probability of returning 10 percent, a 15 percent probability of returning 5 percent, and a 10 percent probability of returning –5 percent. Thus, the estimated return is

$$(0.25 \times 0.15) + (0.50 \times 0.10) + (0.15 \times 0.05) + [0.10 \times (-0.05)] = 9.00 \text{ percent}$$

Identifying potential scenarios and outcomes is typically calculated based on estimates of how well the economy and other macroeconomic factors will perform during the holding period under consideration. The resulting return is simply an estimate, given each economic scenario possible. Monte Carlo computer simulations are sometimes used to help define potential results. All this is done to give investors a better grasp of investment risk and thus allow them to make more informed decisions.

INVESTMENT RISK

Investment risk can be defined in several different ways, as investors view risk differently from one another. Some investors define risk as losing money, while others define risk as being unfamiliar—and therefore uncomfortable—with an investment. Still others define risk as contrarian risk, or the risk investors feel when they are not "following the crowd." Although all the aforementioned definitions of risk are sound, risk is best defined as uncertainty, or the uncertainty that actual investment returns will match expected returns. For example, pension funds and insurance companies view risk as the uncertainty they can meet future benefit obligations.

Viewing risk as the uncertainty of meeting future commitments and funding obligations is a sensible and objective way to view portfolio and investment risk. Future commitments and funding obligations can include paying for college, buying a vacation home, starting a business, or just supplementing social security to pay for living expenses in the golden years.

Taking this concept of risk further, gaps between actual and expected returns can be attributed to volatility of returns over a specific time period. Greater monthly price movement of a particular security—regardless of direction—equates to a higher volatility measure. Higher volatility is considered higher risk, while lower volatility—and therefore more stable prices—is considered lower risk for an investment. Volatility also impacts total performance. Portfolios with greater volatility over multiple periods during one holding period will exhibit lower long-term compounded growth rates of return than portfolios with lower volatility over multiple periods during the same holding period. This is often referred to as the sequence of returns. Thus, it is essential to minimize volatility in your portfolio for maximum performance over time.

Risk management and proper asset allocation help to control both the frequency and the amount of portfolio losses over time. Since you rely on estimates of future returns to design your optimal portfolio, it is critically important that actual returns come close to matching expected returns. Investments with more predictable returns are thus considered lower risk and more favorable for most investors. Conversely, investments with less predictable returns are considered higher risk and typically less favorable for most investors.

Sources of Investment Risk

There are two primary sources of investment risk. The first is called systematic risk, or the risk attributed to relatively uncontrollable external factors; and the second is called unsystematic risk, or the risk attributed directly to the underlying investment. Let's look at systematic risk first.

Systematic Risk

Systematic risk results from conditions, events, and trends occurring outside the scope of the investment. There are four primary types of systematic risk—exchange rate risk, interest rate risk, market risk, and purchasing power risk. At any one point, there are different degrees of each risk occurring. These risks will cause the demand for a particular investment to rise or fall, thus impacting returns.

1. **Exchange Rate Risk:** The risk that the value of an investment will be impacted by changes in the foreign currency market. For example, if you own a foreign asset, then changes in the value of that foreign currency relative to the U.S. dollar will impact your return. If the U.S. dollar increases in value, then your return declines since it will take more foreign currency to buy one U.S. dollar. Conversely, a declining U.S. dollar will increase your return, all else being equal, of course.

2. **Interest Rate Risk:** The risk attributed to the loss in market value for both fixed-income and equity securities due to a change in the general level of interest rates. For bonds and other fixed-income securities, rising interest rates can negatively impact market values. Why? Primarily because as interest rates rise, the availability of more attractive investments with higher yields also increases. For example, if you owned a bond yielding 5 percent and interest rates increased by 1 percent to 6 percent, then the demand for 6 percent bonds will grow and the demand for 5 percent bonds will fall. This translates to lower market values for your 5 percent bond. For equities, changes in interest rates can impact business operations, such as the number of mortgage originations for banks and the number of new home starts for home builders.

3. **Market Risk:** The risk attributed to the loss in market value for individual investments due to price declines in the entire market portfolio. When the overall market falls, then most—but not all—investments decline in sympathy with the overall market. Consider the "flash crash" of 2010, for example. Although an extreme case, few stocks

were up when the Dow Jones Industrial Average was down close to 1,000 points at one time in the day. If you had planned to sell your investment on that day, you were not very happy.

4. **Purchasing Power Risk:** The risk attributed to inflation and the resulting rising prices that erode the real value of an investment over time. This means that $100 today will buy less in one or more years into the future. When prices for goods and services are rising faster than expected, then your ability to sustain your current lifestyle into retirement will be more challenging.

Unsystematic Risk

Unlike systematic risk, unsystematic risk is not attributed to external factors. This source of risk is unique to an investment—such as the debt level of a particular company, the soundness of a company's management team, and the industry in which a company operates. The principal types of unsystematic risk include, but are not limited to, the following:

1. **Business Risk:** The risk attributed to a company's operations, particularly those involving sales and income. For example, persistent declining sales for a specific company can mean the loss of investor confidence followed by a declining stock price.

2. **Financial Risk:** The risk attributed to a company's financial stability and structure, namely the company's use of debt to leverage earnings. Companies with more debt have higher principal and interest payments—which is not a concern during good times. However, during bad times, satisfying higher debt payments can be a significant challenge. As a result, companies with more debt are considered more risky.

3. **Industry Risk:** The risk attributed to a group of similar companies within a particular industry or sector. Investments tend to rise and fall based on what peer companies are doing. A big downside movement in price for one company stock will typically bode poorly for other stocks in that same peer group.

4. **Liquidity Risk:** The risk that an investment cannot be purchased or sold at a price at or near market prices. The more liquid an investment, the easier it is to buy or sell at current market prices. Illiquidity can cause you to sell at a much lower price than originally expected.
5. **Call Risk:** The risk attributed to an event where an investment may be called (i.e., forced to sell back to the issuer) prior to maturity. This may leave the investor unable to reinvest the proceeds at the same or higher interest rate. This risk is associated with fixed-income securities.
6. **Regulation Risk:** The risk that new laws and regulations will negatively impact the market value of an investment. For example, a state government may pass a law requiring manufacturers to add new and costly pollution control systems in their factories. Irrespective of the environmental benefits, adding costly systems could harm a company's financial position, subsequently making it less attractive to investors.

Summing systematic and unsystematic risk equals total risk. Since the goal of asset allocation is to create a well-diversified portfolio, unsystematic risk is considered unimportant because it should be eliminated with proper diversification. Therefore, an optimal portfolio should only possess systematic risk, or risk resulting from market and other uncontrollable external factors.

Measuring Investment Risk

Since different investments have both different types of risk and different degrees of risk, it is essential to quantify risk in order to make comparisons across the broad range of asset classes for better decisions. As mentioned previously, risk is best defined as the uncertainty that actual returns will not match expected returns. Intuitively one can see that the greater the difference between actual and expected returns for an investment, the less predictable and uncertain that investment is considered. This translates into greater risk for investors.

Using historical return data, we are able to measure risk more accurately. Historical volatility data can be obtained using numerous intervals of time—days, weeks, months, and years—with monthly volatility generally used in practice. In simple analysis, averaging the degrees of difference between actual and expected returns for a specific investment gives us the statistical measure called standard deviation. Although we will not get into the technical specifics of how to calculate it, standard deviation is a statistical measure of the degree to which actual returns are spread around the mean actual return. Expressed as a percentage, standard deviation is considered the best—but not sole—measure of risk. A higher standard deviation means higher risk, while a lower standard deviation means lower risk. Unfortunately, calculating standard deviation does not mean the job is finished. Since the price for any security changes over time, so to do standard deviations—they are not static. Some asset classes will change more frequently and to a greater degree than other asset classes.

Volatility typically rises during periods of declining prices and moderates during periods of advancing prices. Historically speaking, even though the volatility of asset classes may change in the short term, volatility ranges have remained relatively stable over the long term. That is good news for investment planning since we are dealing with more predictable inputs.

Since actual returns are impacted by both systematic and unsystematic risks, standard deviation is a measure of total risk. As a result, standard deviation gives an investor a way to evaluate both the risk and return elements of an individual investment. Although standard deviation is one of the best measures of risk, it is by far not without issues. For example, standard deviation may vary from analysis to analysis depending on the holding period duration (in years) selected for comparison. Figure 14-2 shows some actual standard deviations and betas.

RISK AND RETURN TRADE-OFF

Given the direct relationship between risk and return, investors are able to measure this relationship to build a portfolio with the appropriate risk and return trade-off profile. By using what is called the Sharpe ratio, or simply dividing the "excess expected return" of an asset class by its standard deviation (level of risk), we

FIGURE 14-2

Actual Standard Deviations and Betas

ETF	Symbol	Standard Deviation	Beta
Consumer Discretionary Sector SPDR	XLY	27.2	1.16
Consumer Staples Sector SPDR	XLP	14.1	0.59
Energy Sector SPDR	XLE	27.3	0.98
Financial Sector SPDR	XLF	37.6	1.53
Health-Care Sector SPDR	XLV	17.7	0.66
Industrial Sector SPDR	XLI	28.6	1.27
Materials Sector SPDR	XLB	29.9	1.29
Technology Sector SPDR	XLK	23.5	1.01
Utilities Sector SPDR	XLU	16.6	0.55
SPDR S&P 500	SPY	21.76	0.99

Source: Frush Financial Group

are able to ascertain the amount of excess expected return per unit of risk for an asset class. Doing so helps us to compare, contrast, and select asset classes with dissimilar expected returns and levels of risk. Excess expected return is defined as the expected return minus the risk-free rate, or the rate you can earn from investing in U.S. Treasury bills.

Suppose you are evaluating two asset classes for possible investment—asset class A and asset class B. Asset class A has a standard deviation of 6 percent and an excess expected return of 8 percent over the proposed holding period. By dividing the excess expected return of 8 percent by the standard deviation of 6 percent, we find that asset class A has a risk and return trade-off profile of 1.33. Similarly, asset class B has a standard deviation of 4 percent and an excess expected return of 6 percent. This translates into a risk and return trade-off profile of 1.50. As you can see, although asset class A has the higher expected return, it does not provide the highest level of expected return per unit of risk—that prize goes to asset class B.

RISK AND RETURN RELATIONSHIP

Investors who take greater risk should be compensated with greater potential return. Depending on your risk profile, the more risk you assume, the higher your expected return. Of course, there are exceptions to the rules. Aren't there always? To better understand this relationship between risk and expected return, a model called the efficient frontier was developed. The efficient frontier—illustrated by an upward-sloping curved line—represents the investments with the highest risk and return trade-off profiles, or those investments with the highest expected returns for a specific level or unit of risk.

As you can see from Figure 14-3, by moving up the efficient frontier, investments present a greater potential for return, but also come with greater risk. Nevertheless, each point on the efficient frontier exhibits the highest expected total rate of return for the level of risk exhibited. There will be many investments available

FIGURE 14-3

Hypothetical Efficient Frontier

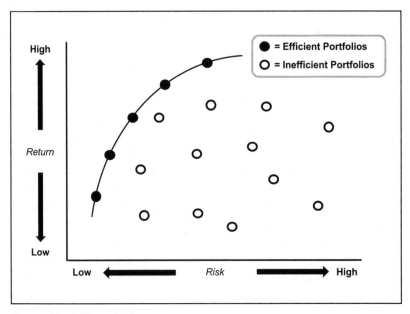

Source: Frush Financial Group

and plotted on the graph, but only those with the best risk and return trade-off profiles will appear on the efficient frontier.

Your objective is to select investments somewhere along the efficient frontier according to your risk and return trade-off profile. Some investors will place their investments near the top of the slope, while others with lower risk and return trade-off profiles will place their investments on a lower part of the slope to the lower left.

Regardless of whether your portfolio is an 80/20, 70/30, 60/40, or 50/50 equity to fixed income, as long as each portfolio combination exhibits the highest expected total rate of return for a given level of risk, then it will be plotted somewhere along the efficient frontier. Portfolios that do not exhibit the highest expected total rates of return per unit of risk will be plotted below the slope of the efficient frontier, and that means a suboptimal or inefficient portfolio. Understanding this relationship between risk and return is critical, as it underlies the process of allocating assets. Without a true understanding of this relationship, you may design a portfolio that either exhibits greater risk than desired or generates lower actual returns given the inclusion of less risky assets. As we will see in the next chapter, the process of asset allocation involves estimating expected returns for each asset class and then determining, within the context of your risk and return trade-off profile, what percentage of the portfolio should be allocated to each asset class.

ASSET CLASSES AND RISK

Different asset classes possess different types and different amounts of risk—including different expected returns. Each type of risk is derived from one or more sources of risk. Regardless of the type and source of investment risk, asset allocation will allow you to control and manage your risk exposure to the best of your advantage.

As previously mentioned, however, it is simply not enough to focus on the merits of one particular asset class since it is how each asset class moves in relation to the other asset classes that truly matters. Regardless of the risk and return potential for each asset class, keep in mind that understanding the asset class's fundamentals and how they impact a portfolio is most important. Figure 14-4 illustrates this all-important lesson.

FIGURE 14-4

Asset Class Risk and Return Trade-Off Profiles

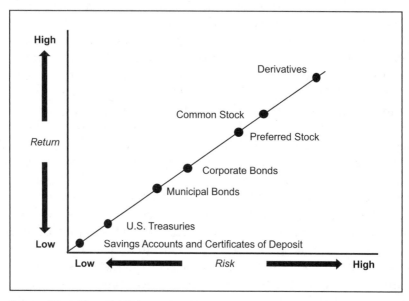

Source: Frush Financial Group

TEN RULES FOR PORTFOLIO RISK REDUCTION

Risk, and the endeavor to control, reduce, or eliminate it, is as old as the financial markets themselves. Regardless of the new technology, the new hot products, or the new financial models, successful investing is all about maximizing the inescapable trade-off between risk and return. The following is a list of 10 reasonable rules you may want to consider for reducing the level of risk in your portfolio.

1. **Understand Your Risk:** Knowing your level of portfolio risk will enable you to make better and more informed decisions. Remember that risk is best defined as uncertainty that actual returns will match expected returns.

2. **Build a Multiasset-Class Portfolio:** Holding multiple asset classes will smooth the volatility risk you would otherwise experience from holding only a minimal number of asset classes.
3. **Target Low Correlations:** Low correlations among asset classes further smooth out volatility risk since lower correlations mean that the prices for two asset classes do not move in tandem with each other.
4. **Add Fundamentally Different Asset Classes:** Asset classes that are fundamentally different exhibit return-enhancement and risk-reduction potential. Hold a combination of these asset classes wherever feasible.
5. **Diversify Each Asset Class:** Diversification is not the same as asset allocation. Diversify each asset class to reduce unsystematic risk, or investment-specific risk unique to single asset classes or investments.
6. **Rebalance Your Portfolio:** Your portfolio asset mix will change over time as stock prices change. To keep this added risk in check, rebalancing back to your original allocations should be done on a frequent basis—at least annually, but better yet quarterly.
7. **Use Common Sense:** When selecting the suitable level of risk for your portfolio, it is more important to be approximately correct than to be precisely wrong.
8. **Hedge Risk:** Although not for all investors, hedging risk with options, swaps, futures, and position neutralizing short sales can protect against severe market declines.
9. **Exercise Discipline:** Employing a steadfast approach will outperform a constantly changing approach any day of the week.
10. **Consider Assistance:** Risk is best managed by experienced people, not financial models. Professional help may provide you with the resources and comfort you need.

## CHAPTER 15

Asset Allocation: An All-Important Overview

Numerous landmark research studies have concluded that how you *allocate* your assets, rather than *which* individual investments you select or *when* you buy or sell them, is the leading determinant of investment performance over time. Not stock picking, nor market timing, nor the latest and greatest hot investment without risk, is the leading determinant of investment performance over time.

No book on exchange-traded funds (ETFs) would be complete without a chapter dedicated to asset allocation. As we saw with the preceding chapter, the relationship between risk and return is central to the investing decision framework. This relationship essentially says that to earn higher levels of return, investors need to assume higher levels of risk. There is simply no other way to accomplish this aim. In addition, investors looking to assume lower levels of risk will typically earn lower rates of return. Asset allocation is very much related to risk and return and the relationship they play in portfolio construction. Investing in ETFs should not be approached as a stand-alone, single investment. Rather, investing in ETFs should be approached as part of the overall picture—a way to enhance and build out asset allocation. It is for this reason that we devote this chapter to the nuts and bolts of asset allocation. For a more detailed discussion of asset allocation, please pick up a copy of *Understanding Asset Allocation* (Frush, McGraw-Hill, New York, 2006).

Asset allocation is best described as the way you optimally divide your investment portfolio and other investable money into different asset classes for maximum benefit. The concept underlying allocating your portfolio in such a way is that by splitting your investment portfolio into different asset classes, you will reduce portfolio risk and enhance your long-term risk-adjusted return. In other words, asset allocation provides you with your best opportunity to earn solid returns over time while assuming the level of portfolio risk most suitable for your unique situation. The allocation of your assets is based on a number of very important factors, such as current financial position, investment time horizon, level of wealth, financial goals and obligations, and risk profile.

There are a few other minor variables, or portfolio allocation inputs, discussed at length later in this chapter. Specifically, the three most important inputs that determine your asset allocation are your financial objectives and obligations, your investment time horizon, and your risk profile. For building an optimal portfolio, your unique risk profile is of utmost importance. Your risk profile includes three variables: your tolerance for risk, your capacity for risk, and your need to assume risk. Much like an army that moves only as fast as its slowest unit, portfolios should be constructed according to the least common denominator for risk of the three components that constitute risk profile.

AL-LOCATION, AL-LOCATION, AL-LOCATION

One of the leading adages of classic wisdom most synonymous with business success is "location, location, location." Nearly everyone has heard of this expression because it is so very true. Building a successful business is not very different from building a successful portfolio. This exact same classic wisdom applies to investment success as well, but expressed with a twist—"al-location, al-location, al-location." Location, or al-location with investing, can mean the difference between success and failure. Before selecting a location, successful business owners do their homework; they do not make ad hoc decisions. As an investor, you should approach your investing in the same manner.

ASSET ALLOCATION ANALOGY

To better help illustrate the significant benefits of asset allocation, let's consider an analogy to hockey. The analogy goes like this. Employing asset allocation is similar to a hockey player wearing protective equipment—helmet, shoulder pads, hip pads, kneepads, etc. If that hockey player were to take off his protective equipment, he could probably skate faster, cut easier, and pass the puck better. As a result, he could become a dominating player. However, it doesn't take a rocket scientist to recognize that not wearing the proper hockey protective equipment is very unwise and foolish. One hit into the boards from an opponent, and you could be out of the game for a very long time, if not forever. No more domination.

Employing proper asset allocation is very similar in nature. An investor who does not wear proper protective equipment may experience uncommonly superior returns for a short period of time, but will eventually take a devastating hit that might crash a portfolio, and possibly severe enough that it won't recover. Taking a serious hit may not happen right away, but it will happen at some point. Think of the dot-com bubble burst in the early 2000s and the market crash of 2008.

FOUNDATION OF ASSET ALLOCATION

Asset allocation is founded on two celebrated and highly influential investment theories. These two are the modern portfolio theory (MPT) and the efficient market hypothesis (EMH), which is essentially a refinement of MPT. These two theories are the most discussed and most widely used theories in all of investment management.

MPT says that investors and portfolio managers should not evaluate each investment on a stand-alone basis. Rather, each investment should be evaluated based on its ability to enhance the overall risk and return profile of a portfolio. For instance, when faced with two investments with identical expected returns but different levels of risk, investors should select the investment that has the lower risk according to MPT. Said from another angle, a rational investor should select the investment with the higher expected return when faced with two investments that have different expected returns but identical levels of risk.

Look at Figure 15-1. When faced with investments A and B, a rational investor will select investment B over investment A because the total return of investment B is higher, with both having the same level of risk. Moreover, when faced with investments B and C, a rational investor will select investment C over investment B because the total risk of investment C is lower, with both having the same total return. Rather simple stuff, but it was revolutionary when first put forth.

FIGURE 15-1

Investment Alternatives and Rational Decisions

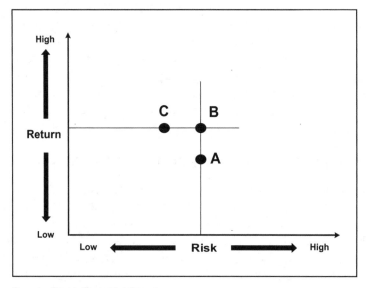

Source: Frush Financial Group

Additionally, MPT introduces the concept of correlation and stresses how it enhances the risk and return profile of a portfolio. The Employee Retirement Income Security Act of 1974, which governs the management of pension funds, emphasizes this point, thus essentially endorsing MPT. Harry M. Markowitz, who was awarded the Nobel Prize in Economics in 1990, is considered the "father of modern portfolio theory" for this work.

Finally, EMH asserts that capital markets are "informationally efficient," meaning one cannot achieve excess risk-adjusted returns consistently over time since the information relied upon to make such a decision is publicly available at the time the investment is made.

EMPIRICAL RESEARCH

Authors Gary P. Brinson, L. Randolph Hood, and Gilbert L. Beebower, in the landmark research study "Determinants of Portfolio Performance" published in the *Financial Analysts Journal* (July–August 1986, pp. 39–44), concluded that asset allocation policy is by far the principal determinant of investment performance over time. Contrary to popular belief at the time—and perhaps still today—the researchers discovered that security selection and market timing determined only a small fraction of investment performance over time.

The aforementioned study was based on the quarterly investment results of 90 large pension funds over a 10-year period from 1974 to 1983. The goal of the study was to determine to what degree asset allocation policy, security selection, market timing, and, to a lesser extent, costs contributed to the investment performance of the pension funds under study.

Asset allocation policy was analyzed within the context of three primary asset classes—stocks, bonds, and cash. For example, one pension fund might have an asset mix of 65 percent stocks, 25 percent bonds, and 10 percent cash, while another pension fund might have an asset mix of 50 percent stocks, 35 percent bonds, and 15 percent cash. Market timing was evaluated by analyzing the changes in asset class weightings over time. For instance, if a portfolio manager altered a pension fund's allocation to the three observed asset classes over a given time period, the researchers interpreted that as an attempt by the portfolio manager to profit from market timing. As you can see from Figure 15-2, asset allocation policy explained 93.6 percent of investment performance, while security selection, market timing, and other factors (including costs) explained 2.5 percent, 1.7 percent, and 2.2 percent of investment performance, respectively.

FIGURE 15-2

Determinants of Investment Performance

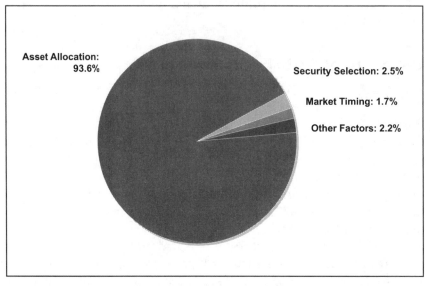

Source: "Determinants of Portfolio Performance" by Gary P. Brinson, L. Randolph Hood, and Gilbert L. Beebower, *Financial Analysts Journal*, July–August 1986

Gary Brinson, Gilbert Beebower, and Brian D. Singer used updated information to conduct a follow-up study. Titled "Determinants of Portfolio Performance II: An Update" published in the *Financial Analysts Journal* (May–June 1991, pp. 40–48), this study arrived at nearly the same conclusion as the previous study. As such, the subsequent study concluded that asset allocation policy is the primary factor explaining investment performance over time. Again, the second study found that security selection and market timing explained only a fraction of investment performance.

As you can see from Figure 15-3, asset allocation policy was found to explain 91.5 percent of investment performance, while security selection, market timing, and other factors explained 4.6 percent, 1.8 percent, and 2.1 percent of investment performance, respectively.

In yet another significant research study, renowned practition-ers Roger G. Ibbotson and Paul D. Kaplan in early 2000 concluded in their study titled "Does Asset Allocation Policy Explain 40, 90, or 100 Percent of Performance?" published in the *Financial Analysts Journal* (January–February 2000, pp. 26–33), that asset allocation pol-icy explains about 90 percent of investment performance over time.

If security selection and market timing do not play a signifi-cant role in determining investment performance over time, a good question to investigate is whether or not individual industries play a role. According to Eugene F. Fama and Kenneth R. French, they generally do not. In their research paper "Industry Costs of Equity," published in the *Journal of Financial Economics* (February 1997, pp. 153–193), the researchers concluded that although spe-cific industries can influence market prices, they do so only in a random and short-term way.

FIGURE 15-3

Determinants of Investment Performance II

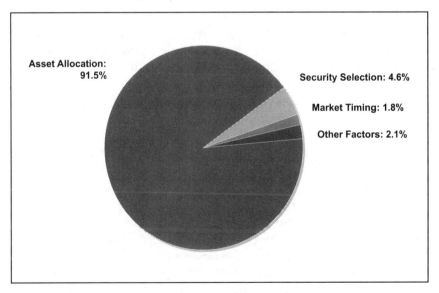

Source: "Determinants of Portfolio Performance II: An Update" by Gary P. Brinson, Gilbert L. Beebower, and Brian D. Singer, *Financial Analysts Journal*, May–June 1991

ADDITIONAL ASSET ALLOCATION CONSIDERATIONS

Portfolios and the asset mix that makes up a portfolio will not remain static over time. At some point in the future your personal situation will change and so too will your asset allocation. There are multiple factors that may change, and each plays a role in determining your optimal asset allocation. In addition to your personal situation changing, market factors impacting your portfolio will also change to some degree over time. These "market-centric" factors include expected total returns, volatility, and trading flexibility. Rest assured, a proper asset allocation policy provides for a quick and easy rebalancing. You will not spend restless nights wondering what to do when changes need to be made.

Importance of Correlation

According to MPT, an optimal portfolio is not just the sum of its parts. Rather, an optimal portfolio is the sum of its synergies. Synergies are created by the interaction of the investments held within a portfolio. This interaction is commonly referred to as correlation and is a critical input to the asset allocation process. *Correlation* is the technical term for measuring and describing how closely the prices of two investments move together over time (see Figure 15-4).

Positively correlated assets move in the same direction, both up and down. Conversely, negatively correlated assets move in opposite directions. Correlations between two assets are expressed on a scale between –1.0 and +1.0. The greater two assets are correlated, or move together, the closer to +1.0. Similarly, the greater two assets move in opposite directions, the closer to –1.0. Two assets that move exactly together have a +1.0 correlation, while two assets that move exactly opposite have a –1.0 correlation. Finally, correlations between –0.3 and +0.3 are considered noncorrelated. This means that the two assets move independently of each other. With noncorrelated assets, when one is rising in price, the other may be rising, falling, or maintaining its current price.

A properly allocated portfolio has a mix of investments that do not behave the same way. Correlation is therefore a variable you need to be concerned with. To maximize the portfolio benefits

FIGURE 15-4

Correlation Impact on a Portfolio

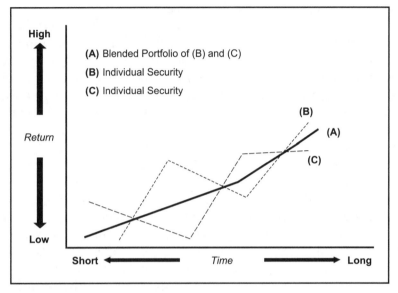

Source: Frush Financial Group

derived from correlations, you will need to incorporate invest-ments with negative correlations, low positive correlations, or even assets that have noncorrelations. By investing in assets with low correlations, you are able to reduce total portfolio risk without materially impacting the expected return of your portfolio.

The greatest portfolio risk-reduction benefits occur during time periods when correlations across the board are low, noncorre-lated, or negative. When correlations increase, risk-reduction ben-efits are partially lost. Over time, some correlations will increase and some will decline.

Since you cannot predict which correlations will change, or to what degree they will change over time, successful investors will allocate to a number of fundamentally different investments to reap the maximum benefits of correlation and its impact on the asset allocation decision.

Time Horizon

Your time horizon is another very important input variable that many investors pay too little attention to. Your time horizon impacts forecasts of expected rates of return, expected volatility, and expected correlations between assets.

As a result of the important role it plays, time horizon is the first constraint that should be identified. Overestimating or underestimating your time horizon can significantly impact how you allocate your assets and thereby impact your risk and return trade-off profile.

The primary role that time horizon plays is to help you select and evaluate the appropriateness of each asset as an investment alternative. Specifically, time horizon helps to determine your balance between equity assets and fixed-income assets. In the short term, equities are simply too volatile and possess too high levels of uncertainty. On the other hand, fixed-income assets are significantly less volatile in the short term and possess much lower levels of uncertainty. As your investment time horizon increases, so too does the probability that equities generate positive returns. Over longer periods of time, equity returns become more stable, with more time for positive equity returns to offset negative equity returns. The returns of equities become significantly clearer and more predictable as your investment time horizon lengthens. The shorter your time horizon, the more emphasis you should place on fixed-income assets. Conversely, the longer your time horizon, the more you should overweight equities.

Asset-Class Behavior

During certain time periods, certain asset classes will perform well, whereas during other time periods, other asset classes will perform well. Unfortunately, we do not know which asset class will perform well during any specific period, and therefore it is vitally important to be invested in multiple asset classes at all times. The benefits of asset allocation and diversification are received when you invest in multiple asset classes where there is a fundamental difference among them. The principal benefit is to enhance the risk-adjusted return of your portfolio. This is referred to as the allocation effect. However, allocating to multiple asset classes does not guarantee consistently higher returns with corresponding low levels of risk.

That simply cannot be accomplished consistently over time. During certain periods, your portfolio will experience strong asset allocation benefits, while during other times your portfolio will experience subdued asset allocation benefits.

Determining your optimal asset allocation comprising multiple asset classes requires a solid understanding of some very important points. First, there is no perfect allocation or perfect plan. There are only good to very good plans that will help you achieve your goals. Second, make sure to learn the key specifics of each asset class, such as general correlations, historical returns, and typical risk levels. Third, understand that forecasting future correlations, returns, risk levels, and price movements—although important—is an extremely difficult endeavor. Leave those tasks to the experts whenever possible. Fourth, a portfolio with more asset classes is more advantageous than a portfolio with fewer asset classes. Last, remember to build a portfolio with an asset allocation that complements your unique situation.

In Figure 15-5, A represents a hypothetical portfolio of large-cap stocks; B represents a hypothetical portfolio of large-cap stocks

FIGURE 15-5

Advantage of Multiasset-Class Portfolios

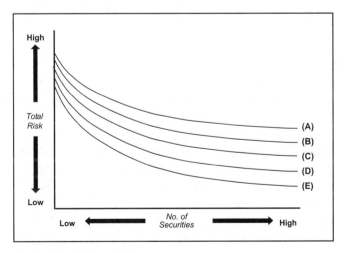

Source: Frush Financial Group

and small-cap value stocks; C represents a hypothetical portfolio of large-cap stocks, small-cap value stocks, *and* corporate bonds; D represents a hypothetical portfolio of large-cap stocks, small-cap value stocks, corporate bonds, *and* real estate; and E represents a hypothetical portfolio of large-cap stocks, small-cap value stocks, corporate bonds, real estate, *and* international stocks.

FACTORS THAT IMPACT YOUR ASSET ALLOCATION

When determining the best asset mix, there are a number of factors to consider. These factors can be classified as either investor-centric inputs or investment-centric inputs. The investor-centric inputs are based on your own attitudes and investment-related objectives and constraints. Investment-centric inputs, on the other hand, are not directly related to you and arise directly from the market and other uncontrollable factors, such as correlations and volatility risk. Below is a discussion of the factors divided into the investor-centric inputs first, with the investment-centric inputs thereafter.

Investor-Centric Inputs

The following section examines specific variables attributed to individual investors that in aggregate impact—along with investment-centric variables—the asset allocation decision and the resulting asset mix of investments.

Risk Profile

Your risk profile is perhaps the most important input to the asset allocation framework. Your risk profile is made up of three similar, yet separate, components. These components include your *tolerance* for risk, your *capacity* for risk, and your *need* for risk. The lowest measure of the three is considered the maximum level of risk you should assume in your portfolio. For example, although an investor may have a high risk tolerance and high capacity to assume risk, that investor may not have the need to assume risk. Why? Many investors have a level of wealth that is more than adequate to fund their lifestyle and goals, now and in the future.

Unfortunately, investor risk profile is difficult to measure for three reasons. First, risk is specific to a situation and not a general rule applicable to all situations. Second, risk is not easily understood, and people therefore act irrationally and unpredictably. Third, an investor's risk profile changes over time; it is not static.

Determining your risk profile is rather subjective and therefore difficult to express as a quantifiable factor. One good solution is to complete a risk profile questionnaire available from most financial services firms.

SMART Goals

Having investment goals and striving to attain those goals will give your investing purpose. Goals will directly impact your asset mix. Do you need money for a new home, or will you be purchasing a new business perhaps? As a result, you may want to overweight fixed income and underweight equities. Conversely, overweighting equities is ideal for the parents saving for a future college education over 10 years away. Matching asset classes to goals is key to achieving long-term investment success. The word *SMART* is oftentimes used to illustrate the five characteristics of well-designed goals.

- **S**pecific: Your goals should be unambiguous, clear, and well defined.
- **M**easurable: Your goals should be quantifiable and calculable.
- **A**ccepted: Your goals should be acknowledged and motivational.
- **R**ealistic: Your goals should be achievable and attainable, but not lofty.
- **T**imely: Your goals should be for a set period, not indefinite.

Investment Objectives

Once you have identified your SMART goals, zeroing in on an investment objective needed to achieve the goals is next. Investment objectives are commonly expressed in performance terms, such as the return an investor may need per year to achieve his or her goals. This is done in order to give you a better perspective on what return you are going to need in order to achieve your SMART goals. Your return objective will then dictate the ideal asset mix of your portfolio.

Investment Knowledge

Time and time again we hear "invest in what you know." Investment titans Warren Buffett and Peter Lynch propagated this belief. The more knowledgeable you are about a specific investment, the more confident and certain you are regarding whether or not that investment is appropriate and suitable. All else being equal, greater investment knowledge means a higher risk profile and the flexibility to construct a portfolio with higher risk.

Current and Projected Financial Position

Your level of wealth plays a significant role in determining your asset allocation. In general, investors with higher levels of wealth tend to have greater risk capacity. Simply put, wealthy investors have more room for error in achieving their goals. Of course, this is not always the case, but as a general rule it usually holds true. Conversely, investors with lower levels of wealth tend to have lower risk capacity.

Time Horizon

The primary consideration of time horizon is to help you determine the portfolio balance between equities and fixed income, namely bonds and cash. All else being equal, the longer your time horizon, the more you should overweight equities and underweight fixed income in your portfolio.

The most pressing type of risk over the long term is purchasing power risk, or the loss in an asset's real value due to inflation. Equities provide the best hedge against this type of risk. In the short term, the most pressing risk is price volatility. Fixed income provides the best hedge against this type of risk.

Income and Liquidity

Your need for current income and liquidity impacts how you allocate your portfolio. Investors that live partly off their portfolios will require highly liquid and higher-than-usual income-paying assets. Furthermore, investors in this position will typically have a much higher need for safeguarding the principal in their portfolios. As a result, overweighting fixed-income assets will be a top priority.

Tax Status and Tax Considerations

For investors with taxable accounts, attention should be given to the tax efficiency of investments. Investors with high federal tax rates will typically find it favorable to invest in tax-exempt municipal bonds rather than taxable corporate bonds. Tax management is very important since taxes on capital gains, interest, and dividends can reduce total portfolio performance—sometimes significantly. Deferring and minimizing taxes are strongly encouraged whenever possible.

The following are three areas related to taxes investors should consider when determining their asset mix:

1. **Capital Gains:** Capital gains taxes are those taxes on the appreciation of an investment that has been sold. Decisions to liquidate investments should be evaluated with respect to their specific tax implications. However, investment decisions take utmost priority over tax considerations. For example, it is not prudent to hold an unsuitable investment just to defer capital gains taxes.

2. **Growth Versus Income:** Taxes on interest and dividends received become taxable in the year received. But gains from the appreciation of an investment are not taxable until they are realized via a sale of the investment. This distinction gives investors some flexibility with determining when and where taxes are paid.

3. **Tax-Exempt Investments:** Depending on your total combined tax rate, it may be ideal to substitute higher-yielding taxable investments, such as corporate bonds, with lower-yielding tax-exempt investments, such as municipal bonds. Why? The after-tax return might be higher with respect to lower-yielding tax-exempt investments than with higher-yielding taxable investments. It's the net return that counts.

Legal and Regulatory Considerations

Legal and regulatory considerations are much more prevalent with institutional investors than with individual investors. However, some of the legal and regulatory considerations you may encounter involve IRA contributions and withdrawals, employee stock option exercises, and challenges of restricted stock. Depending on the specific situation, you may need to build a portfolio with greater liquidity and cash positions.

Unique Preferences and Circumstances

This factor incorporates anything that cannot be categorized elsewhere and is typically unique to a particular investor. Examples of unique circumstances and preferences include the following items:

- Financially supporting a dependent parent or challenged adult child
- Excluding investments in energy or tobacco for socially conscious reasons
- Being restricted from certain investments due to one's job
- Filing for bankruptcy or having excessive debt payments

Investment-Centric Inputs

The following section examines specific factors attributed to individual investments that in aggregate impact—along with investor-centric variables—the asset allocation decision and the resulting asset mix of investments.

Correlations

Correlation is a mathematical calculation used to measure and convey how the prices of two investments move in relation to each other. Your task is to target asset classes that exhibit low, if not negative, correlations with other asset classes. Therefore, allocating to equities, fixed income, and alternative assets is strongly encouraged, as you can gain correlation benefits from these fundamentally different asset classes.

Expected Total Returns

Building an optimal portfolio requires knowledge and application of both current and expected future returns. Without this knowledge and ability to model in expected returns, you might design a portfolio where expected returns are not adequate to reach your SMART goals. Remember, you can't hit a target you are not aiming for.

Risk Management Opportunities

It is important that investors have a grasp of how to manage and control risk when appropriate. This is important because the greater the opportunities to manage risk, the greater the potential to maximize return for the level of risk assumed. Investing in a basket or pool of similar investments minimizes investment-specific risk, or the risk associated with individual investments. Other opportunities for managing risk include the availability of derivatives, specifically put options, and the wherewithal to employ those derivatives. Put options don't mean much if you can't employ them to your benefit.

Inherent Volatility

Inherent volatility is the degree to which the price of an investment changes due to definable characteristics related to the investment. Greater inherent volatility translates into greater risk—and ultimately the need to reduce risk. Inherent volatility can arise from the following characteristics associated with a company's activities:

- Industry or sector
- Sensitivity to interest rates
- Sensitivity to changes in interest rates
- Float or shares outstanding
- Degree of uncertainty in expected returns

Type of Returns

Are you looking for growth or income? How about deferred or immediate earnings? Each asset class can be classified as providing current income, market-value appreciation, or some combination of the two. In consequence, it is important to determine if certain investments match your needs or desire for current income. For instance, S&P 500 ETFs typically pay current income based on the dividends of the stocks in the S&P 500. Conversely, growth ETFs typically pay little to no dividends since growth stocks prefer to reinvest their earnings. For investors desiring current income, knowing the differences among asset classes is important.

Trading Flexibility

You will soon discover—if you have not already—that some asset classes are much easier to trade than others. Depending on their inherent nature, some asset classes are less liquid than others, and that can mean higher trading costs in terms of one-half of the bid-ask spread. In addition, some asset classes are more difficult to invest in due to their availability, such as micro caps, small caps, emerging markets, and commodities.

General Nature

Aside from liquidity, trading costs, and availability as mentioned previously, asset classes also differ in regard to size, differentiation, definability, and completeness. Small differences between asset classes may not be material when determining your asset allocation; however, large differences and many small differences may create a scenario where the asset class is considered fundamentally different from others—a good thing for asset allocation purposes.

SIMPLE WAYS TO DETERMINE YOUR ASSET ALLOCATION

Numerous methods are available to help you design an optimal asset mix. A few of the most common methods include equity overload, simple 110, cash-flow matching, risk avoidance, allocation timing, and custom combination. Note that these methods are very simplistic and do not take into account many of the unique circumstances each investor has—they tend to be very general in nature. Chapters 17 and 18 in this book present multiple sample ETF portfolios for your reference.

Equity Overload

Historically, equity assets have outperformed all other primary asset classes over time. This is the rationale that many investors and financial professionals use to support a portfolio that significantly overweights equities. Volatility risk in such a portfolio can be substantial, however.

Simple 110

This is one of the most commonly employed methods for determining asset allocation, but it is given here with a twist. Under this model, you allocate a percentage to equities and alternative assets based on the equation *110 minus your age*. The remaining portion is allocated to fixed income. For example, a 65-year-old investor would allocate 45 percent to equities and alternatives (110 – 65) and the remaining 55 percent to fixed income. The underlying assumption of this model is that an investor's risk profile—and therefore portfolio risk—will decline with each passing year.

Cash-Flow Matching

Cash-flow matching attempts to match your anticipated future cash inflows with your anticipated future cash outflows. The first step in this complex model is to identify all anticipated future financial obligations. The second step is to identify all anticipated future financial inflows from noninvestment sources, such as wages, social security, and pensions. Third, determine the gap between the two. Fourth, evaluate your current portfolio against what will be needed from your portfolio in the future to fill the gap or gaps. This evaluation will determine what investment performance you must achieve in order to plug the gaps. For example, an investor determines that he will need to earn 6 percent per year in his portfolio to fund his desired retirement. Six percent is a reasonable expectation, and a well-diversified and optimally allocated portfolio should be expected to generate this return over time.

Forecasting skill, lack of preciseness in estimating life expectancy, and uncontrollable or unforeseen market factors are some of the drawbacks of employing this asset allocation method.

Risk Avoidance

Regardless of risk capacity and need to assume risk, some investors simply do not want to take risk (i.e., their tolerance for risk is exceptionally low). They can't stomach it. As a result, overweighting conservative assets is typically the best recipe—something that will help this kind of investor sleep better at night. Although many investors in this situation may feel secure today, they may be jeopardizing a safe and secure retirement. This method is underscored by the application of behavioral finance to investment decision making.

Allocation Timing

Under this method, asset allocations are selected and changes made with modest frequency in the hope of capturing incremental profits. This might include overweighting those asset classes showing the most relative price strength (e.g., the trend is your friend). However, it might also include a contrarian approach of overweighting to asset classes when they are out of favor—such as equities during bearish stock markets—with the hope of selling near the peak when equities are back in favor. This is obviously a market timing strategy and therefore should be approached with care.

Custom Combination

Since many of the methods discussed have one or more drawbacks to them, using a combination may therefore be appropriate. Many financial professionals have gone this route and designed their own unique methods that utilize the best from one or more of the methods. The vast majority employ some sort of cash-flow matching combined with allocation timing. Doing so allows them to establish an asset allocation best suitable for the investor while providing the flexibility to promote their skills in portfolio management—the perceived bread-and-butter way to attract new clients.

THE RIGHT APPROACH

Building and safeguarding a winning portfolio is entirely dependent on how well a portfolio is designed, constructed, and managed. The primary determinant of how well a portfolio eventually performs over time is the asset allocation plan employed.

It is no secret that the majority of portfolio managers do not beat the return of the market each year. Furthermore, according to statistics, those portfolio managers who do beat the market in any given year have a lower probability of beating the market in the following year.

The key to a lifetime of investment success is not complex, nor difficult to understand or apply. The essence of asset allocation is all about gaining and maintaining an edge that will promote long-term investment performance and ensure financial independence, control, and security over time. When designing your portfolio, always remember "al-location, al-location, al-location."

CHAPTER 16

Leading Misconceptions: Separating ETF Fact From Fiction

Given the relatively more recent introduction of exchange-traded funds (ETFs) to the investing marketplace, there are a number of misconceptions investors have due to either a lack of true understanding or a lack of exposure to ETFs—or both. Some of the misconceptions are justifiable; others seem to come out of left field. The majority of these misconceptions center on how ETFs work internally and what benefits and drawbacks they inherently possess. To better help you to understand what ETFs are all about, a chapter on what they *surely are not* may paint a clearer picture and put things in better perspective. The following are some of the more prominent misconceptions about ETFs, with a brief discussion of each.

ALL ETFs ARE FUNDS OR INVESTMENT COMPANIES

Many people casually refer to all exchange-traded portfolios (ETPs) as ETFs. Although this label is not accurate, it has caught on with mainstream investors and is now considered the default and universal generic term for all ETPs. The ETF label is used inappropriately to describe some open-end structured notes, a few grantor trusts, and nearly all commodity-based partnerships and currency pools. In reality, the term *exchange-traded portfolio* is more fitting as an umbrella term, with ETFs a branch of ETPs. I liken this play on labels to mobile phones, where many people still call them cell phones even though "cell" technology is long gone, having become technologically obsolete. Nonetheless, both cell phone and ETF labels are here to stay for the foreseeable future.

ETFs ONLY HOLD STOCKS AND BONDS

The earliest ETFs exclusively held common stock of publicly traded corporations or fixed-income securities from corporations, governments, or federal agencies. Over the years as new innovations in ETFs were made, nontraditional holdings began to appear in ETFs. Currencies and physical commodities were the first alternative investments, followed by futures contracts on commodities. The newest innovation is the holding of swaps to create either leverage or inverse exposure to desired market segments. The actual types of underlying holdings are varied and should continue to grow over time.

ALL ETFs ARE THE SAME

From a 30,000-foot perspective, ETFs may appear the same—especially to the novice investor—but the truth is, given the different legal structures and the different indexes and underlying assets they hold, ETFs are extremely different from one another. Furthermore, even ETFs that track the same index can be different, as they might not employ the same tracking methodology or might have different cost structures. Finally, ETF providers go to great lengths to brand their ETFs and therefore send shareholders the message of how different and better they are from other ETFs.

ETFs ONLY TRACK TRADITIONAL INDEXES

Another leading misconception is that ETFs only track the widely recognizable indexes, such as the S&P 500 and the Dow Jones Industrial Average. Although this was true at the very onset of ETFs, this is nothing close to reality today. Many ETFs do track market indexes, but many now track custom indexes designed by ETF providers to enable the use of active management rather than passive management. Numerous other ETFs track less recognizable market indexes, and others track economic sectors, industry groups, and broad-based styles and sizes.

ETFs ARE ALWAYS PASSIVELY MANAGED

Although many ETFs are passively managed, there are no requirements that ETFs must adhere to any specific management style. Over the last couple of years, actively managed ETFs have grown in number and size, fueled by the tax-efficiency and stocklike tradability benefits that mutual funds do not possess. Within a short time, actively managed ETFs have gone from the design stage to a very robust and hypergrowth market. Think of actively managed ETFs as the top college football player who was recently selected number one in the NFL draft. The player has tons of potential, but just needs more playing time to learn the system, refine his skills, and ultimately dominate the field.

ETFs TRACK ALL EXISTING MARKET INDEXES

A popular fallacy with ETFs is that there is an ETF available for every index, sector, or market segment in existence. This is simply not the case—and far from the truth, for that matter. As of early 2011, there were more than 1,100 ETFs in the marketplace. Many of these ETFs track market indexes, and many track proprietary indexes customized by ETF providers to employ actively managed strategies. Dow Jones Indexes alone boasts over 3,000 indexes, a number still lower than what other index sponsors offer. Thus, the numbers simply do not work out to support the claim for at least one ETF per existing index. Many of the existing market indexes are ignored by ETF providers because they track markets in less-developed countries and regions, such as the Mid-Cap India Index. Even though we have witnessed an explosion in the number of ETFs, the same can be said for market indexes. It's similar to the analogy of a dog chasing its tail.

ETFs ARE HIGHLY COMPLEX

As we all know, many people are uncomfortable with new and unfamiliar things. The same goes for investors and ETFs. As a result, many investors—because they lack familiarity with the investment—view ETFs as being highly complex. The opposite, however, is more accurate, as ETFs are nothing more than accounts or pools of underlying securities. Aside from the more technical creation and redemption processes, ETFs are very similar to mutual funds or portfolios of stocks. ETFs may trade like stocks, but they have more in common with mutual funds—and that should give investors added confidence.

ETFs ARE ONLY SUITABLE FOR SPECULATORS AND MARKET TIMERS

Due to the stocklike tradability of ETFs, many people mistakenly believe that ETFs are much better suited to speculators, market timers, and others with short-term investing time horizons. However, given the more favorable cost structure ETFs have over mutual funds, ETFs are much better suited to long-term investors than are mutual funds. ETFs are tax efficient, charge much lower expense ratios, and do not sock shareholders with flow or subsidy trading costs attributed to shareholders entering and exiting a fund.

ETFs ALWAYS HAVE LOWER EXPENSES THAN MUTUAL FUNDS

For the most part, ETFs are much less costly than comparable mutual funds in nearly all expense categories. However, transacting ETFs does incur trading commissions, unlike mutual funds, which are commission-free when transacted with the fund family. Given the advent of actively managed ETFs, the cost advantage becomes much less clear. Actively managed ETFs require portfolio managers and support staff—which means higher operating costs. These costs must be offset with higher expense ratios. In addition, the more technical actively managed ETFs—specifically leveraged and inverse funds—charge higher expense ratios than one might think. These costs are higher than many no-load actively managed mutual funds. The moral of the story—investors must do their homework to uncover all costs to make smart investing decisions.

ETFs CANNOT OUTPERFORM THE MARKET

Time and time again I hear uninformed investors and investment professionals say you can't make real money in ETFs since they cannot outperform the market. This claim does not take into account the full story of why ETFs are so beneficial. ETFs not only offer lower internal expenses, which adds to the bottom line, but also provide for optimally allocated portfolios. Numerous research studies have concluded that *how* you allocate your investments, rather than *which* individual investments you select or *when* you buy or sell them, is the leading determinant of investment performance over time. ETFs are significantly more asset allocation and rebalancing friendly than stocks or mutual funds. Alternatively, not all ETFs track market indexes that generate beta or market performance. Actively managed ETFs (including leveraged ETFs) were introduced to generate alpha, or to outperform the market. Thus, for investors who are willing to pay higher costs and roll the dice, actively managed ETFs offer the chance to outperform the market.

ETF TRANSPARENCY IS DESIRABLE IN ALL SITUATIONS

Full transparency is very appealing in all cases, isn't it? From one perspective, transparency of market price, net asset value, and underlying holdings is desirable, as it gives shareholders needed information to make comparisons against other ETFs and mutual funds. Unfortunately, full transparency also comes with some unforeseen drawbacks. The specific issue with full transparency arises from trades needed to track underlying indexes. Once an index sponsor preannounces reconstitution to a market index, then speculators—known in practice as scalpers—can front-run the ETF provider by purchasing the security to be added to the index and selling the security to be replaced—all before the index itself is officially reconstituted and ETF providers can subsequently rebalance the holdings. These front-running transactions drive up costs for an ETF that needs to make changes in order to track the underlying market index. This fund-level cost is embedded in the ETF with little to no knowledge of shareholders.

HIGHER ETF TRADING VOLUME MEANS HIGHER LIQUIDITY

What is probably the top misconception with ETFs has to do with trading volume and related liquidity. With stocks, higher trading volumes equate to higher liquidity. Investors mistakenly apply this same logic to ETFs. In addition, some investors believe that higher trading volume also means an ETF is somehow more useful. Neither of these claims is entirely accurate. An ETF's usefulness is not aligned with its trading volume. The inherent benefits of ETFs emphasize tax efficiency, low cost, and stocklike tradability among others. ETF liquidity is not defined by its trading volume as with stocks, but rather is defined by the liquidity of each underlying security. The higher the aggregate liquidity of the underlying securities, the higher the liquidity of the ETF. There are other factors explaining ETF liquidity on the fund level, but they are less impactful.

ETFs DO NOT SCREEN OUT THE DOGS

If you were to listen to financial anchors on various cable networks or radio stations, you would hear some of them slamming ETFs because ETFs include both good and bad companies—they are not selective. Their message is that investors should avoid ETFs and only invest in the common stocks of good companies. In reality, this message has two titanic flaws. First and foremost, if picking the *good* companies were so easy, then why do more than half of professional money managers—backed by highly paid research analysts—not beat the return of their appropriate benchmark each year? Picking high-performance stocks is exceptionally difficult. Selecting stocks by throwing darts often produces better results. Secondly, there is a distinct difference between good companies and good stocks and bad companies and bad stocks. The stock of a good company may be in such high demand that its fundamentals do not justify its current stock price. Furthermore, bad companies can be ignored to such a degree that their stock prices become grossly undervalued.

Traditional Portfolios: ETF Models Based on Life Cycle and Risk Profile

Thus far we have discussed the basics and complexities of exchange-traded funds (ETFs) in addition to reviewing a menu of available investing opportunities. Furthermore, we discussed the importance of asset allocation and investing risk and return. This chapter brings all the previously discussed material together by focusing on the right portfolio for each investor. The material in this chapter emphasizes traditional portfolios based on investing life cycle and risk profile, while the next chapter switches gears and presents specialized portfolios based principally on investor sentiment such as bullish, bearish, or neutral on the market.

The investing life cycle is divided into three primary stages—accumulation, preretirement, and retirement. However, portfolios should not be based solely on life cycle since there are differences among investors in each stage. Some investors may find aggressive portfolios a better fit, whereas other investors will find conservative portfolios more suitable. It is for this reason that we take into consideration risk profile (tolerance for risk, capacity for risk, and need for risk) when identifying a suitable portfolio in each life-cycle stage. We will review each stage and then discuss different portfolio options suitable for an investor in each life-cycle stage.

ACCUMULATION STAGE

People in the accumulation stage are typically in their early to mid careers with long-term investing time horizons. Their net worth, and sometimes their income, is typically small relative to their total debt and other financial obligations. Some people in this group are in their educational years, such as grad school, and may either rent or own their first or second homes. Many people in this group will have student loans, credit card debt, and auto loans or leases and will be burdened by the associated debt payments. Although difficult to do, starting an investment plan in this stage of life is of primary importance. The key for people in this life-cycle group is to begin paying down debt, start saving for retirement, and buy a home, an asset that—the hope is—will appreciate well over time.

People in this group will typically have low to moderate living expenses, although their earnings power is generally lower, but growing. Paying for a mortgage or monthly rent is obviously much easier for two or more people than it is for just one. Another key factor revolves around having a family. Children will add a new complexity to a financial situation whereby expenses will go up and the need to save more will increase dramatically. Of course, having a dual income will help to greatly offset any increase in expenses.

Return Objective

With a long-term investing time horizon, people in the accumulation life-cycle stage should seek total returns by focusing their portfolios on capital gain, growth-oriented assets. At the same time, people in this stage need to be cognizant of current income generation and have a cash reserve to help with immediate and emergency spending needs.

Risk Profile

Due to their long-term investing time horizon, people in this stage have the ability to tolerate a high level of risk. However, some people will not have the stomach or need to assume risk. It is very important that you identify your true risk profile to better enable you to develop a sound financial plan. The Asset Allocator Questionnaire in Appendix B can help with this task.

Optimal Asset Allocation

The optimal mix of assets for people in this life-cycle group significantly overweights equities—both U.S. and international allocations (see Figure 17-1). These equity allocations should be subdivided into different market capitalization sizes for U.S. equities and into developed and emerging markets for international equities. As for fixed income, the proper asset mix should include different market segments with an emphasis on short-term bonds, long-term bonds, and high-yield bonds. TIPs, or Treasury Inflation-Protected Securities, can be added for those investors who are concerned with possible future hyperinflation. Real assets should be included, with priorities given to real estate investment trusts (REITs) and commodities. Given the return-enhancing and risk-reducing benefits of hedge funds to an overall portfolio, hedge fund exposure can be added for moderate to aggressive portfolios. Finally, a cash reserve for emergency situations is ideal and highly encouraged.

FIGURE 17-1

Optimal Asset Mix: Accumulation Stage

ASSET CLASS	Select ETF Options	Conservative Portfolio	Moderate Portfolio	Aggressive Portfolio
U.S. Equities				
Large Cap	VOO, IVV, JKD	10%	10%	15%
Mid Cap	VO, IWR, JKG	10%	10%	15%
Small Cap	VB, IWM, JKJ	5%	10%	15%
International Equities				
Developed Markets	VEU, IOO, EFA	5%	10%	15%
Emerging Markets	VWO, EEM, GMM	5%	10%	10%
U.S. Fixed Income				
Short Term	BSV, CSJ, MBG	10%	5%	0%
Long Term	BLV, LWC, LQD	15%	10%	5%
High Yield	JNK, HYG, ELD	10%	5%	5%

Continued

FIGURE 17-1

Optimal Asset Mix: Accumulation Stage (Cont.)

ASSET CLASS	Select ETF Options	Conservative Portfolio	Moderate Portfolio	Aggressive Portfolio
International Fixed Income				
Developed Markets	BWX, IGOV, BWZ	5%	5%	0%
Emerging Markets	EMB, PCY, DEM	5%	5%	0%
Real Assets				
Real Estate	IYR, VNQ, ICF	5%	5%	7.5%
Commodities	RJI, DBC, DJP	5%	5%	7.5%
Hedge Funds	QAI, ALT, CSLS	0%	5%	5%
Money Markets				
Cash Reserve	———	10%	5%	0%

PRERETIREMENT STAGE

People in this life-cycle group tend to be in their middle to late working years when their time horizon is still relatively long and their need for increased contributions to fund retirement savings is high. As people progress through this stage, their income begins to exceed their expenses, and therefore their capacity to make retirement contributions and pay down debt increases. Many people in this group have already achieved their highest level of education, although that's not always the case, and most people are already in their peak earning years. This is truly the optimal time in one's life to make retirement contributions. If not now, then when?

Many people in this group begin to wonder how much money it will take to sustain their desired level of spending and lifestyle into retirement. A good solution is first to identify how much money you believe you will need during retirement each year based partially on what you are presently spending and then to adjust that figure up or down depending on the desired lifestyle. For example, will you be golfing more or less in retirement? Will you be dining out more or less? After this step, identify all sources of noninvestment and nonpension income per year. Any gaps between what you believe you will need per year and what noninvestment and nonpension sources will provide is the amount per year you will need to plug with investment savings. A certified financial planner professional can help with this task.

People in this life-cycle group will also want to focus on many noninvestment-related tasks to protect their future financial security. These tasks include, but are not limited to, drafting estate planning documents; updating life, disability, and long-term care insurance; and gifting assets to reduce a potential estate tax bill.

Return Objective

Given their relatively long-term investing time horizon, those in the preretirement stage should seek total returns by focusing their portfolios on capital gain, growth-oriented assets. In addition, emphasis should be placed on reweighting to less risky investments as a person progresses through this life-cycle stage. Although some reweighting out of equities and into fixed income should be made, it is important to keep a balanced approach between the two.

Risk Profile

Due to their long-term investing time horizon, people in this stage have the capacity to tolerate above-average levels of risk. Remember, however, that an investor's risk capacity and tolerance for risk should be addressed within the context of their need to assume risk. Just because you have the stomach and capacity to assume more risk does not mean that you should, since you may not need to assume additional risk to achieve your financial goals and objectives. This is a very important consideration.

Optimal Asset Allocation

The optimal mix of assets for people in this life-cycle group will generally emphasize equities. To enhance the risk and return trade-off profile of the portfolio, allocating to multiple asset classes is always ideal. Specifically, allocating to large caps, mid caps, and small caps, as well as allocating to both international developed equities and international emerging markets equities, will maximize a portfolio's risk-adjusted return.

An allocation to fixed income is prudent, as this will decrease volatility risk and enhance risk-adjusted returns. Real assets should be added, with REITs and commodities the top focus. Similar to those in the accumulation stage, preretirees should also allocate anywhere from 5 to 10 percent to cash and equivalents for emergency and perhaps immediate spending needs (see Figure 17-2).

FIGURE 17-2

Optimal Asset Mix: Preretirement Stage

ASSET CLASS	Select ETF Options	Conservative Portfolio	Moderate Portfolio	Aggressive Portfolio
U.S. Equities				
Large Cap	VOO, IVV, JKD	5%	10%	15%
Mid Cap	VO, IWR, JKG	5%	10%	15%
Small Cap	VB, IWM, JKJ	5%	5%	10%
International Equities				
Developed Markets	VEU, IOO, EFA	5%	10%	15%
Emerging Markets	VWO, EEM, GMM	5%	10%	10%
U.S. Fixed Income				
Short Term	BSV, CSJ, MBG	15%	10%	5%
Long Term	BLV, LWC, LQD	20%	10%	0%
High Yield	JNK, HYG, ELD	10%	5%	5%
International Fixed Income				
Developed Markets	BWX, IGOV, BWZ	5%	5%	0%
Emerging Markets	EMB, PCY, DEM	5%	5%	0%
Real Assets				
Real Estate	IYR, VNQ, ICF	5%	5%	7.5%
Commodities	RJI, DBC, DJP	5%	5%	7.5%
Hedge Funds	QAI, ALT, CSLS	0%	5%	5%
Money Markets				
Cash Reserve	———	10%	5%	5%

RETIREMENT STAGE

At some point, many retirees will discover that they have more assets than they will ever need. As a result, some will decide to gift some or most of their assets to heirs or charitable organizations either immediately, throughout their lives, or as bequests. Managing a portfolio for a retiree is different from managing it for an heir or charity; thus a balance must be struck to accommodate both needs.

People in this life-cycle group are in one of the three stages of retirement—early, middle, or late—with time horizons ranging anywhere from 7 to 20 years or more. In addition, although a portfolio may be managed with the short term in mind, a change to a long-term approach can occur when the gifting of assets is desired. For example, if an investor has a $1 million portfolio and desires to gift half of that amount to his or her alma mater in 5 years, then having that portfolio invested only in conservative assets may be a disservice to the university. Over that 5-year period, the portion intended as a gift may experience higher returns if invested partially or wholly in equities. Since universities have long-term time horizons themselves, managing those assets earmarked as gifts is prudent. Plus, a larger gift is a larger tax deduction anyway.

For many retirees, their expenses will exceed their noninvestment income in retirement, which obviously creates a scenario in which living expenses will need to be supplemented by investment and retirement income. Developing a portfolio asset allocation to accommodate this purpose is thus highly desirable.

Return Objective

Given the varying time horizons, retirees should strike a balance between equities and fixed-income investments. Those with longer-term investing time horizons should overweight equities, and those with shorter-term investing time horizons should overweight fixed income. The risk profile of the investor also plays a significant role in the asset allocation and thus the expected portfolio return. Matching expected returns and cash inflows with anticipated financial obligations is a smart move.

Risk Profile

Given a more modest investing time horizon and relatively minimal noninvestment and nonpension income, retirees typically have a lower capacity for risk than both accumulators and preretirees. As a result, the risk profile of retirees tends to be conservative to moderate. People with higher levels of wealth will naturally have a higher capacity for risk, but their tolerance or need may signal a conservative to moderate portfolio. Remember that although you may have the tolerance and capacity for risk, you may not have the need. Taking more risk with no need for additional reward is simply unnecessary risk taking and not especially smart decision making.

Optimal Asset Allocation

The optimal mix of assets for retirees emphasizes a balance between equity and fixed-income assets. For those investors with either longer time horizons or higher risk profiles, a portfolio overweighting equities is prudent. Enhancing the risk and return tradeoff profile should be of primary concern and can be accomplished by adding multiple asset classes. In addition, fixed income should comprise U.S. corporate bonds, high-yield bonds, and international fixed income.

Investing in REITs should be done regardless of the portfolio, whereas investing in commodities and hedge funds should only be included in moderate or, more important, aggressive portfolios. Holding cash is especially vital for retirees and thus highly encouraged (see Figure 17-3).

FIGURE 17-3

Optimal Asset Mix: Retirement Stage

ASSET CLASS	*Select ETF Options*	Conservative Portfolio	Moderate Portfolio	Aggressive Portfolio
U.S. Equities				
Large Cap	VOO, IVV, JKD	5%	5%	15%
Mid Cap	VO, IWR, JKG	5%	5%	10%
Small Cap	VB, IWM, JKJ	0%	5%	10%
International Equities				
Developed Markets	VEU, IOO, EFA	5%	5%	10%
Emerging Markets	VWO, EEM, GMM	0%	5%	10%
U.S. Fixed Income				
Short Term	BSV, CSJ, MBG	20%	15%	10%
Long Term	BLV, LWC, LQD	25%	20%	5%
High Yield	JNK, HYG, ELD	10%	5%	5%
International Fixed Income				
Developed Markets	BWX, IGOV, BWZ	5%	10%	5%
Emerging Markets	EMB, PCY, DEM	5%	5%	0%
Real Assets				
Real Estate	IYR, VNQ, ICF	5%	5%	5%
Commodities	RJI, DBC, DJP	0%	5%	5%
Hedge Funds	QAI, ALT, CSLS	0%	0%	5%
Money Markets				
Cash Reserve	————	15%	10%	5%

## CHAPTER 18

Specialized Portfolios: Bullish, Bearish, Sideways, and Focus Models

For investors who are not interested in employing a traditional portfolio based on life cycle and risk profile, this chapter presents a number of specialized portfolios based on investor sentiment regarding market direction and economic conditions. Some investors want to position their portfolios to take advantage of what they believe will be rising markets, whereas others want to take a contrarian approach and position their portfolios to profit if the market were to fall. Still others may believe that the market could be stuck in a tight trading range for an extended period of time. This group of investors will want to build a portfolio to generate the highest total returns consisting of both market-value appreciation and ordinary income from interest and dividends. There are investors who have an overriding fear of inflation and thus want to protect their portfolios in the best way possible. Finally, there are other investors who believe overweighting alternative assets is the best way to safeguard a portfolio during uncertain economic and geopolitical times.

Irrespective of the type of investor you might be and your thoughts for where the market might be headed, the following models should provide you with ideas for making money under the appropriate scenario. Unlike the previous chapter where the models were well allocated among the primary asset classes and divided into conservative, moderate, and aggressive portfolios, the models in this chapter are more refined and more segmented. As such, there is no consideration for risk profile, and there is no significant emphasis on optimally allocating a portfolio. Rather, each model portfolio incorporates 10 different exchange-traded funds (ETFs) of similar weights for simplicity purposes. Remember, however, that these model portfolios are just that—they are models only. Although these portfolios offer sample holdings, consider your own personal financial situation before moving forward with any of these models. The goal with these models is to develop portfolios using ETFs that generate the highest total rate of return under different future market conditions.

BULLISH MODEL

FIGURE 18-1

Portfolio Composition: Bullish Model

Portfolio Strategy: An aggressive strategy to take advantage of anticipated strong returns in the equity market

#	Symbol	ETF	Expense Ratio	Target Weighting
1	SSO	ProShares Ultra S&P500	0.92%	12%
2	VEU	Vanguard FTSE All-World EX-US	0.22%	12%
3	VWO	Vanguard MSCI Emerging Markets	0.22%	12%
4	IWM	iShares Russell 2000 Index	0.20%	12%
5	JNK	SPDR Barclays Capital High Yield Bond	0.40%	10%
6	TBT	ProShares UltraShort 20+ Year Treasury	0.95%	10%
7	VO	Vanguard Mid Cap	0.12%	8%
8	QQQ	PowerShares QQQ	0.20%	8%
9	GMF	SPDR S&P Emerging Asia Pacific	0.60%	8%
10	DBB	PowerShares DB Base Metals	0.76%	8%
				100%

The bullish strategy accordingly overweights equities, including the use of one leveraged ETF to capture incremental gains. As you can see from Figure 18-1, significant emphasis is placed on international equities with the inclusion of the developed market FTSE All-World Ex-U.S., emerging market, and finally targeted exposure to emerging Asia Pacific. There is some overlapping exposure of the two emerging markets ETFs to gain from this high-growth region. Also included are small caps through the Russell 2000, mid caps through the Vanguard Mid Cap ETF, and the 100 largest stocks in the Nasdaq via the PowerShares QQQ. The SPDR high-yield bond is included since good markets typically favor high-yield bond prices. However, healthy markets can trigger higher interest rates, and for that matter the bullish strategy calls for selling short long-maturity Treasuries. Finally, if the pace of economic activity rises, so too will the demand for base or industrial metals—thus the reasoning behind adding the PowerShares DB (Deutsche Bank) Base Metals ETF.

BEARISH MODEL

FIGURE 18-2

Portfolio Composition: Bearish Model

Portfolio Strategy: A contrarian strategy to protect or profit from an anticipated decline in the equity market

#	Symbol	ETF	Expense Ratio	Target Weighting
1	SH	ProShares Short S&P 500	0.92%	12%
2	MINT	PIMCO Enhanced Short Maturity Strgy	0.35%	12%
3	TIP	iShares Barclays TIPS Bond	0.20%	12%
4	RWM	ProShares Short Russell 2000	0.95%	12%
5	GLD	SPDR Gold Shares	0.40%	10%
6	LSC	ELEMENTS S&P Commodity Trends	0.75%	10%
7	PSQ	ProShares Short QQQ	0.95%	8%
8	WDTI	WisdomTree Managed Futures	0.95%	8%
9	IEI	iShares Barclays 3-7 Year Treasury Bond	0.15%	8%
10	SJB	ProShares Short High Yield	0.95%	8%
				100%

The bearish strategy emphasizes those ETFs that should generate gains when the overall stock market falls. This strategy calls for the addition of three inverse (but not leveraged) ETFs to profit from falling stock prices. In Figure 18-2, these three market indexes include the S&P 500, the Russell 2000 (small caps), and the Nasdaq-

100 (ProShares Short QQQ). The second part of this strategy includes fixed-income ETFs that insulate against a declining stock market, which typically happens as investors seek out safer areas to place proceeds from equity sales. The top two ETFs are the short-maturity PIMCO ETF and the iShares TIPS Bond ETF, which is a Treasury Inflation-Protected Securities (TIPS) fund. Exposure to gold is suggested as a hedge, while the ELEMENTS commodity trends ETF is included since it can go long or short, depending on the price trend of commodities, and thus has the potential to generate gains in falling equity markets. Managed futures are included for their aim to produce absolute, or positive, returns, rather than relative, or market, returns. Selling high-yield bonds short can produce gains since many investors switch from higher-risk high-yield bonds to safer agency and Treasury bonds during economic periods of concern.

SIDEWAYS (NEUTRAL) MODEL

FIGURE 18-3

Portfolio Composition: Sideways Model

Portfolio Strategy: A strategy to generate high total returns through appreciation, but more importantly through consistent dividends and interest

#	Symbol	ETF	Expense Ratio	Target Weighting
1	PBP	PowerShares S&P 500 BuyWrite	0.75%	12%
2	LSC	ELEMENTS S&P Commodity Trends	0.75%	12%
3	AMJ	JPMorgan Alerian MLP Index	0.85%	12%
4	PFF	iShares S&P U.S. Preferred Stock Index	0.48%	12%
5	SDY	SPDR S&P Dividend	0.35%	10%
6	CWB	SPDR Barclays Capital Convertible Secs	0.40%	10%
7	DBV	PowerShares DB G10 Currency Harvest	0.81%	8%
8	DVY	iShares Dow Jones Select Dividend Index	0.40%	8%
9	DOO	WisdomTree Intl. Dividend EX-Financials	0.58%	8%
10	JNK	SPDR Barclays Capital High Yield Bond	0.40%	8%
				100%

The sideways or neutral strategy will overweight those ETFs that either generate abnormally high dividends or can produce gains irrespective of market direction. In Figure 18-3, the BuyWrite

ETF is a covered call strategy for producing income by writing covered calls and collecting the premiums. As mentioned in the previous model, the commodity trends ETF has the potential to generate gains under any equity market scenario, while the JPMorgan ETF is an energy pipeline play that offers high dividends from income collected to move natural gas across pipelines. The preferred stock ETF, S&P Dividend ETF, Dow Jones Select Dividend ETF, WisdomTree International Dividend, and SPDR Barclays Capital High Yield Bond ETF are included to provide higher than normal dividend yields to maximize total returns.

RISING INFLATION MODEL

FIGURE 18-4

Portfolio Composition: Rising Inflation Model

Portfolio Strategy: A strategy to benefit not only when interest rates begin to rise, but also while they are actually rising and sustaining high rates

#	Symbol	ETF	Expense Ratio	Target Weighting
1	STPZ	PIMCO 1-5 Year US TIPS Index ETF	0.20%	12%
2	TBT	ProShares UltraShort 20+ Year Treasury	0.95%	12%
3	BKLN	PowerShares Senior Loan Portfolio	0.83%	12%
4	RJI	ELEMENTS Rogers Intl Commodity	0.75%	12%
5	WIP	SPDR DB Intl Govt Infl-Protected Bond	0.50%	10%
6	JNK	SPDR Barclays Capital High Yield Bond	0.40%	10%
7	DBB	PowerShares DB Base Metals	0.76%	8%
8	VNQ	Vanguard REIT Index	0.12%	8%
9	FIO	iShares FTSE NAREIT Industrial/Office	0.48%	8%
10	VB	Vanguard Small Cap	0.12%	8%
				100%

The rising inflation strategy, illustrated in Figure 18-4, incorporates a number of ETFs that are in favor when investors are concerned with inflation and the loss of purchasing power. As a result, only one traditional equity ETF is included—the small-cap Vanguard fund—with the other nine ETFs consisting of fixed-income, commodities, and REIT ETFs. The PIMCO TIPS ETF speaks for itself, as does the SPDR DB International TIPs ETF. Assets in the PowerShares Senior Loan ETF are tied to market interest rates, which will provide a measure of market-value protection and offer higher interest rates as market rates rise. Since market values of bonds—especially those with long maturities—move inversely to changes in market interest rates, then purchasing the inverse Treasury bond ETF should take advantage of this dynamic. Commodities are included, as they typically do well with rising inflation. Office and rental rates are oftentimes tied to inflation rates, and so REITs have the potential to outperform during high-inflation periods.

ALTERNATIVE ASSET

FIGURE 18-5

Portfolio Composition: Alternative Asset Model

Portfolio Strategy: A disengaged aggressive portfolio of nontraditional assets to profit from rising commodity and real estate values

#	Symbol	ETF	Expense Ratio	Target Weighting
1	RJI	ELEMENTS Rogers Intl Commodity	0.75%	12%
2	RWO	SPDR Dow Jones Global Real Estate	0.50%	12%
3	CCX	WisdomTree Dreyfus Commodity Currency	0.55%	12%
4	USO	United States Oil Fund	0.78%	12%
5	MOO	Market Vectors Agribusiness ETF	0.55%	10%
6	URE	ProShares Ultra Real Estate	0.95%	10%
7	GLD	SPDR Gold Shares	0.40%	8%
8	DBB	PowerShares DB Base Metals	0.76%	8%
9	WDTI	WisdomTree Managed Futures	0.95%	8%
10	COW	iPath DJ-UBS Livestock TR Sub-Index ETN	0.75%	8%
				100%

As exemplified in Figure 18-5, the alternative asset strategy incorporates various commodity classes as well as REITs. The ELEMENTS Rogers ETF is a broadly diversified all-commodity fund with exposure to over 30 different commodity classes. The United States Oil Fund, SPDR Gold, PowerShares DB Base Metals, and iPath Livestock ETFs are included for targeted commodity exposure above and beyond that of the Rogers ETF. Managed futures are added for more professional management of commodity futures. The leveraged ProShares ETF is added for extra exposure to REITs, and the SPDR Dow Jones REIT provides exposure to real estate across the globe. Finally, the currency ETF is added to round out the different types of real asset ETFs included in the strategy.

CHAPTER 19

Future of ETFs: Outlook, Perspectives, and Developing Trends

Exchange-traded funds (ETFs) have become a significant force with investing and wealth management. The growth of the trade in such a short period of time is truly astounding to novice and experienced trader alike. Today, there are more than 1,100 ETFs in the U.S. marketplace with over $1 trillion in assets under management (AuM)—figures that will surely rise going forward. The last 15 or so years have provided the foundation and support for ETFs to grow and flourish—with a bright future ahead. Let's put the past behind us for a moment and think about the future and envision what it may hold for ETF investing.

Many questions quickly surface when we brainstorm all the various possibilities. Will present-day conditions and trends continue into the future, or will they change dramatically—and why? Will ETFs surpass mutual funds in AuM? What new innovation will enhance an already highly favorable investment? One thing is for certain: the ETF marketplace will experience foreseen and unforeseen changes over the next several-plus years. But what will these changes specifically impact, and how will they make that impact? Figure 19-1 illustrates the 11 most impactful changes likely to occur in the future with respect to ETFs and the investing marketplace:

FIGURE 19-1

Probable Future Changes Impacting ETFs

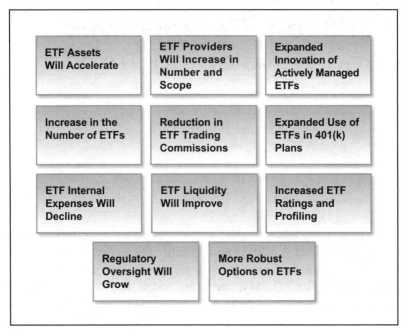

Source: Frush Financial Group

1. ETF AuM WILL ACCELERATE

This assertion is so much common sense that I almost decided to leave it off the list. However, in the spirit of presenting the most impactful future changes with ETFs, I finally resolved to include it. There is no arguing with the fact that ETFs are gaining popularity with investors and financial professionals each and every day. The result, of course, means more assets flowing into ETFs. From a macro perspective, this trend will continue for years to come. Obviously, stock market declines will slow down—if not reverse—the flow of assets into ETFs, but any such occurrence will be transitory in nature. New assets into ETFs will come from two types of sources. First, new assets will flow from virgin money—meaning money that has not been invested before, such as 401(k) contributions that purchase ETFs. Second, new assets will flow out of existing investments, specifically mutual funds, closed-end funds, and even hedge funds. All else being equal, ETFs will continue their charge forward and close the AuM gap with mutual funds.

2. ETF PROVIDERS WILL INCREASE IN NUMBER AND SCOPE

This trend has been developing for some time now, as existing ETF providers expand in size and scope and establish new ETFs for their product offerings. Over the next few years, ETF providers will strive to add more funds and grow their assets in order to gain more favorable economies of scale. With the money many of these ETF providers earn, funding greater expansion will not be especially difficult. This expansion will most likely create mega-ETF providers—with many rivaling the size and scope of powerhouse iShares.

3. EXPANDED INNOVATION OF ACTIVELY MANAGED ETFs

One of the best innovations I have seen over the last couple of years is the creation of bond ETFs with predetermined maturity dates. With these ETFs, all the underlying bonds selected have the same maturity year—so when the ETF terminates, the bonds will pay back par value (face value). The aim is to ease the concern of investors who want to invest in bond ETFs but do not want to lose money if interest rates were to increase and force down the price of bonds over the holding period. This is the type of innovation I envision will continue to grow and gain traction. As mentioned previously throughout this book, the marketplace for ETFs tracking market indexes has been cornered, so to speak, by the largest and most reputable ETF providers. In order to gain new assets, smaller providers will be forced to innovate and develop new ETFs that track custom indexes—and indexes that have not been thought of to date. Commodity-linked ETFs as well as state-specific ETFs will surely draw greater emphasis over time. Although I am a proponent of ETFs that track market indexes, a greater number of ETFs—even if they track custom indexes—will ultimately benefit, rather than hurt, shareholders.

4. INCREASE IN THE NUMBER OF ETFs

The growth in the number of ETFs over the last few years is truly astonishing. Although there has been a noticeable slowdown in the number of ETFs tracking market indexes, there has also been a noticeable increase in the number of ETFs tracking custom indexes. Given the significant amount of AuM in ETFs now and projected to flow into ETFs going forward, providers will continue to innovate and launch new and better ETFs. Many of these new ETFs will catch on with investors, but some will close because the invested assets will not reach critical mass, thus making it financially unfeasible to keep them available.

5. REDUCTION IN ETF TRADING COMMISSIONS

As previously mentioned, one of the primary reasons investors choose ETFs is for the low internal expenses. To attract more assets, ETF providers have been competing with one another by reducing these expenses. At the same time, broker-dealers have also been in competition with one another for investors and took a page out of the provider playbook and began slashing trading commissions. During 2010, Fidelity, Charles Schwab, and Vanguard eliminated their already super-low trading commissions from about $10 per trade on many ETFs. TD Ameritrade took the strategy to new heights by eliminating trading commissions on more than 100 hand-selected nonproprietary ETFs. As a result, self-directed investors have a significant financial incentive to give custody of their portfolios to one of these aforementioned broker-dealers. Although I am skeptical of the broker-dealers to offer select ETFs with no trading commissions forever, I do think this trend will continue over the next several years. At some point, however, broker-dealers may revisit this policy—but not any time soon.

6. EXPANDED USE OF ETFs IN 401(K) PLANS

The use of ETFs is rather pronounced in the traditional investing marketplace. However, the same cannot be said for nontraditional investing such as 529 plans and more importantly 401(k) plans.

Although ETFs have recently made their way into 401(k) platforms, there is still substantial room for expansion. The opportunity is so grand that I liken it to how the young United States more than doubled its size in the early nineteenth century through the Louisiana Purchase from France. When you consider the assets most investors under the age of 50 own, the vast majority of their investable wealth is tied into a 401(k) plan. Yes, investors with 401(k) accounts do have outside investing accounts, but the bulk of investable dollars resides in retirement accounts like 401(k)s. Providers of these plans are keenly aware of the trend toward ETFs and their growing popularity, and thus it is only a matter of time before ETFs are on an equal playing field with mutual funds and index mutual funds inside 401(k) platforms.

7. ETF INTERNAL EXPENSES WILL DECLINE

The question is not if, but how far and how quickly, ETF expenses will decline. Since their inception, ETFs has seen a significant decline in internal expenses, and there is no reason to believe this trend will cease. One of the primary reasons for investing in ETFs is the favorable cost difference—both implicit and explicit—with mutual funds. Providers recognize this shareholder purchasing decision and have reduced ETF expenses to attract additional AuM. There will come a point where cutting fees will lose steam, but I suspect we still have some years to go before this happens. Moreover, actively managed ETFs assess much higher expenses than passively managed ETFs since actively managed ETFs employ custom indexes rather than market indexes and use that fact to justify higher expenses. As with passively managed ETFs, expenses on actively managed ETFs will fall over the next few years, due to the competition for assets and shareholders, many of whom are keenly aware of the expenses and sensitive to overpaying.

8. ETF LIQUIDITY WILL IMPROVE

Liquidity, as defined by the bid-ask spread, is a trading cost for ETF investors (half of the spread paid by buyers and half by sellers). Generally speaking, higher liquidity for any security translates into narrower spreads between the bid and ask prices—a very good thing. As a result, when it comes time to purchase or sell your ETF, you want the narrowest spread possible. The wider the spread, the more you pay to purchase or the less you receive for selling your fund. ETF liquidity is based principally on the liquidity of the underlying securities held in the fund. However, a small amount of liquidity is attributed to trading activity on the fund level as well. Therefore, as the demand for ETFs continues to grow, so too will ETF liquidity.

9. INCREASED ETF RATINGS AND PROFILING

When it comes to research and ratings, the mutual fund trade is light-years ahead of the ETF trade. Although I do not see this gap between the two changing any time soon, I do envision a time when we will have multiple respectable research companies providing ratings and enhanced profiling—far more than exist today.

One of the most interesting and innovative profiling techniques I have seen to date—but has yet to catch on with the mainstream—is the use of strategy boxes (similar to Morningstar asset class boxes) that define single ETFs. This innovation is the brainchild of Rick Ferri of Portfolio Solutions, based in Troy, Michigan. He devotes nearly an entire chapter in his book *The ETF Book* (Hoboken, NJ: John Wiley & Sons, 2009) to this innovation. Over time we will see more and more innovations from various sources, all with the intent to enhance the ETF marketplace.

10. REGULATORY OVERSIGHT WILL GROW

This is another trend that has been ongoing for some time and is fully expected to continue into the foreseeable future. Without a doubt, the Securities and Exchange Commission (SEC) will seek ways to regulate ETFs—especially actively managed ETFs. Tracking a market index is one thing, but managing an ETF according to a custom index is completely different. The SEC wants to be actively engaged with these funds to better protect the general investing public. In addition, ETFs that employ leverage to magnify performance or ETFs that track commodities with futures contracts will see even more scrutiny and tightening of oversight by governmental and industry regulations. Non-ETF scandals such as the Bernie Madoff swindle do not help the cause and only put additional pressure on the SEC to regulate in ways and areas that impose greater burdens on ETF participants.

11. MORE ROBUST OPTIONS ON ETFs

Many of the largest ETFs have underlying call and put options. However, the robustness of each derivative is not the same from ETF to ETF. Moreover, many ETFs simply do not have underlying call and put options assigned to them at all. This will change over time. As more and more shareholders and assets flow into ETFs, so too will the assignment of options to ETFs. When there are only a handful of call options in the nearest contract months for a particular ETF, then liquidity tends to be low and bid-ask spreads wide for those options. Having wide spreads on stocks and ETFs is bad enough, but wide spreads on a much lower priced call or put option is even worse. Nonetheless, the future for the development of calls and puts on ETFs appears to be getting better.

ETF Resources

BOOKS

Abner, David J., *The ETF Handbook*, Hoboken, New Jersey: John Wiley & Sons, 2010.

Appel, Marvin, *Investing with Exchange-Traded Funds Made Easy*, Upper Saddle River, New Jersey: FT Press, 2008.

Delfeld, Carlton T., *ETF Investing Around the World*, Lincoln, Nebraska: iUniverse, 2007.

Dion, Don, and Carolyn Dion, *The Ultimate Guide to Trading ETFs*, Hoboken, New Jersey: John Wiley & Sons, 2010.

Ferri, Richard, *The ETF Book*, Hoboken, New Jersey: John Wiley & Sons, 2009.

Gastineau, Gary L., *The Exchange-Traded Funds Manual*, Hoboken, New Jersey: John Wiley & Sons, 2010.

Groves, Francis, *Exchange-Traded Funds*, Hampshire, U.K.: Harriman House, 2011.

Lofton, Todd, *Getting Started in Exchange-Traded Funds*, Hoboken, New Jersey: John Wiley & Sons, 2007.

Maeda, Martha, *The Complete Guide to Investing in Exchange-Traded Funds*, Ocala, Florida: Atlantic Publishing Group, 2009.

Meziani, A. Seddik, *Exchange-Traded Funds as an Investment Option*, Hampshire, U.K.: Palgrave Macmillan, 2005.

Richards, Jr., Archie M., *Understanding Exchange-Traded Funds*, New York: McGraw-Hill, 2007.

Vomund, David, and Linda Bradford Raschke, *ETF Trading
Strategies Revealed*, Columbia, Maryland: Marketplace
Books, 2006.
Wiandt, Jim, *Exchange-Traded Funds*, Hoboken, New Jersey:
John Wiley & Sons, 2001.
Wild, Russell, *Exchange-Traded Funds for Dummies*, Hoboken,
New Jersey: John Wiley & Sons, 2006.

WEB RESOURCES

Bloomberg: www.Bloomberg.com
CNBC: www.CNBC.com
CNN: www.CNNfn.com
ETF Guide: www.ETFGuide.com
ETF Trends: www.ETFTrends.com
ETF Zone: www.ETFZone.com
Index Investor: www.IndexInvestor.com
Index Universe: www.IndexUniverse.com
Market Watch: www.MarketWatch.com
Morningstar: www.Morningstar.com
Motley Fool: www.Fool.com
MSN: MoneyCentral.MSN.com
Seeking Alpha: www.SeekingAlpha.com
The Street: www.TheStreet.com
Wall Street Journal: www.WSJ.com
Yahoo! Finance: Finance.Yahoo.com/ETF

ETF PROVIDERS

BlackRock (iShares)
525 Washington Boulevard, Suite 1405
Jersey City, NJ 07310
800-iShares
www.iShares.com

Invesco PowerShares Capital Management
301 West Roosevelt Road
Wheaton, IL 60187

800-983-0903
www.PowerShares.com

Van Eck (MarketVectors)
335 Madison Avenue, 19th Floor
New York, NY 10017
800-544-4653
www.VanEck.com

ProFunds Group (ProShares)
7501 Wisconsin Avenue
Bethesda, MD 20814
866-776-5125
www.ProShares.com

Rydex-SGI
P.O. Box 758567
Topeka, KS 66675-8567
800-820-0888
www.Rydex-SGI.com

State Street Global Advisors (SPDRs)
One Lincoln Street, State Street Financial Center
Boston, MA 02111-2900
617-786-3000
www.SSgA.com

The Vanguard Group
P.O. Box 1110
Valley Forge, PA 19482-1110
800-992-8327
www.Vanguard.com

WisdomTree Investments
380 Madison Avenue, 21st Floor
New York, NY 10017
866-909-9473
www.WisdomTree.com

INDEX SPONSORS

Dow Jones Indexes
P.O. Box 300
Princeton, NJ 08543-0300
609-520-7249
www.DJIndexes.com

Morgan Stanley Capital International (MSCI)
One Chase Manhattan Plaza, 44th Floor
New York, NY 10005
888-588-4567
www.MSCI.com

Russell Investments
1301 Second Avenue, 18th Floor
Seattle, WA 98101
866-551-0617
www.Russell.com

Standard & Poor's
55 Water Street
New York, NY 10041
212-438-1000
www.StandardAndPoors.com

Wilshire Associates
1299 Ocean Avenue, Suite 700
Santa Monica, CA 90401
310-451-3051
www.Wilshire.com

BROKERAGE FIRMS

Charles Schwab: www.Schwab.com or 1-866-232-9890
Fidelity Investments: www.Fidelity.com or 1-800-343-3548
Scottrade: www.Scottrade.com or 1-800-619-7283
TD Ameritrade: www.TDAmeritrade.com or 1-800-454-9272
Vanguard Group: www.Vanguard.com or 1-800-319-4254

STOCK EXCHANGES

American Stock Exchange
See New York Stock Exchange

CME Group
20 South Wacker
Chicago, IL 60606
312-930-1000
www.CMEGroup.com

The Nasdaq Stock Market
One Liberty Plaza
165 Broadway
New York, NY 10006
212-401-8700
www.NASDAQ.com

New York Stock Exchange (NYSE Euronext)
11 Wall Street
New York, NY 10005
212-656-3000
www.NYSE.com

FINDING AN INVESTMENT PROFESSIONAL

CFA Institute
560 Ray C. Hunt Drive
Charlottesville, VA 22903-2981
800-247-8132
www.CFAInstitute.org

CFP Board
1425 K Street, NW, Suite 500
Washington, DC 20005
800-487-1497
www.CFP.net

Financial Planning Association
4100 E. Mississippi Avenue, Suite 400
Denver, CO 80246-3053
800-322-4237
www.FPAnet.org

National Association of Personal Financial Advisors
3250 North Arlington Heights Road, Suite 109
Arlington Heights, IL 60004
847-483-5400
www.NAPFA.org

REGULATORY ENTITIES

Financial Industry Regulatory Authority (FINRA)
1735 K Street, NW
Washington, DC 20006
301-590-6500
www.Finra.org

National Futures Association
300 South Riverside Plaza, Suite 1800
Chicago, IL 60606-6615
312-781-1300
www.nfa.futures.org

U.S. Commodity Futures Trading Commission
Three Lafayette Centre
1155 21st Street, NW
Washington, DC 20581
202-418-5000
www.CFTC.gov

U.S. Securities and Exchange Commission
100 F Street, NE
Washington, DC 20549
202-942-8088
www.SEC.gov

Asset Allocator Questionnaire

Asset allocation is the strategy of dividing an investor's wealth among the different asset classes and asset subclasses to achieve the highest expected total rate of return for the given level of risk the investor is willing and able to assume. Empirical evidence has concluded that how you *allocate* your wealth, rather than *which* securities you select or *when* you buy or sell, determines the majority of your investment performance over time.

The Asset Allocator Questionnaire will help you determine your risk profile (tolerance for risk, capacity for risk, and need for risk) and help identify your optimal asset allocation. This worksheet presents a number of questions and, based on your responses, will suggest one of five optimal asset allocations that may be the most appropriate for you. Each optimal asset allocation is designed to give you the highest expected total rate of return for the level of risk you are willing, able, and need to assume.

The optimal asset allocations should not be considered investment advice and should be considered within the context of all relevant investment strategies and when making investment decisions. Last, since your objectives and constraints may change over time, you may want to revisit this questionnaire annually.

1. **What is your investment goal?**

   [A] To make a purchase or pay an expense within three years using a substantial portion of my portfolio

[B] To provide a source of current income (interest and dividends)

[C] To balance capital appreciation with current income

[D] To emphasize capital appreciation over current income

[E] To emphasize aggressive capital appreciation

2. **What is your age group?**

   [A] Under 39

   [B] 40–49

   [C] 50–59

   [D] 60–69

   [E] 70 and over

3. **How much of your portfolio do you anticipate liquidating and using to make purchases within the next five years?**

   [A] 0%

   [B] Between 1% and 15%

   [C] Between 15% and 25%

   [D] Between 25% and 50%

   [E] Between 50% and 100%

4. **Approximately what percentage of your total investment holdings does this portfolio represent?**

   [A] Under 25%

   [B] Between 25% and 50%

   [C] Between 50% and 75%

   [D] Between 75% and 100%

5. **How secure are your future sources of income (employment, investment, retirement)?**

   [A] Very secure

   [B] Secure

   [C] Balanced

   [D] Unsecure

   [E] Very unsecure

6. **How strongly do you prefer securities with lower market-value volatility and lower expected returns over securities with higher market-value volatility and higher expected returns?**

   [A] Strongly prefer

   [B] Prefer

   [C] Indifferent

   [D] Do not prefer

   [E] Strongly do not prefer

7. **When the market is doing well, do you prefer to sell less risky investments and buy more risky investments with the proceeds?**

   [A] Strongly prefer

   [B] Prefer

   [C] Indifferent

   [D] Do not prefer

   [E] Strongly do not prefer

8. **The following chart illustrates potential gains and losses a portfolio may experience over the next five-year period. Please select the potential gain or loss grouping most preferable to you.**

FIGURE B-1

Hypothetical Range of Returns

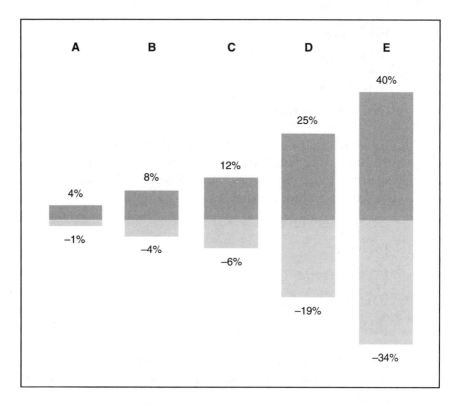

[A] Gains: 4%; losses: −1%

[B] Gains: 8%; losses: −4%

[C] Gains: 12%; losses: −6%

[D] Gains: 25%; losses: −19%

[E] Gains: 40%; losses: −34%

9. **About what percentage of your monthly net income is allocated to paying debt (not including your monthly mortgage payment on your principal residence)?**

[A] Between 0% and 15%

[B] Between 15% and 25%

[C] Between 25% and 50%

[D] Between 50% and 100%

10. **How many dependents do you financially support?**

[A] None

[B] Between one and three

[C] Four or more

11. **What is the size of your emergency fund?**

[A] Do not have one

[B] Between 1 and 3 months of average monthly expenses

[C] Between 4 and 6 months of average monthly expenses

[D] More than 6 months of average monthly expenses

12. **About what percentage of your retirement income do you anticipate coming from this portfolio?**

[A] Between 0% and 15%

[B] Between 15% and 25%

[C] Between 25% and 50%

[D] Between 50% and 100%

13. **What is your experience with equity investments?**

[A] Extensive experience

[B] Moderate experience

[C] Very little experience

[D] No experience

14. What is your experience with fixed-income investments?

[A] Extensive experience

[B] Moderate experience

[C] Very little experience

[D] No experience

15. What is your experience with alternative investments (real estate, commodities, hedge funds)?

[A] Extensive experience

[B] Moderate experience

[C] Very little experience

[D] No experience

16. Please select ONE of the following that best describes your view of portfolio risk.

[A] I prefer investments with low risk.

[B] I mostly prefer investments with low risk, but I am willing to accept some investments with moderate risk.

[C] I prefer a balanced approach of low-, moderate-, and high-risk investments.

[D] I mostly prefer investments with high risk, but am willing to accept some investments with moderate and low risk.

[E] I prefer investments with high risk.

17. How much additional risk are you willing to assume to earn a higher expected total rate of return?

[A] I am willing to accept more risk with all my investments to earn a higher expected total rate of return.

[B] I am willing to accept more risk with a portion of my investments to earn a higher expected total rate of return.

[C] I am willing to accept slightly more risk with all my investments to earn a higher expected total rate of return.

[D] I am willing to accept slightly more risk with a portion of my investments to earn a higher expected total rate of return.

[E] I am not willing to accept more risk to earn a higher expected total rate of return.

SCORE SECTION

For each number below, please circle the letter and corresponding score based on how you answered the aforementioned questions. The blank line at the end should be used to total your score.

1	[A]1	[B]3	[C]6	[D]9	[E]12
2	[A]12	[B]9	[C]6	[D]3	[E]1
3	[A]12	[B]9	[C]6	[D]3	[E]1
4	[A]10	[B]8	[C]6	[D]4	
5	[A]16	[B]13	[C]10	[D]7	[E]4
6	[A]2	[B]5	[C]8	[D]11	[E]14
7	[A]7	[B]6	[C]5	[D]4	[E]3
8	[A]1	[B]5	[C]9	[D]13	[E]17
9	[A]7	[B]5	[C]3	[D]1	

10	[A]5	[B]4	[C]3		
11	[A]2	[B]4	[C]6	[D]8	
12	[A]8	[B]6	[C]4	[D]2	
13	[A]5	[B]4	[C]3	[D]2	
14	[A]5	[B]4	[C]3	[D]2	
15	[A]5	[B]4	[C]3	[D]2	
16	[A]1	[B]5	[C]9	[D]13	[E]17
17	[A]13	[B]10	[C]7	[D]4	[E]1

Total Points = _____

33–58: If your score falls within the range of 33–58, you have a low risk profile and should emphasize aggressive capital preservation.

59–84: If your score falls within the range of 59–84, you have a low to moderate risk profile and should emphasize capital preservation with some growth.

85–121: If your score falls within the range of 85–121, you have a moderate risk profile and should emphasize a balanced approach to capital appreciation and capital preservation.

122–147: If your score falls within the range of 122–147, you have a moderate to high risk profile and should emphasize capital appreciation.

148–173: If your score falls within the range of 148–173, you have a high risk profile and should emphasize aggressive capital appreciation.

OPTIMAL ASSET ALLOCATIONS

The following are five optimal asset allocations that may be the most appropriate for you given the results of your answers. Each optimal asset allocation is designed to provide the highest expected total rate of return for the level of risk you are willing, able, and need to assume.

Scores Between 33 and 58: Aggressive Capital Preservation Portfolio

Equities: 25%
Fixed income: 55%
Cash and equivalents: 15%
Alternative assets: 5%

Scores Between 59 and 84: Capital Preservation Portfolio

Equities: 40%
Fixed income: 45%
Cash and equivalents: 10%
Alternative assets: 5%

Scores Between 85 and 121: Balanced Portfolio

Equities: 50%
Fixed income: 30%
Cash and equivalents: 10%
Alternative assets: 10%

Scores Between 122 and 147: Capital Appreciation Portfolio

Equities: 70%
Fixed income: 10%
Cash and equivalents: 5%
Alternative assets: 15%

Scores Between 148 and 173: Aggressive Capital Appreciation Portfolio

Equities: 70%
Fixed income: 5%
Cash and equivalents: 5%
Alternative assets: 20%

ETF Closures by Year

Exchange-Traded Fund	Symbol
1996	
DB Country Baskets Australia	
DB Country Baskets France	
DB Country Baskets Germany	
DB Country Baskets Hong Kong	
DB Country Baskets Italy	
DB Country Baskets Japan	
DB Country Baskets South Africa	
DB Country Baskets United Kingdom	
DB Country Baskets U.S.	
2002	
iShares DJ U.S. Chemicals Index Fund	IYD
iShares DJ U.S. Internet Index Fund	IYV
iShares S&P/TSE 60 Index Fund	IKC
2003	
Treasury 1 FITR	TFT
Treasury 2 FITR	TOU
Treasury 5 FITR	TFI
Treasury 10 FITR	TTE
2006	
SPDR O-Strip	OOO
2008	
Adelante Shares RE Classics ETF	ACK
Adelante Shares RE Composite ETF	ACB

Exchange-Traded Fund	Symbol
Adelante Shares RE Growth ETF	AGV
Adelante Shares RE Kings ETF	AKB
Adelante Shares RE Shelter ETF	AQS
Adelante Shares RE Value ETF	AVU
Adelante Shares RE Yield Plus ETF	ATY
Ameristock Ryan 10-Year Treasury	GKD
Ameristock Ryan 1-Year Treasury	GKA
Ameristock Ryan 20-Year Treasury	GKE
Ameristock Ryan 2-Year Treasury	GKB
Ameristock Ryan 5-Year Treasury	GKC
Bear Stearns Current Yield	YYY
Claymore/BIR Leaders 50	BST
Claymore/BIR Leaders Mid-Cap Value	BMV
Claymore/BIR Leaders Small-Cap Core	BES
Claymore/Clear Global Vaccine Index	JNR
Claymore/Clear Mid-Cap Growth Index	MCG
Claymore/IndexIQ Small-Cap Value	SCV
Claymore/KLD Sudan Free Large-Cap Core	KSF
Claymore/LGA Green	GRN
Claymore/Robeco Boston Partners Large-Cap Value	CLV
Claymore/Robeco Developed World Equity	EEW
Claymore/Zacks Growth & Income Index	CZG
Elements Australian Dollar ETN	ADE
Elements British Pound ETN	EGB
Elements Canadian Dollar ETN	CUD
Elements Euro ETN	ERE
Elements Swiss Franc ETN	SZE
FocusShares ISE CCM Homeland Security	MYP
FocusShares ISE SINdex	PUF
FocusShares ISE-REVERE WalMart Suppliers	WSI
FocusShares ISE Homebuilders	SAW
HealthShares Autoimmune Inflammation ETF	HHA
HealthShares Cancer ETF	HHK
HealthShares Cardiology Devices Index ETF	HHE
HealthShares Cardiology ETF	HRD
HealthShares Composite ETF	HHQ
HealthShares Dermatology and Wound Care ETF	HRW
HealthShares Diagnostics ETF	HHD
HealthShares Emerging Cancer Index ETF	HHJ
HealthShares Enabling Technologies Index ETF	HHV

Exchange-Traded Fund	Symbol
HealthShares European Drugs ETF	HRJ
HealthShares European Medical Products and Devices	HHT
HealthShares GI/Gender Health ETF	HHU
HealthShares Infectious Disease	HHG
HealthShares Metabolic-Endocrine Disorders ETF	HHM
HealthShares Ophthalmology ETF	HHZ
HealthShares Patient Care Services Index ETF	HHB
HealthShares Respiratory/Pulmonary ETF	HHR
HealthShares Neuroscience ETF	HHN
HealthShares Orthopedic Repair	HHP
Lehman Opta Commodity Index Pure Beta Agriculture Total Return ETN	EOH
Lehman Opta Commodity Index Pure Beta Total Return ETN	RAW
Lehman Opta S&P Listed Private Equity Net Return ETN	PPE
MacroShares Down Oil	DCR
MacroShares Up Oil	UCR
NYSE Arca Tech 100 ETF	NXT
2009	
Bear Stearns Alerian MLP ETN	BSR
MacroShares Down Oil $100	DOY
MacroShares Up Oil $100	UOY
NETS AEX Index	AEX
NETS BEL 20 Index	BRU
NETS CAC 40 Index	FRC
NETS DAX Index	DAX
NETS FTSE 100 Index	LDN
NETS FTSE Singapore Straits Times Index	SGT
NETS FTSE/JSE Top 40 Index	JNB
NETS FTSE-CNBC Global 300 Index Fund	MYG
NETS Hang Seng China Enterprises Index	SNO
NETS Hang Seng Index	HKG
NETS ISEQ 20 Index	IQE
NETS PSI 20 Index	LIS
NETS S&P/ASX 200 Index	AUS
NETS S&P/MIB Index	ITL
NETS TA-25 Index	TAV
NETS Tokyo Stock Exchange REIT Index	JRE
NETS TOPIX Index	NYI
PowerShares Dynamic Aggressive Growth Portfolio	PGZ
PowerShares Dynamic Asia Pacific Portfolio	PUA

Exchange-Traded Fund	Symbol
PowerShares Dynamic Deep Value Portfolio	PVM
PowerShares Dynamic Europe Portfolio	PEH
PowerShares Dynamic Hardware & Consumer Electronics Portfolio	PHW
PowerShares FTSE RAFI Asia Pacific EX-Japan Small-Mid Portfolio	PDQ
PowerShares FTSE RAFI Basic Materials Sector Portfolio	PRFM
PowerShares FTSE RAFI Consumer Goods Sector Portfolio	PRFG
PowerShares FTSE RAFI Consumer Services Sector Portfolio	PRFS
PowerShares FTSE RAFI Energy Sector Portfolio	PRFE
PowerShares FTSE RAFI Europe Small-Mid Portfolio	PWD
PowerShares FTSE RAFI Financials Sector Portfolio	PRFF
PowerShares FTSE RAFI Health Care Sector Portfolio	PRFH
PowerShares FTSE RAFI Industrials Sector Portfolio	PRFN
PowerShares FTSE RAFI International Real Estate Portfolio	PRY
PowerShares FTSE RAFI Telecommunications & Technology Sector Portfolio	PRFQ
PowerShares FTSE RAFI Utilities Sector Portfolio	PRFU
PowerShares High Growth Rate Dividend Achievers Portfolio	PHJ
PowerShares International Listed Private Equity Portfolio	PFP
SPA MarketGrader 100	SIH
SPA MarketGrader 200	SNB
SPA MarketGrader 40	SFV
SPA MarketGrader LargeCap 100	SZG
SPA MarketGrader MidCap 100	SVD
SPA MarketGrader SmallCap 100	SSK
Claymore/Morningstar Manufacturing Super Sector Index ETF	MZG
Claymore/Morningstar Information Super Sector Index ETF	MZN
Claymore/Morningstar Services Super Sector Index ETF	MZO
Claymore U.S.-1—The Capital Markets Index ETF	UEM
MacroShares Major Metro Housing Down	DMM
MacroShares Major Metro Housing Up	UMM
ELEMENTS MLCX Gold Index ETN	GOE
ELEMENTS MLCX Livestock Index ETN	LSO
ELEMENTS MLCX Precious Metals Index ETN	PMY
AirShares EU Carbon Allowances Fund	ASO
PowerShares DB Crude Oil Double Long ETN	DXO
2010	
WisdomTree Earnings Top 100	EEZ
WisdomTree Europe Total Dividend Fund	DEB
WisdomTree International Communications Sector	DGG
WisdomTree International Consumer Discretionary Sector Fund	DPC

Exchange-Traded Fund	Symbol
WisdomTree International Consumer Staples Sector Fund	DPN
WisdomTree International Financial Sector Fund	DRF
WisdomTree International Health Care Sector Fund	DBR
WisdomTree International Industrial Sector Fund	DDI
WisdomTree International Technology Sector Fund	DBT
WisdomTree U.S. Short Term Government Income Fund	USY
Rydex 2x S&P MidCap 400 ETF	SEA
Rydex Inverse 2x S&P MidCap 400 ETF	RRY
Rydex 2x Russell 2000 ETF	RMM
Rydex Inverse 2x Russell 2000 ETF	REA
Rydex 2x S&P Select Sector Energy ETF	RFL
Rydex Inverse 2x Select Sector Energy ETF	RHM
Rydex 2x S&P Select Sector Financial ETF	RTG
Rydex Inverse 2x Select Sector Financial ETF	RRZ
Rydex 2x S&P Select Sector Health Care ETF	RMS
Rydex Inverse 2x Select Sector Health Care ETF	REC
Rydex 2x S&P Select Sector Technology ETF	RFN
Rydex Inverse 2x Select Sector Technology ETF	RHO
Claymore/Delta Global Shipping Index ETF	RTW
Claymore/Zacks Dividend Rotation ETF	RFF
Claymore/Zacks Country Rotation ETF	RPQ
Claymore/Beacon Global Exchanges, Brokers & Asset Managers Index	EXB
Claymore/Robb Report Global Luxury Index ETF	ROB
Grail RP Technology	CRO
Grail RP Financials	IRO
GlobalShares FTSE All-World Fund	OOK
GlobalShares FTSE Emerging Markets Fund	TXF
GlobalShares FTSE All-Cap Asia Pacific EX Japan Fund	GSZ
GlobalShares FTSE All-World EX US Fund	GSO
GlobalShares FTSE Developed Countries EX US Fund	GSW
Geary OOK, Inc.	GSD
Geary TXF Large Companies ETF	GSR
JETS DJ Islamic Market International	JVS
Direxion Daily 2-Year Treasury Bear 3x	TWOZ
Direxion Daily 2-Year Treasury Bull 3x	TWOL
PowerShares Dynamic Healthcare Services Portfolio	PTJ
PowerShares Dynamic Telecommunications & Wireless Portfolio	PTE
PowerShares FTSE NASDAQ Small Cap Portfolio	PQSC
PowerShares FTSE RAFI Europe Portfolio	PEF
PowerShares FTSE RAFI Japan Portfolio	PJO

Exchange-Traded Fund	Symbol
PowerShares Global Biotech Portfolio	PBTQ
PowerShares Global Progressive Transportation Portfolio	PTRP
PowerShares NASDAQ-100 BuyWrite Portfolio	PQBW
PowerShares NXQ Portfolio	PNXQ
PowerShares Zacks Small Cap Portfolio	PZJ

Source: IndexUniverse.com 2011

INDEX

ABOUT THE AUTHOR

Scott Paul Frush, CFA, CFP, is a leading authority on asset allocation policy and portfolio optimization using exchange-traded funds. He has helped investors safeguard and grow their wealth for nearly two decades. Scott is the founder of Michigan-based Frush Financial Group and publisher of the *ETF Market Watch* blog and newsletter.

Scott's professional hallmark is the engineering, construction, and management of highly diversified, low-expense, tax-efficient ETF portfolios under an optimal asset allocation policy and a disciplined rebalancing strategy.

Scott earned a master of business administration degree from the University of Notre Dame and a bachelor of business administration degree in finance from Eastern Michigan University. He holds the Chartered Financial Analyst (CFA) and Certified Financial Planner (CFP) designations.

Scott is the author of five other investing books: *Commodities Demystified* (McGraw-Hill, 2008), *Hedge Funds Demystified* (McGraw-Hill, 2007), *Understanding Hedge Funds* (McGraw-Hill, 2006), *Understanding Asset Allocation* (McGraw-Hill, 2006), and *Optimal Investing* (Marshall Rand Publishing, 2004).

In 2010, Detroit-based *DBusiness* magazine named Scott to its Thirty in Their 30s award list in recognition of his professional achievements before the age of 40. In addition, Scott is the 2007 recipient of *CFA Magazine*'s prestigious Most Investor Oriented award, which recognizes one CFA Institute member who has made outstanding contributions to investor education. In 2008 he was profiled in *Bank Investment Consultant* magazine, which highlighted Scott's expertise with exchange-traded fund portfolios.

The Frush Financial Group Web site is located at www.Frush.com.